Rethinking Gender, Tourism and Hospitality

Rethinking Gender, Tourism and Hospitality

The Sustainable Strategy Dimension

Edited by

Marco Valeri

Associate Professor of Organizational Behaviour, Niccolò Cusano University, Italy

Edward Elgar
PUBLISHING

Cheltenham, UK • Northampton, MA, USA

Published by

Edward Elgar Publishing Limited
The Lypiatts
15 Lansdown Road
Cheltenham
Glos GL50 2JA
UK

Edward Elgar Publishing, Inc.
William Pratt House
9 Dewey Court
Northampton
Massachusetts 01060
USA

Authorised representative in the EU for GPSR queries only: Easy Access System Europe – Mustamäe tee 50, 10621 Tallinn, Estonia, gpsr.requests@easproject.com

A catalogue record for this book
is available from the British Library

Library of Congress Control Number: 2025938983

This book is available electronically in the **Elgar**online
Geography, Planning and Tourism subject collection
https://doi.org/10.4337/9781035350711

MIX
Paper | Supporting responsible forestry
FSC® C013604

ISBN 978 1 0353 5070 4 (cased)
ISBN 978 1 0353 5071 1 (eBook)
ISBN 978 1 0353 7120 4 (ePub)

Printed and bound by CPI Group (UK) Ltd, Croydon, CR0 4YY

Contents

Contributors

Hassan Ali, Research Associate, Eberswalde University for Sustainable Development, Germany

Tanmay Barman, Assistant Professor, Department of Finance and Banking, Gopalganj Science and Technology University, Bangladesh

Filipa Brandão, Assistant Professor, GOVCOPP – Research Unit on Governance, Competitiveness and Public Policies, Department of Economics, Management, Industrial Engineering and Tourism, University of Aveiro, Portugal

Zélia Breda, Assistant professor, GOVCOPP – Research Unit on Governance, Competitiveness and Public Policies, Department of Economics, Management, Industrial Engineering and Tourism, University of Aveiro, Portugal

Bapon Chandra Kuri, Assistant Professor, Department of Tourism and Hospitality Management, Gopalganj Science and Technology University, Bangladesh

Nishita Chatradhi, Policy Advisor and Doctoral Researcher, Government of Alberta, Canada

Carlos Costa, Full Professor, GOVCOPP – Research Unit on Governance, Competitiveness and Public Policies, Department of Economics, Management, Industrial Engineering and Tourism, University of Aveiro, Portugal

Panagiotis E. Dimitropoulos, Assistant Professor, Department of Accounting and Finance, School of Management, University of the Peloponnese, Greece

Margareth Duran-Izquierdo, Researcher, Environmental and Computational Chemistry Group, School of Pharmaceutical Sciences, University of Cartagena, and Arhuaco Teaching and Learning Center, SWAKA, Colombia

João Farinha, Ph.D. Researcher, ISLA Santarém, NECE – Research Centre for Business Sciences, University of Beira Interior and GOVCOPP – Research Unit on Governance, Competitiveness and Public Policies, University of Aveiro, Portugal

Maria de Fátima Pina, Ph.D. Researcher, ISLA Santarém, ISR – UC Institute of Systems and Robotics, University of Coimbra, Portugal

Rogelio Garcia Contreras, Director, Social Innovation Program at the Walton College of Business, Arkansas University, USA

Michelle Maiurro, Ph.D. Researcher, GOVCOPP – Research Unit on Governance, Competitiveness and Public Policies, Department of Economics, Management, Industrial Engineering and Tourism, University of Aveiro, Portugal

Farhad Nazir, CEGOT – Centre of Studies in Geography and Spatial Planning, Faculty of Arts and Humanities, University of Coimbra, Portugal

Panoraia Poulaki, academic teaching staff, University of the Aegean, Greece

Theodoros Rachiotis, PhDC, Department of Physical Education and Sport Sciences, University of Athens, Greece

Carmen Parra Rodríguez, Director, UNESCO Chair on Peace, Solidarity and Intercultural Dialogue, Abat Oliba CEU University, Barcelona, Spain

Shadia Sharmin, Research Assistant, Department of Tourism and Hospitality Management, Gopalganj Science and Technology University, Bangladesh

Durre Shehwar, Lecturer, Department of Tourism & Hospitality Management, University of Baltistan, Pakistan

Lucellys Sierra-Marquez, Researcher, Environmental and Computational Chemistry Group, School of Pharmaceutical Sciences, University of Cartagena, and John Von Neumann Pacific Environmental Research Institute, Cartagena, Colombia

Marco Valeri, Associate Professor of Organizational Behaviour, Niccolò Cusano University, Rome, Italy

Nikolaos Vasilakis, Researcher, Department of History, Ionian University, Greece

Kexin Yuan, Colorado State University, USA

Introduction: *Rethinking Gender, Tourism and Hospitality*

Marco Valeri

This edited book aims to provide a comprehensive collection of chapters, which include new insights into traditional paradigms, approaches, and methods, as well as more recent developments in research methodology on the gender dimension in tourism and sustainability.

Gender inequality in societies, organizational practices, and wider ecosystems has recently come to be debated in the field of tourism and hospitality. The United Nations' 'Transforming Our World: 2030 Agenda for Sustainable Development' (2015) embedded all three pillars of sustainability (economic, environmental, and social) in 17 Sustainable Development Goals (SDGs). SDG 5 specifically focuses on gender equality. This has led policymakers, academics, and practitioners across all kinds of organizations to agree that transformation toward sustainability entails impactful and innovative short-term and long-term efforts, including in regards to gender equality.

The experiences and views of women who engage in sustainable tourism practices are part of a broader framework grounded in complex and multidimensional cultural, social, political, and historical systems. These systems provide a field for action to pursue sustainability via tourism entrepreneurship. As mentioned, this is also encouraged by the UN's 2030 Agenda for Sustainable Development and the SDGs, which are grounded upon a process of contextualization and conceptualization with respect to the links between poverty and gender equality. More specifically, SDG 5 stresses the need for improvement of women's human rights; the re-evaluation, reduction, and addressing of unpaid care work conducted by women and girls; women's full and equal participation in sustainable development as agents and decision-makers in their communities, countries, and the world; the enhancement of leadership experience for women and support for those leaders who defend women's rights and gender equality in parliaments and other public spheres; and the elimination of discriminatory laws alongside the promotion of gender equality and women's empowerment.

Academic debates have offered valuable insights into increasingly complex analyses of gender identities, gender roles, and relations in tourism development policy and practice. In recent years, the "cultural turn" of post-structuralism in tourism studies has encompassed issues such as hegemonic tourism discourses, cultural practices, power inequities, gender identity construction, host and tourist subjectivities, embodiment, and symbolic representation. Researchers often argue a duality in relation to women's changing roles in sustainable tourism entrepreneurship. Other studies on gender and tourism development in Turkey have explored the processes of tourism and socio-cultural change. Thus far, in Turkey, it has mostly been men who have engaged in and dominated entrepreneurial activities and benefited from tourism employment whilst women remained largely excluded from tourism work.

Empirical research revealed another interesting dimension linked to challenging stereotypical labeling against women engaged in sustainable tourism. Some researchers have questioned the idea of a one-way relationship between hosts and guests, with its inherent assumption of local women's complete lack of control and power over their own lives and the dominant empowerment discourse in the field. Scholars rarely challenge sustainable tourism discourse and practice or question it in relation to gender dynamics.

Other researchers have come to the conclusion that tourism has significant potential to contribute to all SDGs in a meaningful manner, provided that we address the issue of gender inequality across all parts of the tourism value chain—in other words, across all highly interconnected members of the ecosystem. This requires developing and exercising agency at both individual and community levels.

STRUCTURE OF THE BOOK

Rethinking Gender, Tourism and Hospitality explores how the interconnections between Sustainable Development Goals (SDGs) and tourism from a gender perspective influence the tourism firm performances. Without tackling gender equality, tourism's potential to support the SDGs will be limited. The book is the result of reflections involving research studies of different countries. The book contains 10 chapters written by 23 authors located in 10 different countries (Bangladesh, Canada,

Colombia, Germany, Greece, Italy, Pakistan, Portugal, Spain, and the USA) and affiliated with a variety of different international universities.

Chapter 1, titled "Integrating Gender Perspectives for Sustainable Practices in Tourism and Hospitality: A Strategic Approach", is written by João Farinha and Maria de Fátima Pina. This chapter explores the critical role of gender dimensions in promoting sustainable strategies within the tourism and hospitality sectors. Recognizing the intersection of gender equality and sustainability, the chapter highlights how integrating gender considerations can enhance long-term economic, social, and environmental outcomes. Through a review of current industry practices and case studies, the research identifies key gender-related challenges and opportunities for sustainable development. A strategic framework is proposed to address these challenges, emphasizing gender-sensitive leadership, inclusive workforce policies, and equitable community engagement. By leveraging gender perspectives, tourism and hospitality businesses can create more resilient, adaptable, and sustainable operations, contributing to the global goals of sustainability and equality.

Chapter 2, titled "Tourism, Sustainability, Empowerment, and Ethnic Women: The Case of Colombia", is written by Lucellys Sierra-Marquez and Margareth Duran-Izquierdo. This chapter aims to analyze tourism initiatives within ethnic groups, evaluating their impact on gender equity and sustainable development. The methodological approach adopted in this study consisted of two stages. In the first stage, a review of scientific databases and government documents was conducted to identify tourism initiatives that are led by women or have a solid impact on female empowerment. The second stage involved the application of a semi-structured questionnaire to women leaders of tourism projects in indigenous and rural communities in order to better explore the relationship between tourism, gender equity, and sustainable development, as well as to understand the limitations and challenges from the participants' experiences in Colombia. Through this methodology, it was possible to identify and document women-led community-based tourism initiatives in ethnic and rural communities in Colombia. These initiatives have significantly contributed to gender equity and sustainable development in the evaluated territories, generating economic benefits, promoting cultural conservation, as well as empowering women and increasing their influence in various areas. Likewise, through interviews, it was possible to confirm that for women, leading tourism initiatives has had a positive impact on key aspects such as female empowerment, gender equity, and education.

Chapter 3, titled "Exploring Intersections: Tourism, Gender and Paths to Peace: The Case of Women in Gambia", is written by Carmen Parra Rodríguez and Rogelio Garcia Contreras. This chapter aims to present a conceptual model that identifies and connects the different approaches and thematic areas in the research field of tourism and gender. The design of the conceptual model is based on data analysis for improving gender mainstreaming in tourism. A set of recommendations to improve employment, entrepreneurship, and leadership prospects for women in the Gambia is provided based on the data analyzed in relation to the situation of women, the social context, and the tourism sector. The presentation of a model focused on the gender perspective in tourism leads to the identification of significant opportunities for work in this area. There are difficulties in accessing real knowledge of women's problems, as Gambia is a country with deep-rooted traditions where men have a central role.

Chapter 4, titled "Contribution of Women's Activity to Development of Agritourism on the Island of Lesvos", is written by Panoraia Poulaki, Theodoros Rachiotis, and Nikolaos Vasilakis. This chapter aims to underscore the significance of women's creativity and involvement in the development of agritourism on the island of Lesvos. It seeks to highlight the notable challenges and opportunities emerging from the growth of agritourism facilitated by female entrepreneurship. The chapter also aims to demonstrate how the blend of female ingenuity and business acumen can create new employment opportunities and drive local and regional development. Initially, a thorough review of the existing literature is conducted to analyze research methodologies utilized in international studies related to this field. This review focuses on the differentiation of gender in entrepreneurship, particularly emphasizing women's participation in the tourism industry. Additionally, it explores the intersection between tourism and agritourism. The primary qualitative research is carried out on the island of Lesvos, investigating the role of women's creativity in agritourism development. The research examines secondary sources discussing women's involvement in entrepreneurship and their impact on the local economy through agritourism. The research highlights the critical role of women in advancing agritourism, showcasing their contribution to economic development and sustainability. The findings reveal that women's entrepreneurship in agritourism significantly enhances local economic growth, providing financial independence and empowerment to women.

Chapter 5, titled "Intersection of Digital Technology, Social Innovation, and Female Entrepreneurship in Tourism: A Theoretical

Review", is written by Michelle Maiurro, Zélia Breda, Filipa Brandão, and Carlos Costa. The objective of this chapter is to provide an analysis of the existing literature on digital technology and social innovation in female entrepreneurship in tourism. It aims to explore the intersections and synergies between these fields, focusing on the contributions of women entrepreneurs to sustainable development. The methodology of this chapter involved analyzing relevant research on the three objects of study. The literature review seeks to understand the scientific and theoretical bases that underpin the construction of knowledge. To this end, the guidelines of a narrative review are used where previously published materials on the topic were searched for in a non-exhaustive way and without the need for rigid systematization for data collection. To collate the relevant literature, several databases were consulted, along with three keywords: digital technology, social innovation, and female entrepreneurship. This chapter integrates theories on these three areas (digital technology, social innovation, and female entrepreneurship) demonstrating how entrepreneurship in tourism can create value and empower women through innovative initiatives.

Chapter 6, titled "Rethinking Gender Bias in China's Tourism and Hospitality Industry: How to Improve Employees' Well-being", is written by Kexin Yuan. This chapter explores strategies to mitigate gender bias in the workplace. Gender stereotypes in China are rooted in historical and cultural evolution, as well as individuals' initial gender cognition shaped within family contexts. These stereotypes, often accompanied by unequal expectations, can generate over-demand for resources or lead to resource misallocation in professional settings. Moreover, unmet gender-based demands in the workplace trigger employee emotional exhaustion, which undermines long-term well-being. Based on Job Demand-Resources Theory and Social Identity Theory, by a focus on cisgender male and female employees (excluding sexual minority groups for the scope of this study), interviews with 15 managers yielded four key findings:

1. Leadership modelling to reset expectations – managers should lead by example to reduce gender-specific role expectations, aligning behavioural norms with competency-based standards.
2. Needs-driven welfare systems – providing beyond expectations resources aligned with employees' needs, while meeting basic demands.

3. Gender identity reconstruction through collaborative structures – organizational strategies should promote cross-gender team collaboration via self-categorization and job role reclassification. This comparative approach dismantles stereotypes by reconstructing professional identities independent of gender labels.
4. Family-concept workplace integration – translating the 'family' paradigm to organizational culture, enterprises can encourage employees to involve family members in company activities and foster open dialogues on work-related topics, thereby mitigating gender role conflicts.

Chapter 7, titled "Nexus of Cultural Heritage Sustainability, Gender Equality, and Tourism in Swat", is written by Hassan Ali, Farhad Nazir, and Durre Shehwar. In line with the UN's SDGs, gender equality, primarily in tourism, is foreseen as a passport to inclusive and holistic societies and, ultimately, a way forward for a sustainable tourism agenda. However, owing to specific disparities, predominantly on socio-economic, socio-geographical, and socio-technological grounds, the duality of gender equality, cultural heritage, and sustainable tourism varies massively. Chapter 7 has corroborated this trilateral nexus and unveiled several themes that highlight the potential and constraints of gender equality in the context of the district of Swat in Pakistan.

Chapter 8, titled "Gender Equality as a Catalyst for Sustainable Development in Tourism and Hospitality", is written by Bapon Chandra Kuri, Tanmay Barman, Shadia Sharmin, and Marco Valeri. The purpose of this chapter is to examine the important role of gender equality in delivering sustainable development in the tourism and hospitality sectors. It aims to provide comprehensive research on how the integration of gender perspectives can enhance strong performance and contribute to achieving the SDGs, in particular SDG 5 (gender equality) and SDG 12b (sustainable tourism). This chapter seeks to address widespread gender inequalities in societies, institutional practices, and wider ecosystems that may constrain the tourism sector's capacity to support the SDGs. Through the relationship between gender tourism and exploring the sustainable development network, this chapter emphasizes the benefits of a gender-inclusive approach. Th authors employ a blended-strategies technique, combining comprehensive literature reviews with empirical studies, consisting of case studies and interviews, allowing for an examination of gender dynamics in tourism through quantitative statistics evaluation and qualitative insights. This chapter demonstrates that gender-inclusive practices empower women, improve decision-making, and challenge traditional stereotypes, ultimately fostering a more inclusive and sustainable tourism and hospitality sector.

Chapter 9, titled "Driving Sustainable Tourism: Female Entrepreneurs' Motivations within the Value Chain", is written by Nishita Chatradhi. The chapter explores the impact of gender on sustainable entrepreneurship in the tourism sector, focusing on how gender influences the motivations, challenges, and successes of female entrepreneurs and their contributions to sustainable development. Utilizing a quantitative approach, the research employs a survey instrument targeting 250 female entrepreneurs across diverse geographical regions, gathered through a purposive sampling strategy. The Entrepreneurial Motivation Scale (EMS) is used to assess motivations, while data analysis is conducted using SmartPLS software. Findings reveal significant gender differences in motivations, with women more often driven by social and environmental concerns. Additionally, female entrepreneurs face greater challenges related to funding access and social norms compared to their male counterparts. Gender-specific support systems, including women-focused networks and mentorship programs, are crucial for women's success. Sustainable tourism businesses led by women demonstrate higher social and environmental impacts, significantly contributing to the SDGs. This chapter enriches the literature on sustainable entrepreneurship, gender studies, and tourism, offering insights for policymakers and support organizations in their development of tailored programs addressing the unique challenges faced by female sustainable entrepreneurs.

Chapter 10, titled "Corporate Sustainability and Board Gender Diversity in the European Hotel Sector: Implications on Financial Performance and Distress Risk", is written by Panagiotis E. Dimitropoulos. The aim of this chapter is to extend the existing literature on the effects of sustainability performance on firms' financial outcomes and viability. Specifically, it examines the impact of environmental and social performance (sustainability) on the financial performance and distress risk of firms operating in the European hotel industry. It also considers board gender diversity as a prominent feature of board governance and its impact on the financial performance and distress risk of hotels. The study employs a quantitative analysis approach with panel data regressions, using financial and sustainability-related data from an unbalanced sample of 579 unique listed hotel firms operating within 32 countries across the European continent over the period 2008–2019. Empirical evidence indicates that sustainability performance and board gender diversity contribute positively to financial performance (measured via Earnings Before Interest and Taxes, EBIT) and viability (reducing distress risk proxied via Altman Z-score). Specifically, hotel firms with increased percentages of board gender diversity experienced a more positive effect on their financial performance and a reduction in their distress risk (higher Z-score), corroborating arguments in the literature referring to the resource-based view of organizations.

1. Integrating gender perspectives for sustainable practices in tourism and hospitality: A strategic approach

João Farinha and Maria de Fátima Pina

1.1 INTRODUCTION

Sustainability has become a central concern in the tourism and hospitality sectors, reflecting broader global efforts to meet the United Nations' Sustainable Development Goals (SDGs). Tourism, in particular, is directly tied to economic, social, and environmental systems, positioning it as a critical area for sustainable development (Gössling & Hall, 2019). The hospitality industry, as a key driver of tourism, contributes significantly to these dynamics. However, sustainability in this field often emphasizes environmental aspects while overlooking social factors, such as gender equality, which is a key component of the SDGs (specifically, SDG 5) (UNWTO, 2021). Integrating gender dimensions into sustainability strategies is crucial because tourism and hospitality industries are major employers of women, and gender inequality persists in the workforce, especially in leadership roles (Baum, 2013). Hence, addressing gender issues is essential not only for promoting equality but also for fostering long-term sustainability in these industries.

Despite growing awareness of the importance of gender equality, current sustainability strategies in tourism and hospitality largely fail to incorporate gender-sensitive approaches. This gap in policy and practice can limit the effectiveness of sustainability initiatives by perpetuating gender-based inequalities and hindering the full realization of social and economic sustainability (Ferguson, 2011). Many businesses within these sectors implement broad sustainability goals but do not adequately consider the specific needs and contributions of women, particularly in areas such as leadership, decision-making, and community engagement.

Without addressing these gender-related challenges, the tourism and hospitality sectors cannot fully achieve their sustainability potential (Seyfi et al., 2019).

This chapter aims to examine the role of gender perspectives in promoting sustainable practices in the tourism and hospitality sectors. Specifically, the objectives are to:

- Explore how gender-sensitive leadership and workforce policies can contribute to the sustainability goals of the tourism and hospitality industries.
- Identify the key challenges and opportunities associated with integrating gender considerations into sustainability strategies.
- Propose a strategic framework that includes gender perspectives in leadership, workforce inclusivity, and community engagement to enhance sustainable practices.

By addressing these objectives, this chapter seeks to offer practical insights and recommendations for businesses in these industries to adopt more gender-inclusive, sustainable operations.

The study employs a qualitative research approach, focusing on a comprehensive review of existing literature and case studies related to gender and sustainability in tourism and hospitality. Case studies from diverse geographical contexts are analyzed to identify patterns and best practices in integrating gender perspectives into sustainability efforts. Key themes such as gender-sensitive leadership, inclusive workforce policies, and equitable community engagement are explored. Additionally, the chapter reviews current industry practices and assesses how these align with SDGs. The qualitative analysis aims to highlight both the challenges and opportunities that gender-inclusive strategies offer for the long-term sustainability of the tourism and hospitality sectors.

1.2 LITERATURE REVIEW

1.2.1 The Intersection of Gender and Sustainability

The integration of gender perspectives into sustainability has been gaining recognition, especially as it aligns with global frameworks like the United Nations' Sustainable Development Goals (SDGs), specifically SDG 5, which aims to achieve gender equality (UNWTO, 2021).

Sustainable development inherently includes economic, social, and environmental dimensions, and the inclusion of gender issues is crucial for achieving a holistic approach to sustainability (Seyfang & Smith, 2007). Research highlights that gender inequality, particularly in decision-making processes, limits the ability of industries, including tourism and hospitality, to achieve their full sustainability potential (Pritchard, 2018).

Women, especially in developing economies, are disproportionately affected by environmental degradation and economic inequality (Elmhirst, 2021). At the same time, women play essential roles in community resilience and environmental stewardship, which are key components of sustainability (Gaard, 2017). Therefore, integrating gender considerations into sustainability efforts, particularly in industries like tourism and hospitality which heavily rely on local communities and environments, is essential for advancing equitable and effective sustainable practices (Gentry, 2020).

1.2.2 Tourism and Hospitality Industry Dynamics

Gender disparities within the tourism and hospitality sectors are well documented, particularly in terms of leadership and workforce participation. According to the International Labour Organization (ILO), while women make up a significant portion of the tourism workforce—around 54%—they are underrepresented in leadership positions (ILO, 2019). Women often occupy lower-paid, lower-status jobs, which limits their influence on decision-making and sustainability strategies (Baum, 2013). Gender biases in recruitment, promotion, and remuneration further exacerbate these inequalities (Mooney & Ryan, 2009).

Leadership roles in the tourism and hospitality sectors remain predominantly male-dominated, with women facing barriers such as the glass ceiling and gendered expectations around work-life balance (Munar, 2019). Studies also reveal that the gendered division of labor in these industries affects not only workforce dynamics but also the broader community impact of tourism. For instance, women are often more engaged in community-based tourism initiatives, which emphasize sustainability, yet they are marginalized in formal decision-making processes that shape industry-wide policies (Ferguson & Alarcón, 2015).

These disparities contribute to a systemic gender gap in both the opportunities available to women and the benefits they derive from sustainable tourism initiatives. Addressing these inequalities requires targeted strategies that promote gender-sensitive leadership and inclusive workforce policies (Sigala, 2021).

1.2.3 Current Sustainable Practices

The integration of gender into sustainable practices within tourism and hospitality is still in its nascent stages. Many sustainability efforts have traditionally focused on environmental issues, such as reducing carbon footprints and minimizing waste, with little attention paid to gender equality (UNWTO, 2021). However, emerging research highlights the importance of incorporating gender-sensitive strategies into sustainability initiatives to enhance their effectiveness (Gentry, 2020).

For example, community-based tourism projects in developing countries often rely on the labor and cultural knowledge of women, yet these contributions are undervalued in formal sustainability planning (Ferguson, 2011). Gender mainstreaming—an approach that assesses the implications of any planned action on both men and women—is increasingly seen as a critical strategy for promoting both sustainability and gender equality (Momsen, 2020). Sustainable tourism models that incorporate gender considerations not only empower women but also contribute to more resilient communities and equitable economic development (Seyfi & Hall, 2020).

Recent studies also emphasize the role of gender-sensitive leadership in advancing sustainability goals. Companies that prioritize diversity and inclusion in leadership tend to perform better in terms of innovation and sustainability outcomes (Munar, 2019). Furthermore, inclusive workforce policies, such as flexible working arrangements and equal pay initiatives, are increasingly recognized as essential for creating sustainable work environments within the tourism and hospitality sectors (Sigala, 2021).

1.2.4 Key Gender-Related Challenges in Tourism and Hospitality

One of the most significant challenges in the tourism and hospitality sectors is the underrepresentation of women in leadership roles. Despite the fact that women constitute more than half of the workforce in these industries, they remain underrepresented in senior leadership and decision-making positions (ILO, 2019). This leadership gap is critical because inclusive leadership has been linked to better organizational performance, including sustainability outcomes (Baum & Cheung, 2015). When women are excluded from leadership, organizations lose the benefits of diverse perspectives, particularly when addressing complex issues like sustainability, which require comprehensive approaches involving economic, social, and environmental factors (Munar, 2019).

Moreover, women's leadership has been shown to positively influence sustainability decisions, as they tend to prioritize environmental stewardship and community well-being, both of which are essential components of sustainable tourism (Sigala, 2021). However, barriers such as the glass ceiling, lack of mentorship, and gender bias in promotions contribute to women's limited access to top management roles (Figueroa-Domecq et al., 2020a). This exclusion hampers progress toward gender equality and diminishes the sector's ability to implement more holistic and inclusive sustainable practices (Madera et al., 2018).

Gender disparities in pay, working conditions, and career advancement continue to pervade the tourism and hospitality sectors. Women are often concentrated in lower-paid, lower-status jobs, such as housekeeping and customer service, where they have limited opportunities for career progression (Ferguson, 2011). According to UNWTO (2021), the wage gap between men and women in tourism remains significant, with women earning, on average, 10–15% less than their male counterparts, even when performing similar roles. This inequity not only affects women's financial independence but also limits their ability to influence sustainability policies and initiatives within their organizations (Costa et al., 2023).

In addition to the pay gap, women in tourism and hospitality often face precarious working conditions, such as temporary contracts, long working hours, and a lack of access to social protections (Gentry, 2020). These conditions disproportionately affect women, particularly in regions where labor laws are weak or poorly enforced. Such inequality in the workforce hinders the potential for inclusive and sustainable development in the industry, as it perpetuates economic instability and reduces women's engagement in sustainability initiatives (Mooney & Ryan, 2009).

Efforts to promote gender equality in the workforce are essential for fostering sustainability, as studies have shown that more equitable workplaces tend to be more innovative and effective in addressing sustainability challenges (Sigala, 2021). Gender-inclusive policies, such as equal pay, flexible working conditions, and mentorship programs for women, can help bridge these gaps and contribute to a more sustainable workforce (UNWTO, 2021).

Cultural norms and gender expectations in different regions significantly influence the participation of women and marginalized genders in the tourism and hospitality sectors. In many parts of the world, traditional gender roles limit women's access to education, training, and employment opportunities, particularly in leadership and technical roles (Figueroa-Domecq et al., 2020a). For instance, in conservative societies where women are expected to prioritize domestic responsibilities over professional careers, their participation in the workforce is often constrained, further perpetuating gender inequality in tourism and hospitality (Baum, 2013).

In regions where tourism plays a major economic role, cultural barriers can also affect the implementation of gender-sensitive sustainability strategies. For example, community-based tourism initiatives often rely on the labor of women for crafting, hospitality services, and local entrepreneurship, yet cultural norms may exclude them from leadership roles or decision-making processes in these projects (Momsen, 2020). This exclusion diminishes the effectiveness of sustainability initiatives, as women's insights, particularly on issues related to community welfare and environmental sustainability, are often overlooked (Seyfi & Hall, 2020).

Addressing cultural barriers requires both institutional and societal changes. Policies that promote gender equality, such as educational programs and training opportunities for women, alongside efforts to challenge and transform gender norms, are essential for ensuring that tourism and hospitality sectors can be inclusive and sustainable (Sigala, 2021). This also involves engaging men and other stakeholders to support gender equality and recognize the value that diverse perspectives bring to sustainable development (UNWTO, 2021).

1.2.5 Opportunities for Gender-Inclusive Sustainability

Women and gender minorities play a pivotal role in fostering innovative sustainability initiatives, particularly in the tourism and hospitality sectors. Research demonstrates that diverse leadership teams—comprising a mix of genders—are better equipped to handle complex challenges, including those related to sustainability (Figueroa-Domecq et al., 2020b). Women, in particular, often bring distinct perspectives on environmental and social responsibility, emphasizing long-term sustainability over short-term profits (Baum & Cheung, 2015). Gender-sensitive leadership can help businesses create more resilient and sustainable strategies, as women leaders are more likely to prioritize inclusive growth, community well-being, and environmental conservation (UNWTO, 2021).

Moreover, recent studies highlight that companies with women in leadership positions tend to perform better in terms of sustainability metrics (Sigala, 2021). Women leaders are often more attuned to the social dimensions of sustainability, such as equitable resource distribution, community engagement, and environmental justice (Costa et al., 2023). Organizations in the tourism and hospitality industries that prioritize gender diversity in leadership are, therefore, more likely to develop and implement innovative sustainability strategies that account for the interconnectedness of economic, social, and environmental factors (Figueroa-Domecq et al., 2020a).

Promoting gender equality in workforce development is essential for advancing sustainability goals in tourism and hospitality. This includes adopting strategies that address gender disparities in hiring, pay, and training. As studies show, women are often overrepresented in low-wage positions while being underrepresented in leadership roles (ILO, 2019). To rectify this imbalance, businesses must implement inclusive hiring practices that actively seek to recruit and promote women and gender minorities to all levels of the workforce (Ferguson, 2011).

Additionally, wage equity is a critical aspect of workforce development. Gender pay gaps remain pervasive in the tourism and hospitality industries, with women earning significantly less than their male counterparts (UNWTO, 2021). Addressing these disparities through transparent pay structures, regular pay audits, and equal pay policies can create a more equitable work environment. Moreover, businesses should invest in training and professional development programs that are accessible to all employees, regardless of gender (Costa et al., 2023). Providing mentorship and leadership training for women and gender minorities can further promote their advancement and representation in decision-making roles, which is essential for fostering a more sustainable and inclusive tourism industry (Sigala, 2021).

Flexible work arrangements and family-friendly policies are additional strategies that can support gender equality in the workforce. By offering flexible hours, remote work options, and parental leave, tourism and hospitality businesses can accommodate the needs of women, particularly those who balance professional and domestic responsibilities (Baum, 2013). These policies not only support gender equality but also contribute to a more motivated and productive workforce, which is crucial for driving innovation in sustainability.

In many developing areas, tourism relies heavily on local communities, and gender-inclusive approaches to community engagement can significantly enhance sustainability. Women, especially in rural and indigenous communities, often serve as cultural custodians and are heavily involved in community-based tourism initiatives (Ferguson & Alarcón, 2015). Gendered approaches to community engagement recognize the distinct contributions of women to sustainable tourism and aim to ensure that they are active participants in decision-making processes.

Community empowerment through tourism can be achieved by creating platforms for women and marginalized genders to share their knowledge and skills in ways that benefit both their communities and the environment (Momsen, 2020). For instance, many ecotourism projects in developing regions are led by women who promote sustainable practices such as organic farming, wildlife conservation, and artisanal crafts (Seyfi & Hall, 2020). These initiatives not only provide women with economic opportunities but also foster stronger community resilience to environmental and social challenges.

Inclusive benefit-sharing mechanisms are another important aspect of gendered community engagement. Tourism enterprises should ensure that both men and women benefit from tourism revenues and development projects, particularly in regions where women are traditionally excluded from financial decision-making (Figueroa-Domecq et al., 2020b). Gender-sensitive approaches to benefit-sharing can help to ensure that tourism supports broader community development goals, such as improved education, healthcare, and infrastructure, which in turn contribute to more sustainable and equitable tourism outcomes (Gentry, 2020).

1.2.6 Strategic Framework for Gender-Integrated Sustainable Tourism and Hospitality

Creating pathways for women and marginalized genders in leadership roles is critical to advancing gender-inclusive sustainability in tourism and hospitality. Gender-sensitive leadership development involves establishing mentorship programs, leadership training, and gender parity in promotion practices to ensure that women and other underrepresented groups are adequately represented at decision-making levels (Baum & Cheung, 2015). These initiatives can help address the current underrepresentation of women in leadership, particularly in higher-level management and executive positions, where sustainability decisions are most impactful (Figueroa-Domecq et al., 2020b).

Companies can also implement leadership quotas or targets to ensure gender diversity at the top while fostering a company culture that values gender-sensitive leadership. Research shows that organizations with diverse leadership teams are more innovative, flexible, and better positioned to address sustainability challenges (Sigala, 2021). Furthermore, gender-sensitive leadership development fosters a more inclusive work environment, leading to improved decision-making processes that prioritize long-term sustainability over short-term gains (UNWTO, 2021).

Promoting gender equality in the workforce is essential for the long-term sustainability of the tourism and hospitality sectors. Policies that ensure fair pay, work-life balance, and professional growth for all genders are key components of inclusive workforce development. Fair pay policies, such as conducting regular wage audits and enforcing equal pay for equal work, are necessary to close the gender pay gap, which remains a persistent issue in tourism and hospitality industries worldwide (ILO, 2019). By ensuring equitable compensation, companies not only foster employee satisfaction but also create a more sustainable and motivated workforce (Costa et al., 2023).

Work-life balance policies, including flexible work schedules and parental leave, are also essential for supporting women and other marginalized genders in the workforce. Tourism and hospitality industries, which often involve long hours and unpredictable shifts, can benefit from implementing policies that allow employees to manage both professional and personal responsibilities (Baum, 2013). Furthermore, offering continuous professional development opportunities for all employees, regardless of gender, ensures that everyone has equal access to career growth and leadership pathways (Ferguson & Alarcón, 2015). These strategies not only promote workforce inclusion but also enhance the overall sustainability of tourism and hospitality operations by cultivating a more engaged and diverse talent pool.

Incorporating gender considerations into community engagement practices is essential, especially when collaborating with local populations in tourism-dependent regions. A gender-sensitive approach to community engagement ensures that women and marginalized genders have equal opportunities to participate in and benefit from tourism development (Figueroa-Domecq et al., 2020a). Women, in particular, often serve as key stakeholders in community-based tourism initiatives, playing critical roles in cultural preservation, environmental conservation, and local entrepreneurship (Seyfi & Hall, 2020). However, traditional gender roles can limit their involvement in decision-making processes, resulting in an unequal distribution of tourism benefits.

To address this, tourism enterprises should actively involve women and marginalized genders in project planning and implementation, ensuring that their voices are heard and their contributions are valued. Gender-sensitive benefit-sharing mechanisms, such as ensuring equal access to financial resources, training, and leadership positions, can enhance community resilience and contribute to the overall sustainability of tourism initiatives (Momsen, 2020). Furthermore, gender-sensitive community engagement practices can foster greater social cohesion, reduce inequalities, and create more inclusive and sustainable tourism models that benefit all members of the community (Gentry, 2020).

To ensure the success of gender-integrated sustainability strategies, it is essential to implement robust monitoring and evaluation mechanisms that track progress toward gender-inclusive goals. One of the most effective ways to do this is through the collection and analysis of gender-disaggregated data (Sigala, 2021). Gender-disaggregated data allows organizations to assess how different gender groups are impacted by tourism policies and practices, helping to identify areas where inequalities persist and where further action is needed (UNWTO, 2021).

By regularly tracking key indicators, such as gender representation in leadership, pay equity, and participation in community engagement, tourism and hospitality organizations can measure their progress toward gender-inclusive sustainability goals. This data can also be used to inform policy adjustments, ensuring that strategies remain aligned with both gender equality and sustainability objectives. Additionally, the transparent reporting of gender-disaggregated data fosters accountability and encourages continuous improvement in gender-sensitive sustainability practices (Costa et al., 2023).

Collaboration between industry stakeholders, government, and non-governmental organizations (NGOs) is crucial for advancing gender-sensitive sustainability strategies in tourism and hospitality. Public-private partnerships (PPPs) offer a platform for sharing knowledge, resources, and best practices, enabling more effective implementation of gender-inclusive policies (Ferguson & Alarcón, 2015). Governments can provide the necessary regulatory frameworks and incentives for businesses to adopt gender-sensitive practices, while NGOs can offer expertise in gender equality and sustainable development (Baum & Cheung, 2015).

For instance, partnerships between tourism companies and local NGOs can support gender-inclusive community engagement initiatives by providing training, resources, and support for women-led tourism enterprises (Seyfi & Hall, 2020). Similarly, collaboration with governments can lead to the development of gender-sensitive national tourism policies, which promote equal opportunities for all genders in the tourism workforce and leadership (Figueroa-Domecq et al., 2020a). Through these partnerships, tourism and hospitality businesses can leverage collective expertise to create more sustainable, gender-inclusive operations that contribute to broader social and environmental goals.

1.3 STRATEGY FRAMEWORK FOR GENDER-INTEGRATED SUSTAINABLE TOURISM AND HOSPITALITY: A MODEL PROPOSAL

To achieve sustainable development in the tourism and hospitality sectors while promoting gender inclusion, we propose a comprehensive strategic framework that integrates gender-sensitive approaches into the industry's sustainability efforts. This model is structured around five key pillars: Leadership Development, Workforce Inclusion, Community Engagement, Monitoring and Evaluation, and Public-Private Partnerships (Figure 1.1). These components are interlinked, supporting each other

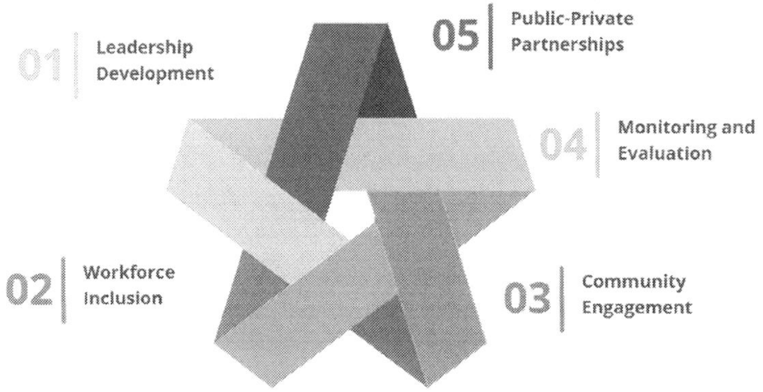

Source: Author's own elaboration.

Figure 1.1 *Key pillars of the model*

to create a sustainable and gender-inclusive environment. Below is an explanation of each component within the framework.

1.3.1 Gender-Sensitive Leadership Development

This pillar focuses on creating pathways for women and marginalized genders to assume leadership and decision-making roles within tourism and hospitality organizations. Leadership diversity is crucial for fostering innovative sustainability solutions, as diverse teams bring a broader range of perspectives and ideas. The key elements are:

- Mentorship and leadership training: Establish mentorship programs that focus on developing leadership skills among women and marginalized genders.
- Leadership quotas/targets: Set measurable goals for increasing the representation of women in leadership and management roles.
- Inclusive company culture: Develop a company culture that values diverse leadership styles, encouraging inclusive and empathetic decision-making.

Rationale: Research shows that gender-diverse leadership teams are better positioned to address sustainability challenges and promote long-term, inclusive growth (Baum & Cheung, 2015). Leadership training and mentorship can close the gender gap in decision-making roles, allowing women and marginalized genders to influence sustainable practices within the organization (Sigala, 2021).

1.3.2 Workforce Inclusion Strategies

This pillar addresses the need for inclusive workforce policies that promote fair pay, career advancement, and work-life balance for all genders. Ensuring gender equity in the workforce is essential for building a strong foundation for sustainability within the organization. The key elements are:

- Fair pay and wage equity: Implement wage audits and equal pay policies to eliminate gender-based pay gaps.

- Flexible work arrangements: Offer flexible hours, parental leave, and family-friendly policies to accommodate the diverse needs of the workforce.
- Professional development opportunities: Provide training, leadership courses, and clear career progression pathways for all employees, with a focus on underrepresented groups.

Rationale: A gender-inclusive workforce creates a more dynamic, engaged, and innovative environment that enhances sustainability. Fair pay and work-life balance policies help retain talent, while professional development ensures all employees can contribute to the organization's long-term goals (ILO, 2019).

1.3.3 Community-Centric Approaches

This pillar ensures that gender considerations are embedded in community engagement, particularly when working with local populations in tourism development. Sustainable tourism must benefit the communities it operates in, and gender-sensitive approaches can empower marginalized groups within those communities. The key elements are:

- Inclusive community participation: Ensure women and marginalized genders have equal opportunities to participate in tourism development decisions and initiatives.
- Gender-sensitive benefit sharing: Implement fair and transparent systems that ensure all community members, regardless of gender, benefit equally from tourism revenues and opportunities.
- Support for women-led initiatives: Invest in women-led community projects that promote sustainability, such as ecotourism or cultural preservation programs.

Rationale: In many regions, women play central roles in cultural and environmental preservation. Gender-inclusive community engagement fosters stronger community relations and ensures that tourism development benefits all segments of the population, making it more socially and economically sustainable (Figueroa-Domecq et al., 2020a).

1.3.4 Monitoring and Evaluation Mechanisms

This pillar emphasizes the need for robust monitoring and evaluation systems that track progress toward gender-integrated sustainability goals. Collecting gender-disaggregated data ensures that organizations can measure their impact on gender equality and sustainability over time. The key elements are:

- Gender-disaggregated data collection: Regularly collect and analyze data on gender representation, pay equity, and community engagement.
- Sustainability and gender audits: Conduct audits that assess both the sustainability and gender inclusivity of business practices.
- Transparent reporting: Publicly share progress reports to foster accountability and promote continuous improvement in gender-inclusive sustainability efforts.

Rationale: By tracking gender-specific outcomes, tourism and hospitality organizations can identify gaps, address inequalities, and refine their sustainability strategies. Transparent reporting of gender-disaggregated data encourages accountability and helps the organization stay aligned with both gender equality and sustainability goals (UNWTO, 2021).

1.3.5 Public-Private Partnerships

Collaboration between industry stakeholders, governments, and non-governmental organizations (NGOs) forms the foundation for advancing gender-sensitive sustainable strategies. These partnerships are essential for pooling resources, sharing knowledge, and promoting inclusive growth across the sector. The key elements are:

- Collaborative policy development: Work with governments and NGOs to create gender-sensitive policies that promote sustainability across the industry.
- Industry-wide standards for gender inclusion: Establish industry-wide standards for gender-inclusive practices in hiring, leadership, and community engagement.

- Capacity building programs: Partner with local organizations to develop programs that support women and marginalized groups in tourism-related industries.

Rationale: Public-private partnerships help leverage resources and expertise from different sectors to implement gender-sensitive sustainability initiatives. Collaboration ensures that policies are scalable and aligned with broader national and global development goals (Ferguson & Alarcón, 2015).

1.3.6 Strategic Framework Model Summary

- Leadership Development: Fostering women and marginalized genders into decision-making roles ensures diverse leadership that supports sustainability.
- Workforce Inclusion: Fair policies in pay, work-life balance, and career growth create a gender-equal workforce, driving innovation and sustainability.
- Community Engagement: Embedding gender-sensitive practices in community relations ensures equitable benefits for all genders in local tourism development.
- Monitoring and Evaluation: Regular data collection on gender impacts ensures accountability and continuous improvement in sustainable practices.
- Public-Private Partnerships: Collaborative efforts across sectors enable broader implementation and scaling of gender-integrated sustainability strategies.

This framework forms a cyclical and interdependent system, where each element supports and enhances the others. As organizations integrate these pillars into their operations, they create a sustainable tourism and hospitality model that promotes both gender equality and long-term environmental, economic, and social sustainability.

1.4 CASE STUDIES

In this section, we present some successful gender-inclusive sustainable initiatives, lessons learned from failures and challenges, and finish with some key takeaways from case studies.

1.4.1 Successful Gender-Inclusive Sustainable Initiatives

In what follows, we explore three examples of successful gender-inclusive sustainable initiatives.

1.4.1.1 The Intrepid Group: Gender equity in leadership and community empowerment

The Intrepid Group, a leader in sustainable tourism, has made significant strides in gender inclusion by promoting women into leadership roles and supporting local women-led initiatives. As part of their commitment to gender equity, the company introduced a target to achieve a 50% female leadership ratio by 2020, which they successfully met (Intrepid Group, 2020). Additionally, they established women-only tours in traditionally male-dominated regions such as the Middle East and North Africa, providing opportunities for female guides and local businesswomen to benefit from tourism. These gender-inclusive initiatives have not only promoted female leadership within the company but also empowered women in the communities where the tours take place, contributing to broader gender equality and sustainability goals (Intrepid Group, 2020).

Impact: The Intrepid Group's focus on gender equity in leadership and community empowerment has led to an increase in women's participation in tourism in regions where their involvement was previously restricted. This approach has fostered economic sustainability by creating new opportunities for women to participate in and benefit from the tourism industry (UNWTO, 2021).

1.4.1.2 Costa Rica's Certification for Sustainable Tourism (CST): Integrating gender in national tourism policy

Costa Rica's Certification for Sustainable Tourism (CST) program is another successful case of gender integration into sustainability practices. CST evaluates tourism businesses based on their environmental, social, and economic sustainability, including gender inclusion. For instance, some certified businesses have adopted inclusive hiring practices that prioritize gender equality and have partnered with local women's cooperatives to provide job opportunities in ecotourism and hospitality (Blázquez-Salom et al., 2020).

Impact: The program has contributed to the economic empowerment of women, particularly in rural and indigenous communities, by offering them employment opportunities in sustainable tourism. This model demonstrates how national tourism policies can successfully integrate gender considerations into broader sustainability goals, serving as a benchmark for other countries (UNWTO, 2021).

1.4.1.3 Soneva Resorts: Women's empowerment and environmental sustainability

Soneva Resorts, located in the Maldives and Thailand, have incorporated gender-inclusive practices into their sustainability strategies. The resorts employ a significant number of women in leadership positions and promote female entrepreneurship by collaborating with local women on sustainable craft projects sold at their properties. Additionally, Soneva's commitment to environmental sustainability—such as operating on renewable energy and reducing single-use plastics—intersects with its gender inclusion efforts by ensuring that women are actively involved in these initiatives (Cioccarelli, 2023).

Impact: The integration of gender into Soneva's sustainability model has empowered local women economically while simultaneously contributing to environmental conservation. By fostering partnerships with local women and incorporating them into their sustainability strategy, Soneva has built a more inclusive and resilient business model.

1.4.2 Lessons Learned from Failures and Challenges

In what follows, we analyze three examples of lessons learned from failures and challenges.

1.4.2.1 Overlooking gender in ecotourism projects: The case of Nepal

A study on ecotourism projects in Nepal highlighted the challenges that arise when gender issues are not adequately addressed in sustainability efforts. Many projects aimed at promoting community-based ecotourism in rural areas failed to include women in decision-making processes, despite women being key contributors to environmental conservation and local economies (Giri & Darnhofer, 2010). This exclusion not only reinforced existing gender inequalities but also limited the overall success of the projects. Without women's involvement, critical local knowledge related to sustainable resource use and cultural preservation was overlooked, ultimately undermining the sustainability goals of the initiatives.

Impact: The failure to account for gender disparities in ecotourism development weakened both community participation and long-term sustainability. As a result, several projects were abandoned or failed to deliver the promised economic and environmental benefits. This case underscores the importance of incorporating gender perspectives from the planning stages of sustainable tourism projects to ensure inclusive and effective outcomes (Giri & Darnhofer, 2010).

1.4.2.2 Unintended consequences of gender-neutral policies in the Caribbean

In the Caribbean, several tourism initiatives aimed at promoting sustainability adopted gender-neutral policies, which inadvertently reinforced existing gender inequalities. For example, in one case, efforts to promote eco-lodges and nature reserves failed to account for the fact that women had less access to land ownership, financial resources, and formal employment than men (Momsen, 2020). This meant that while the projects generated economic growth, the benefits were disproportionately captured by men, exacerbating gender-based economic disparities.

Impact: The failure to recognize and address gender inequalities in access to resources led to unintended consequences, such as the exclusion of women from economic opportunities and the reinforcement of patriarchal structures. This example highlights the need for explicitly gender-sensitive policies in sustainable tourism initiatives to ensure that all community members benefit equitably (Momsen, 2020).

1.4.2.3 Community-based tourism in South Africa: Gender inequality in benefit distribution

In South Africa, several community-based tourism (CBT) projects aimed at promoting sustainability have faced challenges related to gender inequality in the distribution of tourism benefits. In many cases, men have controlled the decision-making processes and received the majority of financial rewards, despite women doing most of the work in managing lodges, preparing food, and organizing cultural experiences (Scheyvens, 2011). These gendered power dynamics have led to frustration among women participants and, in some cases, the collapse of CBT projects due to internal conflicts and a lack of cooperation.

Impact: The lack of gender-sensitive approaches in South African CBT projects has highlighted the need for equitable benefit-sharing mechanisms and inclusive decision-making processes to ensure long-term sustainability. This case illustrates how ignoring gender disparities in tourism development can lead to project failures and reinforces the necessity of integrating gender perspectives into all aspects of sustainability planning (Scheyvens, 2011).

1.4.3 Key Takeaways from Case Studies

The successes and failures of gender-inclusive sustainable initiatives in tourism and hospitality underscore the importance of integrating gender considerations into every stage of sustainability planning. Successful cases, such as the Intrepid Group, Costa Rica's CST, and Soneva Resorts, demonstrate that gender-sensitive approaches can lead to enhanced sustainability outcomes, both socially and economically. On the other hand, failures in Nepal, the Caribbean, and South Africa reveal that neglecting gender issues can undermine sustainability goals and perpetuate existing inequalities. Moving forward, tourism and hospitality businesses must adopt gender-sensitive frameworks to ensure that sustainability efforts benefit all stakeholders, regardless of gender.

1.5 IMPACT OF GENDER INTEGRATION ON SUSTAINABILITY GOALS

Integrating gender perspectives into sustainability strategies in the tourism and hospitality industries has a profound impact on achieving comprehensive social, economic, and environmental outcomes. Gender inclusion improves the scope and effectiveness of sustainability initiatives by ensuring that all members of society, regardless of gender, are actively engaged in and benefit from sustainable development.

1.5.1 Social Outcomes

Gender-inclusive strategies in tourism and hospitality promote social equity by providing opportunities for women and marginalized genders to participate in decision-making processes, leadership roles, and economic activities. This inclusion enhances social cohesion within communities, as it empowers women to take active roles in shaping their futures. Research indicates that women's participation in sustainable tourism projects leads to greater community development, improved living standards, and strengthened social ties (Momsen, 2020). For instance, in rural tourism initiatives where women have been engaged in leadership or entrepreneurship, communities have witnessed more equitable access to resources, increased local investment in social services, and heightened gender awareness (Figueroa-Domecq et al., 2020a).

1.5.2 Economic Outcomes

Economic sustainability is strongly tied to the equitable distribution of resources and opportunities. Gender-sensitive strategies foster economic growth by enabling more women to enter the workforce, access better-paying jobs, and contribute to local economies. Women's participation in tourism and hospitality enterprises has been shown to increase household income and create economic diversification in many regions, especially in rural areas where other economic opportunities may be limited (Baum & Cheung, 2015). By closing the gender pay gap and ensuring equal career advancement opportunities, companies can boost employee morale, reduce turnover, and increase productivity, which are all key components of long-term economic sustainability (UNWTO, 2021).

1.5.3 Environmental Outcomes

Research suggests that gender-inclusive approaches also contribute positively to environmental sustainability, as women, particularly in rural and indigenous communities, are often the primary stewards of natural resources (Scheyvens, 2011). Women bring valuable knowledge about local ecosystems and sustainable resource management, which can be harnessed in the development of eco-friendly tourism and hospitality initiatives. When women are involved in environmental conservation and decision-making, it often leads to more effective and sustainable environmental practices. For instance, women's leadership in community-based ecotourism projects has resulted in improved conservation of natural habitats and resources (Giri & Darnhofer, 2010). Gender-inclusive environmental sustainability initiatives have been especially successful in regions like Southeast Asia, where women-led organizations have implemented programs to reduce plastic waste and promote responsible tourism. These initiatives have not only addressed environmental challenges but also provided income-generating opportunities for women, further enhancing the socio-economic sustainability of these communities (Intrepid Group, 2020).

1.6 GLOBAL AND LOCAL PERSPECTIVES

The effectiveness of gender-inclusive sustainability strategies varies significantly across global and local contexts, as regional differences shape both gender dynamics and the feasibility of implementing such strategies.

Local cultural norms, economic conditions, and political environments all play a role in determining how gender-inclusive policies are adopted and enforced.

1.6.1 Global Perspective

Globally, there is growing recognition of the importance of integrating gender into sustainability frameworks. International organizations, such as the United Nations World Tourism Organization (UNWTO) and the International Labour Organization (ILO), emphasize the need for gender equality in achieving the Sustainable Development Goals (SDGs), particularly SDG 5 (Gender Equality) and SDG 8 (Decent Work and Economic Growth). According to the UNWTO's 2021 report, tourism is one of the few sectors where women's participation in the workforce is often higher than in other industries, but significant gender disparities remain in leadership positions, wage equality, and access to resources (UNWTO, 2021). In regions such as Europe and North America, gender-sensitive policies are more likely to be enforced due to supportive legal frameworks and broader cultural acceptance of gender equality (Figueroa-Domecq et al., 2020b). However, even in these regions, challenges persist, particularly in addressing unconscious biases that hinder women's access to leadership roles.

1.6.2 Local Perspective

At the local level, cultural norms and societal expectations often have a significant influence on the success of gender-inclusive sustainability initiatives. In many parts of the world, particularly in developing countries, deeply ingrained gender roles and patriarchal structures continue to limit women's participation in the tourism and hospitality sectors. For example, in parts of the Middle East, South Asia, and Africa, cultural restrictions on women's mobility and access to education and employment create barriers to their involvement in sustainable tourism (Baum & Cheung, 2015).

However, there are successful examples where gender-sensitive strategies have been adapted to fit local contexts. In Nepal, for example, despite initial resistance, community-based tourism projects have successfully incorporated gender-inclusive approaches by providing women with leadership training and creating opportunities for them to participate in decision-making (Giri & Darnhofer, 2010). These initiatives have not only improved women's socio-economic standing but also fostered more inclusive and sustainable tourism models. Similarly, in Latin America, local tourism operators have worked with indigenous women to develop culturally appropriate ecotourism projects that empower women economically while preserving traditional knowledge and environmental sustainability (Scheyvens, 2011). These cases highlight the importance of contextualizing gender-inclusive strategies to ensure their success in different cultural and economic environments.

1.7 CONCLUSION

The integration of gender perspectives into sustainability strategies has demonstrated substantial benefits in the tourism and hospitality sectors, enhancing social, economic, and environmental outcomes. While global recognition of the importance of gender inclusion continues to grow, regional and local differences significantly influence the implementation of these strategies. Gender-sensitive approaches must be tailored to fit specific cultural, economic, and political contexts to ensure their success. The examples of both global successes and local challenges underscore the importance of adopting a flexible, context-driven approach to integrating gender into sustainability efforts, ensuring that no one is left behind in the pursuit of sustainable development.

Also, the integration of gender perspectives into the tourism and hospitality sectors is critical for achieving comprehensive sustainability goals. This analysis has demonstrated that gender-inclusive strategies foster improved social, economic, and environmental outcomes. Socially, these strategies empower women and marginalized genders, providing them with opportunities for leadership, decision-making, and economic independence, which contributes to greater community cohesion. Economically, gender equality in the workforce enhances productivity, increases household income, and creates opportunities for more diverse local economies, especially in rural areas. Environmentally, women's traditional roles as stewards of natural resources often lead to more sustainable environmental practices when they are included in decision-making processes.

Furthermore, the global recognition of the intersection between gender and sustainability is growing, but regional and cultural differences significantly affect the implementation of gender-sensitive strategies. Successful cases from organizations such as the Intrepid Group and Costa Rica's Certification for Sustainable Tourism highlight the positive impacts of gender-inclusive initiatives. However, failures, such as those in Nepal and the Caribbean, where gender issues were neglected, demonstrate the risks of ignoring gender considerations in sustainability planning. Therefore, some policy recommendations are:

1. Strengthen gender-sensitive leadership development: Tourism and hospitality businesses should prioritize leadership training and mentorship programs for women and gender minorities to address the current leadership gap. Public and private sector collaborations can foster pathways for diverse leadership, ensuring that gender considerations are embedded in decision-making processes.
2. Implement gender-inclusive workforce policies: Employers should enforce fair pay, gender-sensitive hiring practices, and equal opportunities for career advancement. Creating flexible work environments that consider work-life balance, especially for women, will encourage more gender diversity across all levels of the workforce. This also includes focusing on closing the gender pay gap, a persistent issue in tourism and hospitality industries globally.
3. Adopt gender-centric community engagement: Community-based tourism initiatives must integrate gender perspectives into their engagement and benefit-sharing models, ensuring that women and other marginalized genders are actively involved. This approach will help reduce local gender disparities and ensure that all community members benefit equitably from tourism revenue.
4. Ensure gender-disaggregated data for monitoring and evaluation: Policymakers and tourism organizations should collect and analyze gender-disaggregated data to track progress on gender equity in sustainability initiatives. Monitoring mechanisms can help identify gaps in implementation and enable stakeholders to adjust strategies based on measurable results.
5. Promote public-private partnerships: Collaboration between governments, NGOs, and the private sector can promote gender-sensitive policies and encourage knowledge sharing. Public-private partnerships have the potential to develop comprehensive strategies that address local gender dynamics while contributing to global sustainability goals.

1.7.1 Future Research Directions

While progress has been made in integrating gender into sustainability frameworks, significant gaps remain in the literature and in practice. Future research should focus on:

1. In-depth regional studies: Understanding how local cultural and societal norms affect the success or failure of gender-inclusive sustainability strategies in different parts of the world, particularly in regions with deeply entrenched gender inequalities.
2. Impact of gender-inclusive technology in tourism: Investigating how technological advancements, such as digital platforms and automation, influence gender dynamics in tourism and hospitality. This includes exploring how technology can be leveraged to create more equitable opportunities for women in the sector.
3. Longitudinal studies on gender-inclusive initiatives: Future research should track the long-term impact of gender-inclusive policies on both sustainability outcomes and gender equality in tourism and hospitality. Longitudinal data would provide valuable insights into how gender-sensitive strategies evolve and contribute to overall sustainability over time.
4. Intersectionality in tourism and hospitality: More research is needed on the intersection of gender with other forms of identity, such as race, class, and disability, in the context of sustainable tourism and hospitality. Understanding how multiple identities intersect can provide a more nuanced view of equity challenges and help in designing more inclusive policies.
5. Evaluating the role of gender in crisis management and recovery: The impact of crises, such as the COVID-19 pandemic, on gender disparities in tourism and hospitality should be further examined. Research should explore how gender-inclusive approaches can enhance resilience in crisis situations and contribute to more equitable recovery efforts.

Therefore, integrating gender perspectives into tourism and hospitality sustainability strategies is essential for creating equitable, resilient, and sustainable operations. The evidence shows that gender inclusion not only benefits women and marginalized genders but also contributes to the overall success of sustainability initiatives, leading to better social, economic, and environmental outcomes. Policymakers, industry stakeholders, and researchers must continue to prioritize gender-inclusive practices and explore innovative approaches to closing gender gaps in leadership, workforce participation, and community engagement. By addressing these challenges, the tourism and hospitality sectors can move closer to achieving their sustainability goals while promoting global gender equality.

REFERENCES

Baum, T. (2013). *International Perspectives on Women and Work in Hotels, Catering, and Tourism*. Geneva: International Labour Organization.

Baum, T., & Cheung, C. (2015). Women in tourism and hospitality: Unlocking the potential in the talent pool. *Worldwide Hospitality and Tourism Themes, 7*(3), 244–256.

Blázquez-Salom, M., Blanco-Romero, A., Vera-Rebollo, F., & Ivars-Baidal, J. (2020). Territorial tourism planning in Spain: From boosterism to tourism degrowth? In: *Tourism and Degrowth,* 20–41. Routledge. https://doi.org/10.1080/09669582.2019.1675073.

Cioccarelli, E. (2023). *Aligning Luxury With Responsibility: An In-Depth Study of ESG Implementation and Communication in Boutique Hotel.* Master's thesis, Universidade Catolica Portuguesa (Portugal).

Costa, C., Seeyitoglu, F., Malta, A.M. & Martins, M. (2023). Gender (in)equality and work-life (im)balance in tourism and hospitality labour: Perspectives of tourism organisations in Portugal. *Tourism and Hospitality Management, 29*(4), 623–626. https://doi.org/10.20867/thm.29.4.8.

Elmhirst, R. (2021). Gender and environmental sustainability. *Geoforum, 122*, 10–20. https://doi.org/10.1016/j.geoforum.2021.03.003.

Ferguson, L. (2011). Promoting gender equality and empowering women? Tourism and the third Millennium Development Goal. *Current Issues in Tourism, 14*(3), 235–249. https://doi.org/10.1080/13683500.2011.555522.

Ferguson, L., & Alarcón, D. M. (2015). Gender and sustainable tourism: Reflections on theory and practice. *Journal of Sustainable Tourism, 23*(3), 401–416. https://doi.org/10.1080/09669582.2014.957208.

Figueroa-Domecq, C., Palomo, J., Segovia-Pérez, M., & Muñoz-Mazón, A. (2020a). Gender mainstreaming in sustainable tourism. *Journal of Sustainable Tourism, 28*(7), 1040–1056.

Figueroa-Domecq, C., Pritchard, A., Segovia-Pérez, M., Morgan, N., & Villacé-Molinero, T. (2020b). Tourism gender research: A critical accounting. *Annals of Tourism Research, 52*, 87–103. https://doi.org/10.1016/j.annals.2015.03.001.

Gaard, G. (2017). Ecofeminism and climate change. *Women's Studies International Forum, 49*, 20–33. https://doi.org/10.1016/j.wsif.2017.09.001.

Gentry, K. M. (2020). Engendering tourism: Gender and development in a global local world. *Tourism Geographies, 22*(1), 120–142.

Giri, K., & Darnhofer, I. (2010). Outmigrating men: A window of opportunity for women's participation in community forestry? *Scandinavian Journal of Forest Research*, *25*(9), 55–61.

Gössling, S., & Hall, C. M. (2019). *Tourism and Sustainability: Development, Globalisation and New Tourism in the Third World* (4th ed.). Oxon: Routledge.

International Labour Organization (ILO) (2019). *Women in Business and Management: The Business Case for Change*. Geneva: ILO.

Intrepid Group (2020). Gender equality in travel and tourism leadership. https://www.intrepidtravel.com.

Madera, J. M., Dawson, M., Guchait, P., & Belarmino, A. M. (2018). Strategic human resources management research in hospitality and tourism: A review of current literature and suggestions for the future. *International Journal of Contemporary Hospitality Management*, *30*(1), 48–67.

Momsen, J. H. (2020). *Gender and Development*. Oxon: Routledge.

Mooney, S., & Ryan, I. (2009). A woman's place in hotel management: Upstairs or downstairs? *Gender in Management*, *24*(3), 195–210. https://doi.org/10.1108/17542410910950877.

Munar, A. M. (2019). The gender gap in tourism leadership. *Journal of Sustainable Tourism*, *27*(7), 999–1016.

Pritchard, A. (2018). Predicting the next decade of tourism gender research. *Tourism Management Perspectives*, *25*, 144–146. https://doi.org/10.1016/j.tmp.2017.11.014.

Scheyvens, R. (2011). Exploring the tourism-poverty nexus. *Current Issues in Tourism*, *14*(3), 243–247. https://doi.org/10.1080/13683500.2011.555522.

Seyfang, G., & Smith, A. (2007). Grassroots innovations for sustainable development: Towards a new research and policy agenda. *Environmental Politics*, *16*(4), 584–603. https://doi.org/10.1080/09644010701419121.

Seyfi, S., & Hall, C. M. (2020). Gender, tourism and development in Iran: Challenges, opportunities and prospects. *Journal of Sustainable Tourism*, *28*(9), 1377–1396. https://doi.org/10.1080/09669582.2020.1747475.

Seyfi, S., Hall, C. M., & Shabani, B. (2019). Decentralisation and tourism: Localisation of tourism development in Iran. *Journal of Sustainable Tourism*, *27*(5), 688–703.

Sigala, M. (2021). Gender issues in tourism: A strategic framework for empowering women through tourism entrepreneurship. *Journal of Sustainable Tourism*, *29*(3), 413–434.

United Nations World Tourism Organization (UNWTO) (2021). *Global Report on Women in Tourism – Second Edition*. Madrid: World Tourism Organization.

2. Tourism, sustainability, empowerment, and ethnic women: The case of Colombia

Lucellys Sierra-Marquez and Margareth Duran-Izquierdo

2.1 INTRODUCTION

Tourism is a key strategic activity in the global economy, given its significant contribution to employment, trade, and infrastructure. In an area that demands high competitiveness and sustainability, the policies implemented by destinations play a crucial role. Ensuring that sustainable development and the effective involvement of local communities become the primary focus of this activity is essential (Quang et al., 2023).

Tourism also plays a key role in achieving the Sustainable Development Goals (SDGs) from the UN 2030 Agenda for Sustainable Development. This sector significantly contributes to various goals, such as sustainable consumption and production patterns (SDG 8) and the protection of marine life (SDG 14) (Fernández-Torres et al., 2021). Additionally, it has the capacity to influence gender equality (SDG 5), promoting the empowerment of women, especially in local communities (Trupp & Dolezal, 2020). By incorporating gender issues into its policies, tourism can generate decent jobs, foster the active participation of women, and promote female entrepreneurship in local destinations (Lasisi et al., 2020). However, tourism is also considered a major threat to wildlife ecosystems (Tolvanen & Kangas, 2016) and local communities (Lukman et al., 2022).

Colombia, the second most biodiverse country in the world with significant biocultural wealth, has seen tourism emerge as a vital economic driver. The figures show a remarkable recovery after the COVID-19 pandemic; by 2023, non-resident visitors increased by 26.6% compared to

2022 (MINCIT, 2023). Thus, tourism represents a vital source of foreign exchange, employment, and contribution to GDP, especially in rural areas and ethnic communities. In this context, it is important to highlight that a report by the 'Fundación Foro Nacional por Colombia' (2019) indicates that, despite this growth, more than 70% of the revenue generated by community-based tourism is still captured by mass tourism actors, and only a small percentage of those benefits actually reach rural or ethnic communities.

The growth of tourism presents challenges in terms of environmental sustainability, social equity, and cultural preservation in the country's main destinations, with the empowerment of local communities from a social, political, and economic perspective being the main objective (Lukman et al., 2022). Sustainability should not only be seen as the need to protect natural capital; it must also involve local social and cultural development, harmonizing the interests of the communities, including ethnic communities.

In this context, the empowerment of ethnic women becomes crucial, with tourism serving as an invaluable tool and opportunity for their development. These women, who have faced structural marginalization (Vergel Barrera et al., 2021), find in tourism access to empowerment through training, economic and social opportunities, networking, and the elimination of inequality and extreme poverty. Furthermore, in many cases, they reinforce their cultural identity and contribute to the preservation of their traditions. However, for tourism to function as an effective empowerment tool, it is essential to manage initiatives that integrate tourism and gender equity as unified and cross-cutting concepts. In this way, tourism policies and projects will not only promote economic development but also address gender inequality and foster the equitable participation of women in this sector (Moreno Alarcón, 2014).

In conflict and vulnerable contexts, gender inequalities tend to intensify. Ethnic women live in vulnerable environments and face multiple layers of discrimination, including racial, socio-economic, participation, and resource access inequalities, as well as gender inequality (Wei et al., 2024). As a result, gender equity remains an even less accessible concept, limiting women's participation in economic recovery initiatives and their ability to develop on equal terms within their communities.

In Colombia, the tourism sector accounts for around 3.6% of Gross Domestic Product (GDP) and generates approximately 1.5 million direct and indirect jobs. The sector is experiencing growth in community-based, nature, and rural tourism. These tourism modalities have created spaces for the direct involvement of communities in managing tourism activities, also addressing the gender gaps faced by rural and ethnic women in the country. Women's participation in this type of tourism, which in some cases allows them to assume leadership and management roles, has enabled them to develop skills and earn their own income, boosting their empowerment in contexts where power and gender dynamics have limited their opportunities. This transformation contributes to greater gender equity, strengthens social fabric, and promotes sustainable practices, benefiting both communities and the local economy (UN Women, 2024).

This chapter employs an exploratory analysis to provide current evidence on the connections between tourism, sustainability, gender equality, and the empowerment of ethnic women in Colombia. Through specific case studies, this chapter will analyze the role of sustainable tourism as a driver of empowerment for ethnic women in Colombia and discuss the necessary actions to promote equitable and sustainable development. Ultimately, it will explore how tourism can be a powerful tool for social change and ethnic female empowerment in the Colombian context.

2.2 METHODOLOGY

The methodology for gathering information for this chapter was developed in two phases:

Phase 1: Literature Review

This phase included academic studies and tourism initiatives related to sustainability and women's empowerment, particularly in ethnic communities in Colombia.

Selection criteria

The selected studies encompassed publications from 2000 to 2024 in indexed journals, with a primary focus on sustainable tourism, the participation of ethnic women, and economic and cultural empowerment in Colombia. Additionally, the review incorporated tourism initiatives developed by non-governmental organizations (NGOs), public entities, and community associations, provided that a gender component was included.

Information sources

The search for academic studies was conducted in scientific databases such as Scopus, Web of Science, and Google Scholar. For tourism initiatives in Colombia, data collection included reports from NGOs, websites of community projects, and international cooperation programs related to tourism and gender.

Search strategy

The literature review phase included a set of keywords such as "sustainable tourism," "female empowerment," "Indigenous communities," and "SDGs in Colombia". The analysis involved an exhaustive review of the references in the selected articles to ensure the inclusion of all relevant studies.

Data analysis and evaluation

The categorization and analysis of the information were carried out manually, identifying key themes such as "gender and tourism," "sustainability practices," "challenges faced by ethnic women," and "empowerment policies". For the tourism initiatives, the impacts were evaluated using criteria such as female participation, changes in leadership roles, and the sustainability of the projects. Finally, it is important to mention that the main limitation of the review is the limited availability of empirical studies on the empowerment of ethnic women in Colombian tourism, reflecting a need for broader research in this area.

Phase 2: Interviews with Female Leaders in the Tourism Sector

The second phase of this research focused on conducting semi-structured interviews with female leaders from ethnic or rural communities who actively participate in the tourism sector. These interviews aimed to explore in depth their experiences, challenges, and opportunities.

Participant selection

The selection criteria for completing the survey were to lead or have led sustainable tourism projects in ethnic communities. Thirty women were selected through purposeful sampling.

Design of the interviews

The interviews were conducted using a Google Forms questionnaire (Annex 1) with questions about participation in tourism, empowerment, challenges, and sustainability.

Procedure

The questionnaire was distributed online, allowing flexibility in participation.

Analysis of results

A qualitative manual analysis was conducted to identify common themes related to empowerment and barriers in sustainable tourism.

2.3 RESULTS AND DISCUSSION

Literature Review

The tourism projects mentioned in Table 2.1 highlight tourism as a key tool for female empowerment. Through these initiatives, women have developed more inclusive and sustainable tourism practices, enabling them to take leadership roles in the sector while gaining economic independence and strengthening their roles in decision-making within their communities.

Many of these initiatives also promote the elevation of ancestral worldviews and local traditions to visitors, fostering a type of tourism based on cultural education. These activities, in the long term, encourage the identity and appreciation of Indigenous people and communities.

However, it is important to emphasize that the positive impact of tourism on female empowerment largely depends on factors such as structured governance, social capital, and equitable distribution of resources to ensure that female empowerment is sustainable and truly transformative.

Survey Results

The survey conducted was aimed at ethnic or rural women working and engaging in tourism, specifically those with leadership roles in their communities and tourism ventures. A total of 23 tourism leaders completed the survey. Various types of entrepreneurship have always existed within ethnic communities, helping sustain traditional economies and ecologies. In this way, the adoption of Indigenous tourism can also play

Table 2.1 Study of initiatives related to women and tourism in Colombia

Study/project title	Objective or purpose	Gender perspective/empowerment and sustainability	Bibliography
Community-based tourism, social capital, and governance of post-conflict rural tourism destinations: The case of Minca, Sierra Nevada de Santa Marta, Colombia	Contributes to the theoretical and empirical analysis of the relationships between community-based tourism, social capital, and governance in post-conflict contexts.	This study demonstrates that tourism barely benefits communities when there is insufficient social capital and unstructured governance due to the low presence of the government.	Rocca and Zielinski, 2022
Chachita Ecotourism Lodge in Nuquí, Chocó	To offer tourism and gastronomic services led primarily by women.	Women's leadership in tourism and business management.	https://ue.parquesnacionales.gov.co/?portfolio=posada-ecoturistica-chachita-sas
Chira Tuse Ethno-Tourism Route	To showcase other aspects of the municipality through the Indigenous worldview, gastronomy, birdwatching, handicrafts, and the community's own history.	Led by the Indigenous Cabildo Nueva Isla of Valle del Guamuez, Putumayo, allowing active participation and leadership of Indigenous women in local tourism.	https://www.mincit.gov.co/prensa/noticias/turismo/mujeres-colombianas-protagonizaran-nuevo-turismo

Study/project title	Objective or purpose	Gender perspective/empowerment and sustainability	Bibliography
Native Inns of San Andrés, Providencia, and Santa Catalina	Strengthen the economy of the Raizal people by supporting local entrepreneurs in designing cultural and nature tourism offers under the community tourism model.	Support, education, and transformation of daily activities into sources of employment and economy, involving women in leadership activities.	https://www.posadasnativas.co
You, Woman	Opportunities for the development and internationalization of women-led entrepreneurial projects in the tourism industry.	Sustainability in integrating community tourism with local cultural practices.	https://procolombia.co/sala-de-prensa/noticias/procolombia-impulsa-el-liderazgo-femenino-en-el-turismo
Wayúu Women in Tourism (La Guajira)	Develop cultural and sustainable tourism in the Wayúu territory, promoting women's participation in managing and promoting regional tourist attractions.	Training in leadership, business management, and preserving local culture. Ecotourism that respects the Wayúu worldview and the conservation of the La Guajira desert.	https://www.radionacional.co/cultura/mujeres-wayuu-las-manos-que-tejen-la-vida
Ecotourism with Entrepreneurial Women in Choco	Offer tourist experiences in the Choco region, focusing on biodiversity, led by Afro-Colombian women.	Afro-Colombian women manage accommodations, wildlife watching, and local crafts, strengthening their economic autonomy.	https://sicec.eu/article/99/

Study/project title	Objective or purpose	Gender perspective/empowerment and sustainability	Bibliography
Wirakoku Foundation: Tourism in the Kogui Indigenous Community (Sierra Nevada de Santa Marta)	Develop a tourism model that respects the nature and ancestral culture of the Kogui, Arhuaco, Wiwa, and Kankuamo Indigenous peoples.	Indigenous women actively participate in managing and promoting tourism, transmitting their worldview and ancestral practices.	https://www.instagram.com/wirakoku/
The Women of the San Juan River (Choco)	Promote ecotourism in the Río San Juan region, an area rich in biodiversity, with a focus on Afro-Colombian communities.	Afro-Colombian women lead tourist activities, generating income and increasing their autonomy.	https://www.portafolio.co/tendencias/mujeres-sostienen-familias-artesanias-111142
Land of Women (Cabo de la Vela, La Guajira)	Promote ecotourism in Cabo de la Vela, with a focus on strengthening the role of Wayúu women in tourism.	Wayúu women are involved in organizing and promoting tourism, generating income.	https://news.un.org/es/story/2022/05/1508782
Raizal Women in Tourism (San Andres, Providencia, and Santa Catalina)	Develop cultural and ecological tourism on the islands, with an inclusive focus on Raizal women.	Raizal women lead tourism initiatives, promoting their Afro-Caribbean culture.	https://colombiavisible.com/las-mujeres-raizales-que-con-artesanias-preservan-su-identidad-y-crean-espacios-seguros/

Source: Prepared by the authors based on a literature review.

this same role (Scheyvens et al., 2021). Figure 2.1 shows the ethnic affiliation of the participants, with 50% being Indigenous women, followed by women from rural or farming communities (40%).

When addressing the issue of the type of tourism or activities developed by the communities, the results indicate that cultural and community-based tourism, particularly in relation to ethnic communities, is the most predominant form (Figure 2.2). This type of tourism not only allows communities to share their rich cultural heritage and traditions, but it also fosters meaningful exchanges between visitors and residents. Moreover, by focusing on the unique aspects of each community, it strengthens the preservation of their identities and customs, while generating sustainable economic opportunities.

Formality in tourism activities represents one of the sector's main challenges, as its adoption not only strengthens business structures but also enhances the economic and social benefits that can be derived from them. Figure 2.3 illustrates the level of formality achieved by businesses led by women, highlighting significant progress in this area. In particular, it is noted that 74% of the participants hold a formal role, indicating growing inclusion and empowerment of women in the tourism industry.

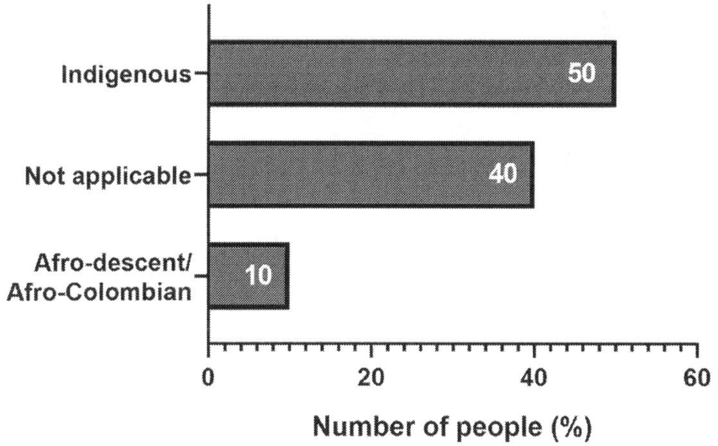

Source: Prepared by the authors.

Figure 2.1 *Ethnic affiliation of the women participants in the survey*

Source: Prepared by the authors.

Figure 2.2 *Word cloud with the main tourism activities led by ethnic women in Colombia*

This progress not only contributes to the sustainability of the sector but also lays the foundation for a more equitable and prosperous future.

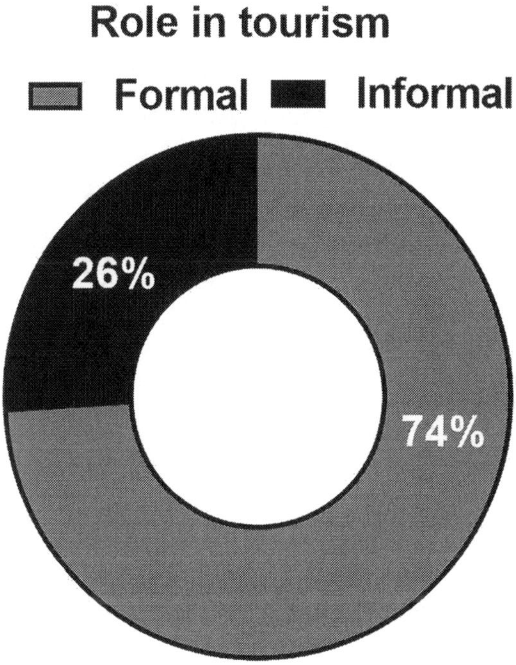

Source: Prepared by the authors.

Figure 2.3 *Formality of women-led tourism initiatives*

The survey included a component aimed at assessing tourism as a tool for empowerment from a gender perspective, analyzing its specific impact on ethnic women (see Figure 2.4). The results reveal that these women have experienced a notable increase in their financial independence, with 87% acknowledging this benefit. Furthermore, 74% report an improvement in their quality of life, while 78% have experienced greater recognition of their role within their community. Although these are important findings, it is essential to note that, while the participating women have improved their economic situation by meeting their basic needs, this does not imply an equitable distribution of resources between women and men—a situation that is crucial to promote sustainability and social justice (UN Women, 2024).

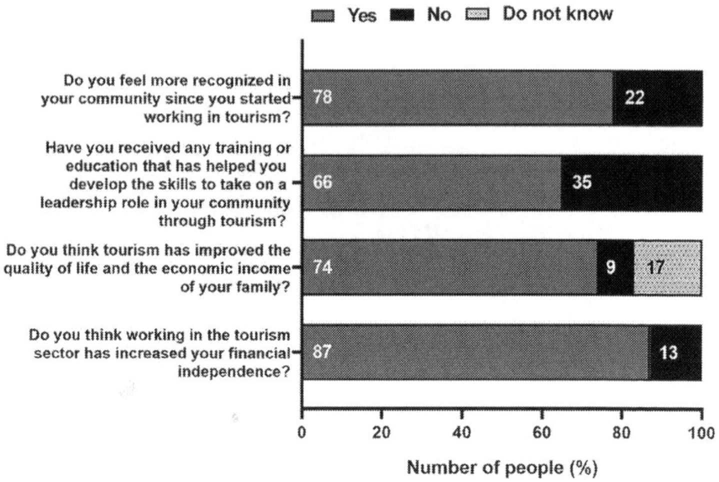

Source: Prepared by the authors.

Figure 2.4 Empowerment component and gender perspective in tourism

In this same context of empowerment, training plays a crucial role in promoting female participation and leadership across various sectors. While the majority of the survey respondents reported having received some form of training, 35% indicated that they had no access to any kind of training. This highlights the urgent need to continue creating learning and training opportunities, especially in rural areas where access to these resources is even more limited. This is key to the role of women's leadership in fostering community autonomy and a sense of community (Silva Dos Santos et al., 2024). Strengthening skills, building capacities, promoting digital literacy to manage tourism businesses, and recognition of the importance of Indigenous peoples by destination authorities and the tourism sector in general are also crucial.

In analyzing the gender equity component in the tourism sector, which aimed to address the influence of gender dynamics in the industry and focused on the specific experiences and challenges women face, it was observed that 61% of the respondents perceive that men predominantly hold decision-making roles in the tourism sector of their communities.

While this figure reflects inequality, it has improved compared to other studies, suggesting progress toward inclusion.

Tourism has emerged as a crucial platform for women to assert and promote their rights, achieving a significant positive impact in 91% of cases, particularly in regards to cultural and gender identity. This dynamic highlights how participation in the tourism sector not only fosters economic empowerment but also allows women to bring visibility to their reality.

However, despite these achievements, 52% of the interviewees reported experiencing discrimination in the tourism sector due to their gender. This data reveals the persistence of barriers that limit equal opportunities (see Figure 2.5).

The final component concerned limitations and challenges, and aimed to identify and analyze the barriers and challenges faced by women in the tourism sector in Colombia, with the purpose of understanding how these limitations affect their professional development and empowerment.

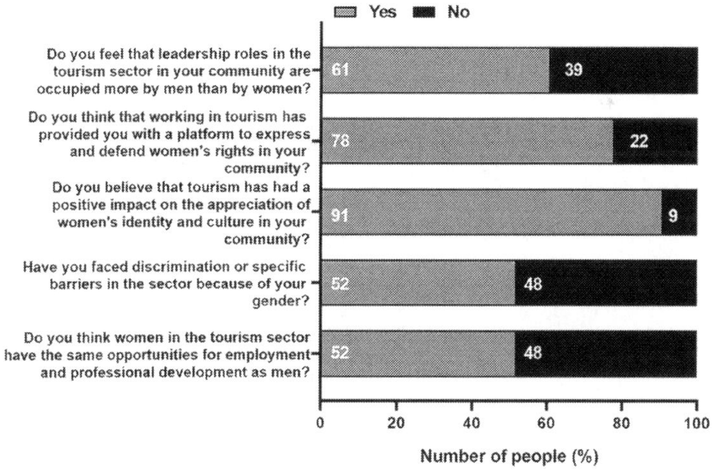

Source: Prepared by the authors.

Figure 2.5 *Gender equity component*

Regarding the perception of the effectiveness of government policies on gender equity, 52% of participants (see Figure 2.6) noted that progress has been made, with the potential for further change. This highlights the fundamental need to integrate gender policies with the country's tourism policies in order to align these efforts for the empowerment and gender equity of women. Achieving tourism sustainability is very difficult if the gender focus is not integrated into its development.

Regarding the availability of support networks and mentorship within their communities, a remarkable 83% of respondents stated that these networks do exist, which is a promising indicator of solidarity and community-based support among women. Nevertheless, this underscores the need to further strengthen and expand these networks, providing more structured education, training, and mentorship opportunities so that women can build careers and access leadership and managerial roles in both tourism and their communities.

Additionally, when asked about the recognition of their contributions to community tourism, 56% of participants expressed feeling unappreciated, suggesting a general perception of invisibility in their roles and efforts. Finally, 61% of respondents stated that domestic responsibilities

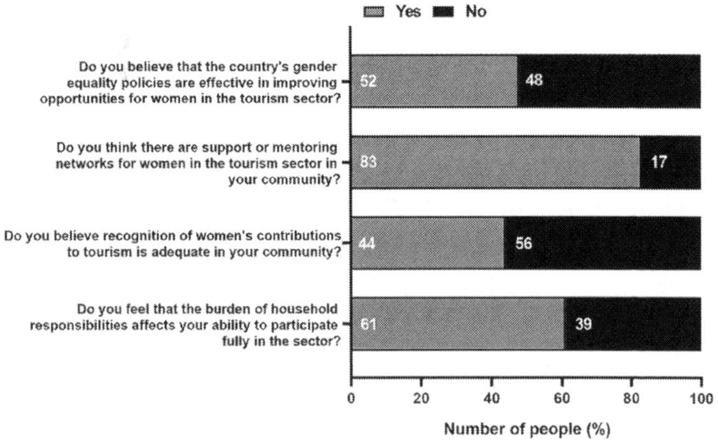

Source: Prepared by the authors.

Figure 2.6 *Challenges for the tourism sector in empowerment and gender equity*

negatively affect their participation in the sector, limiting their opportunities for growth and continuity in the tourism industry.

2.4 CONCLUSIONS

In Colombia, community-based tourism led by women has proven to be an effective means of promoting their empowerment. By taking the initiative in the creation and management of tourism projects, women have enhanced their economic independence and strengthened their participation in decisions that affect their communities.

To continue advancing gender equity in the tourism sector, it is essential that public policies not only promote economic growth but also integrate gender equity and sustainability as core principles. Only in this way can tourism be developed responsibly and in a manner that benefits all stakeholders, especially women.

Despite the progress made, women, particularly those from rural and ethnic communities, continue to face significant obstacles. Structural inequalities related to gender and ethnicity hinder their access to leadership roles and participation in the opportunities that tourism provides, limiting their ability to influence the development of their communities.

Training in key areas such as leadership, tourism enterprise management, and the preservation of local culture, along with the establishment of support networks, is crucial to transforming power structures within communities. These efforts not only enhance women's skills but also enable them to challenge the traditional barriers that have limited their development and access to opportunities.

For the benefits of tourism to reach all parties equitably, tourism policies must focus on ensuring that women, especially in rural and ethnic communities, receive a fair share of the generated income. This will contribute to a tourism development model that is not only economically viable but also socially just, promoting equal opportunities and the well-being of all community members.

REFERENCES

Fernández-Torres, Y., Gutiérrez-Fernández, M., & Gallego-Sosa, C. (2021). Environmental performance of the tourism sector from a gender diversity perspective. *International Journal of Environmental Research and Public Health*, *18*(16), 8834. https://doi.org/10.3390/ijerph18168834.

Fundación Foro Nacional por Colombia (2019), https://foro.org.co/revista/.

Lasisi, T. T., Alola, A. A., Eluwole, K. K., Ozturen, A., & Alola, U. V. (2020). The environmental sustainability effects of income, labour force, and tourism development in OECD countries. *Environmental Science and Pollution Research*, *27*, 21231–21242.

Lukman, K. M., Uchiyama, Y., Quevedo, J. M. D., & Kohsaka, R. (2022). Tourism impacts on small island ecosystems: Public perceptions from Karimunjawa Island, Indonesia. *Journal of Coastal Conservation*, *26*(3), 14. https://doi.org/10.1007/s11852-022-00852-9.

MINCIT (2023). Informe mensual de turismo. https://www.mincit.gov.co/estudios-economicos/estadisticas-e-informes/informes-de-turismo/2023. https://www.mincit.gov.co/getattachment/estudios-economicos/estadisticas-e-informes/informes-de-turismo/2023/diciembre/oee-yv-turismo-diciembre.pdf.aspx.

Moreno Alarcón, D. (2014). El camino del turismo con igualdad El caso de Cartagena de Indias, Colombia. *Memorias: Revista Digital de Historia y Arqueología desde el Caribe*, *23*, 26–51. http://www.scielo.org.co/scielo.php?script=sci_arttext&pid=S1794-88862014000200003&lng=en&tlng=es.

Quang, T. D., Nguyen, Q. X. T., Nguyen, H. V., Dang, V. Q., & Tang, N. T. (2023). Toward sustainable community-based tourism development: Perspectives from local people in Nhon Ly coastal community, Binh Dinh province, Vietnam. *PLOS One*, *18*(10), e0287522. https://doi.org/10.1371/journal.pone.0287522.

Rocca, L. H. D., & Zielinski, S. (2022). Community-based tourism, social capital, and governance of post-conflict rural tourism destinations: The case of Minca, Sierra Nevada de Santa Marta, Colombia. *Tourism Management Perspectives*, *43*, 100985.

Scheyvens, R., Carr, A., Movono, A., Hughes, E., Higgins-Desbiolles, F., & Mika, J. P. (2021). Indigenous tourism and the sustainable development goals. *Annals of Tourism Research*, *90*, 103260.

Silva Dos Santos, C., Lugosi, P., & Hawkins, R. (2024). Trust, traditions and Indigenous women's leadership in sustainable tourism management. *Journal of Sustainable Tourism*, *33*(1), 1–17.

Tolvanen, A., & Kangas, K. (2016). Tourism, biodiversity and protected areas: Review from northern Fennoscandia. *Journal of Environmental Management*, *169*, 58–66. https://doi.org/10.1016/j.jenvman.2015.12.011.

Trupp, A., & Dolezal, C. (2020). Tourism and the sustainable development goals in Southeast Asia. *ASEAS-Austrian Journal of South-East Asian Studies*, *13*(1), 1–16.

UN Women (2024). The gender snapshot 2024. https://www.unwomen.org/en/resources/gender-snapshot?gad_source=1&gclid=CjwKCAiAxKy5BhBbEiwAYiW--9C5I7x7pa1Dvc_2OcyQ68NsDHyqkjVl1wGujAy5fb59kjXbsXG12hoC3RMQAvD_BwE.

Vergel Barrera, M. D., Muñoz, M., & Ximena, L. (2021). Mujer indígena, desigualdad social y quebrantamiento de sus derechos. *Novum Jus*, *15*(1), 251–275. https://doi.org/10.14718/novumjus.2021.15.1.11.

Wei, A., Zhang, Y. B., Robertson, E., Steen, J., Mushquash, C., & Wekerle, C. (2024). Global Indigenous gender concepts, gender-based violence and resilience: A scoping review. *Child Abuse & Neglect, 148*, 106185.

ANNEX 1

Survey

Women, Tourism, Sustainability, and Gender Perspective in Colombia

Objective

This survey aims to explore the experiences and challenges of women working in the tourism sector in Colombia, with a special focus on sustainability, women's empowerment, and gender equity. It seeks to understand how tourism has impacted their lives and how it contributes to the personal, social, and economic development of women in various communities, especially ethnic ones.

Demographic Information

What is your age?

- What is the name of your community/neighborhood/locality?
- Do you belong to an ethnic community? If yes, indicate which one: Indigenous Black Afro-descendant / Afro-Colombian Raizal / Palenquera Roma (Gypsy) Not applicable
- Is your work in the tourism sector formal or informal? Formal / Informal

Empowerment

- What is your role in tourism?
- Briefly describe the activities you perform in the tourism sector (e.g., guiding, hospitality, hiking, cultural tourism).
- How long have you been working in the tourism sector? Less than 1 year / Between 1 and 5 years / More than 5 years
- Do you consider that working in the tourism sector has increased your financial independence? Yes / No

- Do you think tourism has improved your family's quality of life and income? Yes / No / Not sure
- Have you received any training that has helped you develop leadership skills in your community through tourism? Yes / No

Gender Perspective

- Do you feel more recognized in your community since you started working in tourism? Yes / No
- Do you think women in the tourism sector have the same employment and professional development opportunities as men? Yes / No
- Have you faced discrimination or specific barriers in the sector due to your gender? Yes / No
- Do you think tourism has had a positive impact on valuing women's identity and culture in your community? Yes / No
- Has your work in tourism given you a platform to express and defend women's rights in your community? Yes / No
- Do you feel that leadership roles in the tourism sector in your community are more often held by men than by women? Yes / No

Limitations and Challenges

- Do household responsibilities affect your ability to fully participate in the sector? Yes / No
- Do you think women's contributions to tourism are adequately recognized in your community? Yes / No
- Are there support or mentorship networks for women in the tourism sector in your community? Yes / No
- Do you believe that national gender equality policies are effective in improving opportunities for women in the tourism sector? Yes / No

3. Exploring intersections: Tourism, gender, and paths to peace: The case of women in The Gambia

Carmen Parra Rodríguez and Rogelio Garcia Contreras

3.1 INTRODUCTION

Travel and tourism have been proven to provide women with more opportunities for empowerment compared to other industries, giving the sector increased responsibility for the advancement of women (Inda, 2016, p. 47). According to the UN Global Report on Women in Tourism by the World Tourism Organization, tourism provides better opportunities for women's participation in the workforce, women's entrepreneurship, and women's leadership than other sectors of the economy. For example, the report found that women were nearly twice as likely to be employers in the tourism sector than in any other industry (Ireland, 1993).

However, women are also more likely to be involved in tourism due to the unique characteristics of the tourism sector (Kinnaird & Hall, 1996, p. 99; Figueroa-Domecq & Segovia-Pérez, 2020). The barriers to entry are low, particularly in terms of skill requirements and capital. There is less emphasis on formal education and training and greater emphasis on personal and hospitality skills (Mooney, 2020; Zhang, 2021). There are increased options for entrepreneurship that do not require heavy start-up financing. Moreover, the nature of the work can be quite flexible in terms of working hours and part-time or full-time employment (Bianchi and De Mans, 2021). However, jobs in tourism are also likely to be low-earning, with businesses being smaller, less well-capitalized, and informal.

The Gender Assessment of the Tourism Sector in The Gambia aims to document the existing gender disparities and key gendered challenges in tourism for inclusive economic growth in The Gambia. Tourism is the second largest contributor to The Gambia's GDP and a key source of job creation. The assessment in this chapter aims to understand women's participation in the tourism sector in The Gambia where gender gaps are among the widest in the region and the world. More specifically, it aims to demonstrate the gender disparities in participation and earnings; assess the underlying barriers and binding constraints to women's participation and better economic outcomes in tourism; and provide targeted recommendations to be incorporated into the implementation of the World Bank Tourism Diversification and Resilience in The Gambia project (P177179),[1] as well as create a knowledge base for future interventions.

The chapter explores key issues in women's employment, entrepreneurship, and leadership within the tourism sector while examining cross-cutting factors that impact women's economic opportunities as well as their decision-making capabilities, such as policy and institutional environment, social norms, and education (Markussen and Røed, 2017). To guide policies and programs within tourism that aim to enhance women's economic empowerment, the chapter also analyzes wage employment, self-employment, and leadership in different trades as their interventions and stakeholders could be different. Policies, social norms, and education are analyzed as important contextual factors determining outcomes in these three areas. In addition, the chapter unpacks the impact of diversification of tourism activities, such as ecotourism and conference tourism, on women's economic outcomes.

3.2 METHODOLOGY

3.2.1 Framework

The gender gap analysis examines women's participation in tourism through three lenses: employment, entrepreneurship, and leadership. Employment and entrepreneurship are seen as principal objectives for increasing women's participation and earnings in tourism (Kimbu & Ngoasong, 2016). They are treated separately as the stakeholders and interventions can be quite different. For example, how to encourage hotels to hire more women staff requires a different intervention than

---

1 https://projects.worldbank.org/pt/projects-operations/project-detail/P177179.

how to encourage hotels to procure from women-owned enterprises. The third pillar, leadership, is seen both as an enabling factor that can support bringing about the proper policies needed to support women's employment and entrepreneurship but also as a key outcome on its own. While assessing the status of women in leadership roles within tourism and more broadly, women's presence in wider decision-making mechanisms is also taken into consideration.

The ecosystem and stakeholder assessment examines the enabling environment through three cross-cutting areas: policy and institutional environment, social norms, and tourism education. These are explored as the key external factors contributing to women's outcomes in employment, entrepreneurship, and leadership.

Table 3.1 covers the framework and key areas to examine the barriers and binding constraints to growing women's participation in the sectors of employment, entrepreneurship, and leadership.

3.2.2 Data Collection

The first step in the assessment was desk research. The World Bank Group's Gender Data Portal,[2] UNDP's Gender Development Index,[3] World Economic Forum's Global Gender Gap Report,[4] and the Women, Business and the Law report also from the World Bank Group[5] provided useful initial background information on how The Gambia was performing on gender equality. The National Tourism Strategy, National Gender Strategy, and Country Partnership Framework[6] provided an understanding of the broader policy landscape of the country. The assessment also took note of descriptive statistics on gender gaps shared in country surveys or in other surveys such as World Bank Enterprise Surveys.[7]

Recent research conducted in The Gambia contributed invaluable insights to the gender assessment of the tourism sector. Some of these resources include The Gambia Poverty and Gender Assessment

---

2 https://genderdata.worldbank.org/en/home.

3 https://hdr.undp.org/gender-development-index#/indicies/GDI.

4 https://www.weforum.org/publications/global-gender-gap-report-2023/.

5 https://wbl.worldbank.org/en/wbl.

6 https://www.worldbank.org/en/projects-operations/country-strategies.

7 https://www.enterprisesurveys.org/en/enterprisesurveys.

Table 3.1 Gender assessment framework for the tourism sector

Gender assessment of the tourism sector	Employment	Entrepreneurship	Leadership
What are the gender disparities?	Gender disparity in participation and earnings The type of jobs (high value vs low value) and composition in sub-sectors	Gender disparity in participation and earnings The type of businesses (informal, micro, etc.) and the info on sub-sectors	Where/how do women participate in leadership and decision-making in the tourism sector? How does this compare to men?
What are the key issues / barriers?	Key issues: • Supply side (e.g., transport, childcare, training, safety) • Demand side (e.g., employer bias, hiring practices, legal barriers)	Key issues: • Skills • Access to finance • Access to markets • Networks • Information	Key issues: • Gender discrimination • Skills shortages at managerial levels • Sexual harassment
Ecosystem factors (cross-cutting) • Policy and institutional environment • Social norms and gender-based violence • Education and skills	–	–	–

Gender assessment of the tourism sector	Employment	Entrepreneurship	Leadership
• Who are the key stakeholders? • Other policy stakeholders and community organizations	• Hotels (hiring) • MSMEs • Training institutions	• Women-led businesses • Hotels and other larger firms (procuring) • Intermediaries	• Government agencies • Associations • Political representation

Source: Author's own.

2022,[8] Policies for Sustainable and Inclusive Private Sector-led Growth: Achieving Sustainable and Inclusive Growth in The Gambia,[9] and the Project Appraisal Document of The Gambia Tourism Diversification and Resilience Project (P177179)[10] among others.

Following the desk research, the assessment undertook a mapping of the stakeholders with a few important considerations. First, the authors identified a number of actors in the five economic activities that generate revenues and income in the tourism sector (transport, accommodations, excursions, food and beverage, and shopping). Depending on the size of each sub-economic activity and the conditions in the field, the authors interviewed a representative number of stakeholders to reflect diversity of experience and opinion. In addition, relevant stakeholder suggestions by the Project Implementation Unit of the current Gambia Tourism Diversification and Resilience Project were included in the list. Finally, the assessment tried to ensure a balance of female and male participants in the stakeholder meetings.

Key informant interviews and focus group discussions were conducted in The Gambia in May 2023. The 22 organizations interviewed included industry associations, training institutes, direct tourism service providers in accommodation, tour excursions, crafts sellers, hotel and restaurant personnel, enablers, development partners, and NGOs. In addition, the authors interviewed multiple hotel staff, fruit sellers, and tour guides, and conducted a focus group with women entrepreneurs in different industries across the tourism value chain, facilitated by The Gambia Women's Chamber of Commerce.

The in-person assessment also resulted in the collection of data from tourism organizations such as The Gambia Tourism Board and The

---

8 https://documents.worldbank.org/en/publication/documents-reports/documentdetail/099530111032210190/p1771390c18b5d0c60896b0a2b66d6e4f32.

9 Policies for Sustainable and Inclusive Private Sector-led Growth Achieving Sustainable and Inclusive Growth in The Gambia, https://mocde.gov.gm/wp-content/uploads/2023/10/PRIVATE-SECTOR-DEVELOPMENT-AND-EMPOWERMENT-STRATEGY-2024-Through-ICTs.pdf.

10 https://documents.worldbank.org/en/publication/documents-reports/documentdetail/764921654609947116/gambia-tourism-diversification-and-resilience-project.

Gambia Tourism and Hospitality Institute. Though available to a certain extent, finding sex-disaggregated data was a challenge throughout the assessment. The in-country assessment filled some gaps in data and provided a complementary analysis, but more data will need to be systematically collected to shed light on the issues women face in the tourism industry as well as any progress made going forward.

The assessment's focus was less on rural areas and more on urban tourism centers, though it investigated community-based tourism in rural areas, which carries a potential for tourism and women's economic opportunities in The Gambia. The in-person consultations mostly took place around more urbanized centers such as Serrekunda and Banjul, except for in the case of a few eco-lodges that were visited where staff were interviewed. Even though the assessment has not conducted in-depth interviews in villages, there were interviews that took place around Kunta Kinteh Island and with community-based tourism actors such as the Institute of Travel and Tourism of The Gambia. The assessment recognizes the key linkages, especially agricultural, between the rural economy and the tourism ecosystem. Where necessary, the analysis tried to fill in the gaps with the study Barriers to Economic Empowerment of Rural Women in The Gambia,[11] which has a strong focus on rural women and findings from relevant key informant interviews.

Table 3.2 covers stakeholder consultations, especially tourism providers operating in The Gambia in services, public sector, associations, and training institutes.

3.3 THE GAMBIA CONTEXT

3.3.1 Tourism in The Gambia

Tourism is an important contributor to the GDP and a source of jobs in The Gambia, but the sector lags behind its competitors due to fewer arrivals, shorter stays, and lower expenditures. This mainly results from limited diversification in source markets, distribution channels, and product offerings, leading to high seasonality, modest spillover effects, and susceptibility to climate risks and shocks. Pre-pandemic, tourism's

[11] https://documents.worldbank.org/en/publication/documents-reports/documentdetail/099810001222232967.

Table 3.2 *Stakeholder consultations – The Gambia, direct tourism service providers*

Accommodation	African Princess Hotel
Tour excursions	Sunset Beach Hotel Ocean Bay Hotel Footsteps Eco Lodge Kairaba Hotel
Food and beverage	Timotours (local tour) Discovery Tours
Shopping	Senegambia Craft Market Focus Group Entrepreneurs
Public sector	The Gambia Tourism Board The Gambia Tourism and Hospitality Institute National Center for Arts and Culture Ministry of Health
Industry associations	The Gambia Chamber of Commerce and Industry The Gambia Women's Chamber of Commerce The Gambia Hotel Association
Training institutes	The Gambia Tourism and Hospitality Institute Tourism of The Gambia (ITTOG) CSC Gambia (Cruise recruitment)

Source: Author's own.

direct contribution to GDP was estimated to be between 12 and 16%. Tourism supported over 42,000 jobs directly and another 40,000 jobs indirectly (UNDP, 2020).[12] It generated an annual US$85 million in foreign exchange earnings, making it the country's number one foreign exchange earner.[13] High seasonality variation—with passenger arrivals in the low season at about 40% of the high season—is a critical issue impacting employment and earnings.

Despite its rich asset base, The Gambia has barely diversified away from "sun and sea" tourism into other areas such as ecotourism and

[12] https://www.undp.org/es/publicaciones/informe-anual-del-pnud-2020.

[13] WB The Gambia Poverty & Gender Assessment (2022), https://documents1.worldbank.org/curated/en/099530111032210190/pdf/P1771390c18b5d0c60896b0a2b66d6e4f32.pdf.

culture tourism. According to the World Economic Forum's Travel and Tourism Development Index, The Gambia ranks 62 out of 140 countries when it comes to the total number of known fauna species and 58 on the attractiveness of natural assets index. It is also among the countries with the highest number of United Nations Educational, Scientific and Cultural Organization (UNESCO) sites in the Sub-Saharan region, with two cultural heritage sites (Stone Circles of Senegambia and Kunta Kinteh Island), and one intangible expression (the "Roots" Festival commemorating the experiences of the descendants of African slaves who were taken from the region during the transatlantic slave trade). Nevertheless, tourist sites are currently in a state of poor maintenance and require substantial enhancements, a challenge addressed by the World Bank's Tourism Diversification and Resilience in The Gambia project. Furthermore, the country's infrastructure needs improvements and is under the looming threat of climate change. Erosion has affected the UNESCO site of Kunta Kinteh Island, shrinking its size annually and endangering its integrity and tourism value. And, considering that over half of the nation's population resides in urban regions and around 80% of the urban population is situated within a 20 km range of the Atlantic coast, the anticipated increase in sea levels presents a significant peril.

3.3.2 Status of Women in The Gambia

The gender gap in The Gambia is substantial. According to the 2023 World Economic Forum Global Gender Gap Report, the country ranks 119th out of 146 countries in gender equality. In the UNDP Gender Inequality Index (GII), which analyzes three dimensions—reproductive health, empowerment, and the labor market—The Gambia ranks 153rd out of 170 countries. More broadly, in the UNDP Human Development Index (HDI), which measures progress in basic dimensions of human development, The Gambia ranks 174th out of 191 countries and is placed in the low human development category.

Women and girls in The Gambia confront a complex web of challenges. Limited access to education persists, with factors like poverty, early marriage, and cultural norms hindering girls' enrollment and retention in schools. According to World Bank Gender Data Portal,[14] only 51% of women can read and write compared to 62.5% of men. The gap in

[14] https://genderdata.worldbank.org/en/home.

adult literacy between men and women is larger than the gap in the Sub-Saharan Africa aggregate. Child marriage remains prevalent, disrupting education, endangering young mothers, and perpetuating poverty and gender inequality. Despite the criminalization of female genital mutilation (FGM) in The Gambia, the practice remains common. About 50% of girls aged 0–14 years have undergone FGM, and one in every two women endorses the practice.[15]

Women lack access to paid work, and labor market opportunities are particularly limited for young women. In The Gambia, the labor force participation rate (the proportion of the population aged 15 and older that is economically active) among females is 57.3% and among males is 65.8% for 2022, according to the World Bank Gender Data Portal. Women are 3.7 times more likely to be unpaid helpers in family businesses and 26% times more likely to be engaged in subsistence agriculture, according to the World Bank Gender and Poverty Assessment. Most women are in vulnerable employment, which means they are less likely to have formal work arrangements, social protection, and safety nets to guard against economic shocks; thus, they are more likely to fall into poverty. Vulnerable employment among women is 81.3% and among men is 62.7% in The Gambia for 2019, according to the World Bank Gender Data Portal.

The level of women's involvement in decision-making and leadership roles in The Gambia continues to be limited. Women in The Gambia rank 132nd out of 146 countries in regards to their political empowerment, according to the 2023 World Economic Forum Global Gender Gap Report. Women's roles are often delineated by traditional gender norms, impacting their access to education, employment opportunities, and decision-making power. Gender-based violence is also a prevalent issue; one in four women has been subjected to physical and/or sexual violence by a current or former intimate partner.

In the domain of self-employment, where a significant number of women are involved, women face difficulties in opening bank accounts and accessing formal credit due to underlying constraints that disadvantage women.

[15] https://www.unicef.org/gambia/press-releases/its-past-time-silence-men-and-boys-too-must-stand-against-fgm.

3.3.3 Tourism Segments in The Gambia

By far the most predominant tourism sector, the beach—"sun and sea"—is still the main attraction for about 80% of tourists. The sector is heavily reliant on international tour operators (ITOs), which bring in 50–70% of all tourists, control 70% of all air access and international marketing, and contribute 85% of all hotel revenues (The Gambia Country Partnership Framework).[16] Tourists predominantly come from select markets in Europe—particularly the UK and Netherlands. This assessment analyzes women's participation in the hotels' workforce and the role of women-led businesses in hotel value chains.

The diversification of the tourism offering in The Gambia, especially *conference tourism*, *ecotourism*, and *community-based tourism*, could lead to promising economic outcomes for women, both in terms of improving women's employment and women-led Micro, Small Medium Enterprises (MSMEs) accessing new markets, contributing to inclusive economic growth opportunities (Anyanwu & Augustine, 2013). Due to limited diversification, distribution channels, and product offerings, The Gambia currently lags behind its competitors. Diversification carries new possibilities for women's economic involvement in the sector while also broadening the sector and boosting the economy.

Ecotourism combines well with community-based tourism, creating additional employment opportunities for women, such as birdwatching tours, cooking demos, etc. This is in line with various studies which show that women could be psychologically, socially, economically, and politically empowered by their participation in ecotourism ventures (Deori & Das, 2013; Irandu & Shah, 2014). Ninki Nanka Trail, which offers community-based tourism in rural communities along the Gambia River, was designed to promote travel during the low season, between May and October. Its focus is on sustainable tourism to benefit host communities, businesses, and the environment. The Gambia Tourism Board has a code of conduct for Ninki Nanka Trail tour operators, both domestic and international, including a condition to be an ethical business with decent employment practices and to maintain a policy on gender equality and decent working conditions.

---

[16] https://documents.worldbank.org/en/publication/documents-reports/documentdetail/450591652556583165/gambia-country-partnership-framework-for-the-period-fy22-26.

Research shows that developing nature-based and sustainable tourism could also help attract high-value tourism. Recent World Bank consumer research on three key European outbound markets (Germany, Sweden, United Kingdom), which are also important for Gambian tourism, identified five market segments among travelers.[17] Three of these segments, which account for 66% of respondents, focus on nature-based and sustainable tourism and are the highest spending of all traveler types. These tourists actively seek distinctive experiences, aspire to connect with local communities and enterprises, view travel as a means of education, and are committed to sustainable practices. Attracting more of these tourist segments by changing the marketing strategy and increasing the supply of active, nature-based experiences, coupled with targeted strategies to employ women, could positively impact women both as producers of local goods and services and as actors in community-based and ecotourism.

3.4 DATA ANALYSIS

3.4.1 Gender Disparity in Employment

There are five key economic activities that generate revenues and income in the tourism sector – transport, accommodations, excursions, food and beverage, and shopping. Women's participation within each of these activities varies, as do the explanations and interventions needed. In all key economic activities of Gambian tourism, male workers are employed at higher numbers than women, with the gender gap smaller for part-time work in some activities. Women constitute 35% of all full-time employees in the tourism sector compared to 65% of men, with a resulting gender gap of 30 percentage points. The gender gap in employment drops for part-time work. Women comprise 42% and men make up 58% of part-time employees, resulting in a smaller gender gap of 16 percentage points.

Two-thirds of the tourism jobs are heavily concentrated in accommodations, accounting for 64% of men's and 58% of women's tourism employment. In part-time work, the gender gap in employment in accommodations drops to 3 percentage points, showing that women are more likely to be hired as part-time employees in hotels and other

[17] https://www.worldbank.org/en/publication/wdr2022.

accommodation establishments. The next largest employment area is food, beverage, and entertainment. This accounts for nearly a quarter of tourism jobs and close to one-third of women's employment in the sector.

Hotels constitute more than one quarter of all accommodation jobs, but only one third of hotel employees are female. Women work as receptionists, waitresses, housekeeping staff, or as managers in HR, finance, and marketing. They are more likely to be part-time or paid seasonal workers. Among the large hotels, data collected by one study shows that women represent, on average, 15% of the workforce, ranging from a minimum of 4% to a maximum of 35%.

Transport and excursions are heavily male-dominated. According to 2018 data, 85% of full-time and 89% of part-time workers in transport are male. Excursions are also male-dominated, with almost all tour guides being male in the country. Being a tour guide is seen as almost impossible once a woman is married or has children, mainly due to the long hours involved and also due to the possibility that clients are only male. However, there is female ownership of tour operator outfits.

3.4.2 Gender Disparity in Entrepreneurship

Women show strong willingness to participate in the hospitality industry, given that their enrollment rates in The Gambia Tourism and Hospitality Institute are higher than men. However, this is not translating to employment in the hotel industry, due to a combination of key supply- and demand-side barriers identified. Female labor force participation could remain low due to a lack of skills, assets and networks; time-based constraints; limited mobility; gender discrimination in hiring and promotion; and restrictive gender norms (Halim et al., 2023). The key informant interviews suggest that women are switching to alternative jobs or self-employment due to an interplay of factors.

The restricted hours that women typically work within the tourism and hospitality sector might potentially result in a bias towards selecting male candidates over female ones. Most businesses have a policy of not hiring women for shifts after 4 pm. Though this is not a legal requirement, it is a de facto practice due to a variety of cited reasons, including safety and cultural norms. As a result, this might be leading to a preference in hiring men as there is greater flexibility in employing men for both day and night shifts.

Tourism businesses might be favoring women for part-time work over full-time work also partially due to maternity policy. Businesses in The

Gambia are legally obligated to implement a 6-month paid maternity leave policy for female employees. Paid paternity leave is available for up to 10 days for fathers. Some interviews suggest that this results in favoring women for part-time work or male candidates over female ones. In other countries, such as São Tomé and Príncipe, this maternity leave bias is eliminated as it is social security that pays for the leave rather than the companies. The Women, Business and the Law (2023) report lists "laws affecting women's work after having children" as one area for improvement to enhance legal equality for women in The Gambia. Offering only leave for mothers, especially above a threshold of 30 weeks, can be correlated with fewer women in the workforce (Del Rey et al., 2021). Studies show that a smaller gap between mothers' and fathers' leave is associated with a higher female labor force participation rate.

While stigma is key, it is vital to recognize that safety concerns in regards to late-hour shifts are also likely to contribute to low levels of women's participation. Transportation takes up a significant portion of income of all hotel staff, but safety in the late hours can be an additional constraint, especially for women. Traveling home can require 2–3 stops and street lighting is cited to often be insufficient. According to the Gallup World Poll in 2021,[18] 69% of women in the country declared not feeling safe walking alone at night in the city or area where they live, while only 39% of men said the same. This is much higher than the Africa average, where 49% of women in the country declared not feeling safe walking alone at night. To tackle this challenge, some larger hotels arrange transportation options for staff, but this is not the case for all establishments and is often expressed as an issue by hotel staff.

Women lack information about lucrative tourism jobs and prior experience. In The Gambia, women's lack of information about lucrative tourism jobs and their lack of prior experience or training seem to contribute to low female participation in some roles. For example, interviews with staff from tourism organizations revealed challenges with recruiting female tour guides, where cultural norms and women's lack of information about the trade were cited as the two main challenges. Tour companies prefer candidates with prior tour experience, and since it is a male-dominated trade, women have difficulty breaking into it. Research shows that providing early exposure to and training in male-dominated

---

18 https://www.gallup.com/analytics/318875/global-research.aspx.

sectors, and information about trade earnings could support women to cross over into more male-dominated roles and sectors.[19]

The seasonality of work also makes it difficult for women to participate if there is no income for half the year. As women are more likely to be on part-time contracts, they are less likely to stay on the payroll of larger hotels all year round. As a result, many women switch to self-employment to stay economically engaged year-round and to control their working hours as well.

Micro, small, and medium-sized enterprises (MSMEs) play a key role in the economy as wage opportunities are scarce in The Gambia. MSMEs in The Gambia contribute about 20% of GDP and employ approximately 60% of the urban labor force. Nine in ten businesses are micro businesses, i.e., either one-person businesses or family businesses.[20] Moreover, they constitute a crucial source of work for Gambian youth (those aged 18–35 years), who own more than 40% of MSMEs. Approximately one in six women and one in four men aged 15 to 64 is the owner of her/his own business.

Despite the prevalence of self-employment among women, women own smaller businesses compared to men, employ fewer people, and have lower profits than male-led businesses in The Gambia. According to The Gambia Poverty and Gender Assessment 2022, 83.4% of female-led businesses were just one-person businesses compared to 63% of male-led businesses. Close to 2% of female-run businesses were small, while 12% of male-run businesses were small. Less than 1% of female-run businesses are medium or large.[21] The same assessment shows that median monthly profit was 3000 GMD for a female-led business, while it was 5000 GMD for a male-run business, demonstrating a profit gap.

As the literature shows, the gender gap in business performance is attributed to the gender-related limitations that women encounter when

[19] Breaking Barriers: Female Entrepreneurs Who Cross Over to Male-Dominated Sectors report, https://www.worldbank.org/en/topic/gender/publication/breaking-barriers-female-entrepreneurs-who-cross-over-to-male-dominated-sectors.

[20] The Gambia Poverty & Gender Assessment 2022, https://documents1.worldbank.org/curated/en/099530111032210190/pdf/P1771390c18b5d0c60896b0a2b66d6e4f32.pdf.

[21] The Gambia Poverty & Gender Assessment 2022 notes that these are estimations based on LFS 2018 and looks at ages 15 to 64.

initiating, maintaining, and expanding their businesses. In Sub-Saharan Africa, women are more likely to be entrepreneurs than men, and yet their businesses earn only two-thirds the profits of their male-owned counterparts (World Bank, 2019).[22] The significant gender gap in earnings is not a result of inherent variations in the skills of male and female entrepreneurs. Instead, there are multiple underlying contextual constraints such as legal discrimination, social norms, and the risk of gender-based violence; endowments such as education/skills, confidence/risk preferences, finance and assets, and networks and information; and, finally, household-level constraints such as care and allocation of factors of production.

Increased revenue of tourism-related MSMEs is a key country priority, as also indicated in the Country Partnership Framework. The MSMEs within the sectors of accommodation, food and beverage, and travel and tours have exhibited a higher level of economic activity. Nevertheless, the presence of exclusive agreements between ITOs, accommodation providers, and ground tour operators has limited the potential for numerous MSMEs to partake in the existing tourism value chain. Furthermore, the impacts of COVID-19 have rendered many businesses in the tourism sector susceptible to concurrent shocks in both supply and demand.

Women are craft sellers, beach fruit sellers, tour operators, and restaurant owners and contribute indirectly to the tourism sector as vegetable and food suppliers, with their catering, beauty and skin care, and fashion businesses. Economic activities in the tourism industry are often intertwined with other sectors. The transport sector is heavily male-dominated. There is a large share of women's participation in the crafts market, however mainly for beaded jewelry, cloth, and baskets. In beauty, there is an increasing number of women entrepreneurs who use the local plants/trees of the country to make oils, such as baobab oil.

3.4.3 Leadership and Decision-Making

Women's participation in decision-making and leadership remains low in The Gambia. While the United Nations at the 1995 Beijing Conference on Women set a gender quota of 30% for women's representation in decision-making processes, the actual representation of women in leadership roles falls far below this standard (Segovia-Pérez et al. 2019). Women

22 https://www.worldbank.org/en/publication/wdr2019.

constitute only 8.6% of the Gambian parliament, while 91% of the parliamentarians are men, ranking The Gambia 168th out of 186 countries worldwide. This falls behind the Sub-Saharan Africa average as well as the world average.[23] In the executive, only three of the 22 ministers in the current Cabinet are women, at the local level eight out of 120 councilors are female, and among traditional council leadership only 13 of the 1,887 *Alikaalo*[24] are female. Women represent a full 57% of the registered electorate in The Gambia, but they play mostly supporting roles, e.g., as voters and party organizers and mobilizers. Often, when a woman and a man want to run for the same political party, the woman is asked to step aside to make room for the man.[25]

Leadership positions in the upper echelons of companies are lacking in terms of female representation (Moreno Alarcón, 2018). According to World Bank Enterprise Surveys in 2018, only 10% of firms have a female top manager and 17% of all firms have female participation in ownership. These are significantly lower than the Sub-Saharan Africa average, which is 16% for top management and 31% for female ownership.

None of the leading tourism organizations in the ecosystem are headed by women, though women have a presence at other levels. Even though tourism globally provides better opportunities for women's leadership than other sectors of the economy, none of the key public tourism players such as The Gambia Tourism Board, The Gambia Tourism and Hospitality Institute, and National Center for Arts and Culture (NCAC) are headed by women. On the private sector side, female representation has been better. There is some female presence among general managers (GMs) of hotels; approximately 3–4 out of some 40 hotels have a woman GM. Aside from GMs, women are often managers in back-office positions such as accounting and sales. Additionally, The Gambia Hotel Association and the Travel and Tourism Association of The Gambia have had women in leadership positions at various times in their history.

---

[23] IPU Parline (December 2022), Monthly ranking of women in national parliaments, https://data.ipu.org/women-ranking?month=6&year=2023.

[24] The *Alikaalo* is the traditional Gambian village chief of the founding family; however, today they are elected.

[25] Summary Report: A Conversation on the Political Empowerment of Women in The Gambia. https://gambia.un.org/en/194076-conversation-political-empowerment-women-gambia.

Gender norms, discrimination, and stereotypes, combined with forms of gender-based violence such as sexual harassment, are some factors that contribute to keeping women from leadership positions. In The Gambia, about three-quarters (74%) of citizens say women should have the same chance as men to run for political office. Economically better-off citizens (86%) and those with post-secondary education (84%) are more likely to agree with this view. However, 60% of Gambians think that if a woman runs for public office, she will likely be criticized or harassed by others in the community, and 40% think she will probably face problems with her family. Cultural phenomena have created the stereotype "impression that men are superior and women are inferior" and a "socialization process [that] has also led men and women to perceive men as leaders and women as supporters". These perceptions are alleged to "put women in the private sphere as wives, mothers and daughters and men in the public domain of decision-making", as well as in the economic and political arenas.

3.5 CONCLUSION

To enhance gender mainstreaming in tourism within The Gambia, a holistic set of policy recommendations spanning employment, entrepreneurship, leadership, and public policy has been outlined.

3.5.1 Employment

Improving women's employment and earnings in tourism requires addressing both demand-side constraints and biases, as well as supporting women's willingness and capacity to enter into tourism. Encouraging female employment will require addressing some of the financial concerns, safety infrastructure, and cultural norms. Specific recommendations include:

- Recognizing hotels with high levels of female staff, female managers, and those offering paid maternity leave to encourage and incentivize hotels to hire and retain female staff. Moreover, such recognition would resonate well with ecotourists, who are more sensitive to socially sustainable lodgings.
- Creating an inclusive work environment through measures such as implementing anti-harassment laws and systemic mechanisms for

reporting and dealing with abusive behavior, so that women feel protected in the sector.

- Showcasing the diversity of employment opportunities within the hospitality sector at the high school level to help overcome the stigma of the sector and encourage women to enter the sector.
- With almost all hotel employees going through The Gambia Tourism and Hospitality Institute Hospitality School and relying on their placement, ensuring that women are placed at equivalent rates to their enrollment numbers would reduce bias and increase confidence. Incorporating personal initiative training and other gender-sensitive training into their offerings would also improve earning outcomes for women.
- Improving women's earnings by increasing their training, particularly in management skills but also in the culinary arts. The general shortage of management skills in the tourism sector, plus the current drain caused by the cruise industry, has opened an opportunity to onboard women employees who are more likely to stay on than their male counterparts.

3.5.2 Entrepreneurship

Limited markets and lack of skills are key hindrances to women-owned businesses in The Gambia. Improving access to markets and helping women to serve both domestic and tourist markets—especially given the high-low swings of the tourism season—can make businesses more sustainable. Likewise, skill development and support to expand offerings, particularly in locally produced products but also in higher skilled jobs, such as event planners and marketing and logistics staff in the conference tourism sector, could open more opportunities for women entrepreneurs. Recommendations to support women entrepreneurs include:

- Providing training and market connections to hotel value chains. There are various opportunities in hotel sourcing from more staple products, such as eggs and poultry (which often face shortages) and tropical fruits, to other niche agricultural products, such as unique high-end vegetables, provided hotels and chefs are also onboarded to diversify their menu offerings.
- Facilitating partnerships with grocery stores and hotels to sell locally made items, such as honey, jams, snacks, scrubs, etc. In addition,

providing training and packaging support to women entrepreneurs to improve the quality and presentation of their products. Technical assistance could also be paired with financial assistance.

- Engaging with craftswomen on how to expand or customize their offerings to bring in higher revenues, for example through conduct training workshops for skill development in new artisan offerings.
- Providing an elevated artisan craft space for locally produced products and unique handicrafts, in part to resolve the low turnover constraints of the existing craft stalls, but also to provide a centralized space for more innovative entrepreneurs and artisans to sell their products.
- Given the pervasive use of cell phones, creating a platform to connect women entrepreneurs to training and marketing events. E-commerce is just starting to take off, and helping women access and market on these platforms can broaden their sales and client outreach.
- Providing training programs that tackle both hard and soft skills. Personal initiative training is one key curriculum that could be added to the program to encourage more innovation.

3.5.3 Leadership, Public Policy, and Support

Mainstreaming gender in tourism will require leadership in bringing together different stakeholders and getting their buy-in for the changes. While women's role in The Gambia's tourism sector is gradually improving—with more women entering upper management in hotels, as well as in key tourism and business associations—translating that to better results on the ground will take additional actions, such as:

- Making informed policy decisions. More gender-disaggregated data is needed in the tourism sector, particularly data on earnings. While there is information on employment in tourism, data on businesses or self-employment in tourism is less available, providing an incomplete view.
- Increasing the placement of women managers in government agencies related to tourism.
- Identifying best practices from hotels that have sought gender diversity and incentivizing others to replicate.

- Developing a strategy to expand and advertise community-based tourism, which could open pathways for women, particularly in more rural areas of the country.
- Strengthening the legal and regulatory environment faced by women in relation to their economic participation. The Women, Business and Law (WBL) analysis shows that areas of improvement include: enacting legislation protecting women from sexual harassment in employment and adopting criminal or civil penalties for sexual harassment in employment.
- Tackling offenses in the tourism industry by implementing measures such as a specialized hotline for gender-based violence (GBV) incidents within the sector. This will enhance the current response systems for GBV and ensure the availability and accessibility of information regarding GBV and support services for survivors, complementing other ongoing initiatives.

This comprehensive approach aims to create a more inclusive and diverse tourism sector in The Gambia, fostering economic empowerment and equitable opportunities for women.

REFERENCES

Anyanwu, J. C., & Augustine, D. (2013). Gender equality in employment in Africa: Empirical analysis and policy implications, *African Development Review*, *25*(4) 400–420.

Bianchi, R. V., & De Mans, F. (2021). Tourism, inclusive growth and decent work: A political economy critique. In: *Justice and Tourism. Principles and Approaches for Local-Global Sustainability and Well-Being*, edited by Tazim Jamal, James Higham. Oxon: Routledge, 1–19.

Del Rey, E., Kyriacou, A. & Silva, J.I. (2021) Maternity leave and female labor force participation: Evidence from 159 countries. *Journal Population Economics*, *34*, 803–824.

Deori, S., & Das, N. (2013). Ecotourism in wetland environment: A case study of Deepar Beel Wildlife Sanctuary. *Revista Brasileira de Ecoturismo*, *6*(2), 354–365.

Figueroa-Domecq, C., & Segovia-Pérez, M. (2020). Application of a gender perspective in tourism research: A theoretical and practical approach. *Journal of Tourism Analysis*, *27*(2), 251–270.

Halim, D., O'Sullivan, M. B., & Sahay, A. (2023). Increasing female labor force participation. *World Bank Group Gender Thematic Policy Notes Series*.

Inda, N. (2016). La perspectiva de género en investigaciones sociales. In En Verschuur, C. (ed.) *Des brèches dans la ville: Organisations urbaines, environnement et transformation des rapports de genre.* Geneva: Graduate Institute Publications, 37–54.

Irandu, E. M., & Shah, P. (2014). The role of ecotourism in promoting women empowerment and community development: Some reflections from Kenya, *Journal of Tourism and Hospitality Management*, *2*(6), 245–259.

Ireland, M. (1993). Gender and class relations in tourism employment. *Annals of Tourism Research*, *20*(4), 676.

Kinnaird, V., & Hall, D. (1996). Understanding tourism processes: A gender-aware framework. *Tourism Management*, *17*(2), 95–102.

Kimbu, A. N., & Ngoasong, M. Z. (2016). Women as vectors of social entrepreneurship. *Annals of Tourism Research*, 60, 63–79.

Markussen, S., & Røed, K. (2017). The gender gap in entrepreneurship – the role of peer effects. *Journal of Economic Behavior and Organization*, *134*, 356–373.

Mooney, S.K. (2020). Gender research in hospitality and tourism management: Time to change the guard. *International Journal of Contemporary Hospitality Management*, *32* (5) 1861–1879.

Moreno Alarcón, D. (2018). Feminist perspectives in the development of action plans for tourism. In: Cole, S. (ed.) *Gender Equality and Tourism: Beyond Empowerment.* Wallingford, UK: CABI, 24–33.

Segovia-Pérez, M., Figueroa-Domecq, C., Moraleda, L., & Muñoz, A. (2019). Incorporating a gender approach in the hospitality industry: Female executives' perceptions. *International Journal of Hospitality Management*, *76*(A), 184–193.

The 2023 Women, Business and the Law report lists https://openknowledge.worldbank.org/entities/publication/e0437bc9-bac8-4486-959e-5be1dd45f253.

UNWTO (n.d.) https://www.unwto.org/.

Travel & Tourism Development Index 2024, https://www.weforum.org/publications/travel-tourism-development-index-2024/.

Zhang, J. (2021). A qualitative comparative analysis of tourism and gender equality in emerging economies. *Journal of Hospitality and Tourism Management*, *46*, 284–292.

4. Contribution of women's activity to development of agritourism on the island of Lesvos

Panoraia Poulaki, Theodoros Rachiotis, and Nikolaos Vasilakis

4.1 LITERATURE REVIEW

4.1.1 Agritourism – International and Greek Area

Agritourism combines the activities of agriculture with tourism, offering visitors the opportunity to have authentic experiences in the countryside and get to know the local culture and tradition (Adams, 2008). Agritourism can be defined as tourism activities that take place in rural areas and include staying on farms, engaging in agricultural activities, and consuming local products.

Agritourism can be traced back to ancient times when people traveled to learn about different agricultural practices and to exchange knowledge and technologies. In modern times, agritourism began to develop systematically after the Second World War, when rural areas faced serious economic problems and were looking for new sources of income (Wall, 2004). There is a growing demand for experiential and authentic experiences, as visitors want to actively participate in rural activities and learn about local traditions and practices (Poulaki et al., 2021a). There is a growing emphasis on sustainability and environmental awareness, with agritourism destinations promoting environmentally friendly practices.

Agritourism is a key driver for promoting sustainable development in rural areas, providing multiple benefits for both the local community and the environment. It also contributes to the diversification of farmers' incomes and to strengthening the local economy by creating new jobs and attracting tourism expenditure (Knowd, 2001). Many farms involved in agritourism preserve traditional practices and buildings, providing visitors with knowledge and experiences of the history and culture of the area, thus enhancing the cultural identity of the community (Ndlovu & Rogerson 2004).

Agritourism promotes education and understanding of agriculture and rural life. It also enhances social cohesion and cultural heritage by preserving and promoting customs and traditions (Amaral & Edgar, 2010). Agricultural EU policies have encouraged a shift from traditional production models to more complex business models in Europe, with agritourism being a primary element of this transition.

Italy and France were among the first countries to strongly promote agritourism by offering visitors the opportunity to participate in rural activities. Italy, in particular, is a model for the development of rural tourism (Šostar et al., 2024). The development of this form of tourism began in the 1980s. Agritourism has grown significantly due to the country's rich cultural and gastronomic heritage. Agritourism businesses offer a combination of agricultural and tourist services. The state has contributed to the development of agritourism through rural tourism organizations such as Terra Nostra, Turismo Verde, and Agriturist, which organize and promote agritourism businesses and provide professional training. Agritourism accommodations in Italy include reconverted castles, autonomous farmhouses, and rooms in farmhouses near farmland or urban areas (Porcaro, 2009). The income of many Italian farmers is fully dependent on agritourism, making it an important area of growth and innovation for business activity.

In France, agritourism is also well developed, with many farms offering gastronomic experiences, accommodation, and participation in rural activities (Knowd, 2001). This form of tourism has developed rapidly. The state contribution has been strong, with various practices to encourage farmers to switch to agritourism. One important body is Bienvenue à la ferme, founded in 1988 and currently involving 10,000 farmers, which helps to organize and promote agritourism businesses in terms of services and products. Agritourism accommodation in France is characterized by its long stretches of land next to roads or rivers.

Germany also has a long tradition of agritourism, with over 150 years of history, due to people's desire to visit non-industrial areas. Agritourism facilities include farmers' houses, farmhouses, or campsites next to farmland with various activities such as horse riding, fishing, and cycling.

Agritourism also began to develop in the United States in the 1960s in the form of "farm and ranch hospitality". At the same time, other forms of this type of tourism began to appear, such as agricultural and rural tourism (Pittman, 2006; Brown & Reeder, 2007). In the United States, agritourism often takes the form of educational tours, farm visits, and sales of local products directly to consumers, while in Canada agritourism includes activities such as winery tours, participation in farm work, and accommodation in farmhouses (Busby & Rendle, 2000).

Many rural businesses can be considered as agritourism, such as farms offering accommodation, bed and breakfasts, barns, camps, ranches, etc. (Ollenburg, 2006). Agritourism emerged in Australia in the 1970s, where farm women played an important role in the development of this form of tourism. It developed into a multi-dimensional business activity that usually takes place in non-urban areas, offering visitors the experience of rural life. In addition to the contribution of women, the state has played a key role in the development of rural tourism in Australia by dynamically supporting the primary sector with subsidies (O'Halloran et al., 2000). There are more than 700 farms in Australia that provide agritourism services catering to the needs of thousands of visitors. These farms are divided into full-time, part-time, retirement, and lifestyle categories, and offer activities such as domestic animal husbandry, dairy farming, and crop cultivation.

In India, agritourism activities include traditional experiences such as participating in farm work and staying on farms. Agritourism in China began to emerge in the 1980s and was mainly driven by government initiatives aimed at poverty reduction. In China, agritourism is growing rapidly, with agritourism farms offering activities such as tea harvesting, rice farming, and learning about traditional Chinese agriculture (Ying & Zhou, 2007; Gao et al., 2008). The development of agritourism in China contributed to the emergence of *Nongjiale*, also known as the "happy farmer's house". *Nongjiale* combines elements of local cultural heritage with the natural environment of the area where they are embedded. In China, there are over 20,000 to 30,000 *Nongjiale* communities in each province. The contribution of rural tourism to the Chinese economy is very significant, and it has provided positive impacts both economically and socially. Agritourism has helped to boost local economies by providing new sources of income for farmers and enhancing rural development. Through *Nongjiale*, farmers have been able to offer hospitality, local products, and cultural experiences to visitors, enhancing sustainable tourism development and protecting cultural heritage. Agritourism in China continues to grow with local communities adapting to changes and innovating to attract more visitors.

In Greece, agritourism began to gain ground in the 1980s with the support of European funding programs and the promotion of rural areas as tourist destinations. Agritourism in Greece seems to have started after 1983, as a result of a series of socioeconomic changes in the 1980s. An important contribution to this was made by the country's accession to the European Economic Community.

The European Union has contributed significantly to the development of rural tourism in Greece through funding programs. In the 1980s, the Mediterranean Integrated Programmes (MIPs) played a key role in boosting employment. In the 1990s, programs such as LEADER (Liaison Entre Actions de Développement de l'Économie Rurale), and others subsidized by the Greek state, contributed to the development of rural tourism (European Commission, 2023). In the last 20 years, these programs have been implemented through the National Strategic Reference Framework (NSRF) (European Commission, 2021). The creation of the first women's agritourism cooperatives, initiated by women and supported by various entities—including the General Secretariat for Equality and Human Rights, the Greek National Tourism Organisation, the Employment Organisation of Labour Force (OAED in Greece), and other bodies—was also crucial to the development of agritourism in Greece.

An important initiative/action of the state mechanism was the creation of the Organized Rural Area Development Programs (OPAX). These programs were designed to support remote rural areas, with the Ministry of Agriculture as the main body, and started in 1999. OPAX aimed to reduce the isolation of mountainous areas, level out local inequalities, and promote less developed areas by highlighting their competitive advantages.

The Ministry of Rural Development and Food announced the launch of a new grant program entitled "Green Rural Tourism" in 2022. With this program, it aims to strengthen the position of farmers, promote environmentally friendly innovations, and develop experiential agritourism and sustainable development within the region (ESPA.io., n.d.). The region of Pelion provides a successful example of agritourism development, having benefited significantly from initiatives such as Green Rural Tourism. Its traditional architecture, local gastronomy, and natural beauty have made it a popular destination for tourists year-round (Viljoen & Tlabela, 2007).

Agritourism plays a particularly important role in the region of Crete. Through agritourism activities, local populations can preserve and highlight their traditions, and tourists can expect to experience local festivals, traditional songs, and dances. Tourists also participate in activities such as the preparation of Cretan food using traditional recipes and local products (Poulaki, et al., 2021b). Crete offers a variety of agritourism experiences that can meet the needs and interests of every visitor, such as participating in olive harvesting and olive oil production, and visiting local wineries for wine tasting. Several traditional farms and houses in Crete have been converted into guesthouses and accommodation, offering visitors the opportunity to live in an authentic Cretan environment. The first operational agritourism destination in Crete is the settlement of Milia, founded in 1993. It is one of the most well-known agritourism destinations internationally. It is a purely agritourism-based enterprise located in the mountains of the prefecture of Chania and was originally redeveloped from the homonymous settlement, which had been deserted. The picturesqueness of the settlement has been preserved, and the accommodation has the necessary facilities to meet basic needs. The appearance of both the exterior and the interior are influenced by the local traditional aesthetics. Various activities, such as hiking, cooking, preparation of local products with raw materials from the settlement, and excursions to nearby destinations, accompany a pleasant stay in the 13 wood and stone houses (Milia Mountain Retreat, n.d.).

Another agritourism business on the island of Crete is the Enagron accommodation in the village of Axos in the prefecture of Rethymno, which has been active in the area for more than 20 years. It started to operate as private accommodation serving the needs of its owners for rest and contact with nature, and in the process, it began operating as hospitality accommodation (Enagron Ecotourism Village, n.d.). The business was included in the LEADER 2 program, from which it received funding and which resulted in it taking the form it does today. It is a unique farm with a vineyard, garden, animal area, dining room, cafeteria, swimming pool, and spa area. The building coexists harmoniously with the surrounding environment and perfectly combines the rural lifestyle with comfort and luxury. The agritourism activities allow visitors to either participate in or watch the production of goods, such as raki or cheese, using materials from the farm and the wider region. The farm attracts visitors mainly from Europe but also from Crete itself (Ecotourism Greece, n.d.).

Another interesting Greek agritourism business is the Perleas Guesthouse in Kampos on the island of Chios. The agritourism enterprise has restored the mansion "Perleas", which was built in 1640, and turned it into a guesthouse. The accommodation has eight luxurious rooms that are decorated with handmade furniture, and breakfasts made with products from the estate are provided to the guests. The mansion is surrounded by a garden where organic citrus trees blossom, and visitors are given the opportunity to take care of the trees and harvest the fruits (Perleas Mansion, n.d.).

When comparing Greece with other European countries, where agritourism is more developed, it is evident that it is necessary to create a national plan for the strategic policy development and management of agritourism in the country (Poulaki et al., 2021a).

4.1.2 Female Entrepreneurship and Agritourism

Female entrepreneurship provides the possibility of an identity and offers actions, acquiring the characterization of the "process of socialized character" (Drakopoulou-Dodd, Anderson, 2007; Poulaki, et al, 2021a). Female entrepreneurship is theoretically part of a globalized economic context, a context that in recent years has caused a homogenization in the productive and cultural sector at the international level as well as a similarity of characteristics in each state or destination (Carpio et al., 2008; Poulaki, et al., 2021a).

In many European regions, there is environmental and cultural diversity which offers the possibility of developing new employment opportunities for women. This concerns both urban areas and areas where organic agricultural production flourishes, where women acquire new roles with important professional activities (Ventura, 1994; Poulaki et al., 2021a). Gender and female creativity play an important role in the promotion of agritourism, as women entrepreneurs create in an innovative way, utilizing their imagination and exploiting the combined and unique resources they have (Poulaki, et al., 2021a).

The review of the literature highlights the aspirations of female entrepreneurship that contribute to the development of agritourism both internationally and in Greece. Many researchers have addressed the specific research field of female entrepreneurship from the perspective of female creativity, focusing on their creative imagination (Al-Dajani & Marlow, 2013; Poulaki, et al., 2021a). The social system is often gender-bound due to the integration of institutionalized structures, preventing women from realizing new ideas and creating businesses (Welter, 2011; García & Welter, 2013; Poulaki et al., 2021a). There are many references to international examples of female entrepreneurship related to gender correlation and tourism development, how their well-being is achieved, and therefore their "empowerment" through development programs (Poulaki et al., 2021b).

The dynamic presence of female creativity in Greece and in the world of entrepreneurship appears in the 1980s with women entrepreneurs engaged in agricultural life and entrepreneurship, founding the first women's cooperatives, with a great example being that of the island of Lesvos and specifically the Municipality of Petra. The involvement of women in the business world is intense. An important role is played by tourism that creates jobs and contributes fundamentally to the development and competitiveness of several regions (Camisón et al., 2017) with huge social and cultural benefits beyond economic development for a tourist destination (Hieu & Rasovska, 2017; Poulaki, et al., 2021a; Rachiotis & Poulaki, 2024a).

Tourism at the international level, due to its flexibility, capacity, and its particularities, strengthens the unequal division of labor and the income criteria of women (Peeters, Ateljevic, 2009; Poulaki et al., 2021a). The motivation is quite great for women to engage in agritourism. Gender balance at both the professional and personal levels is a key concern of the European Union (Mills et al., 2014). In many European countries, visitors are strongly motivated to participate in agricultural activities and get to know the wealth of agricultural cooperatives. Female participation in cooperatives at both local and regional scales offers further value to a tourist destination (Poulaki, et al., 2021b).

4.1.3 Case Study – Island of Lesvos

Lesvos, the third-largest island of Greece and one of the largest in the Mediterranean, is in the northeastern Aegean Sea. The island is known for its rich history and culture. Lesvos has a Mediterranean climate with mild winters and warm summers, suitable for tourism and agricultural activities. The biodiversity of Lesvos is extremely rich with more than 1,000 species of plants and over 200 species of birds, and is an important destination for birdwatching. The wetlands of the Gulf of Kalloni and Polihnitos are characteristic and attract numerous bird species. It offers unique experiences to its visitors, combining natural beauty, traditional lifestyle, and local flavors (Discover Greece, n.d.). In recent years, there has been a shift towards special and alternative forms of tourism with an emphasis on agritourism, which can contribute to the economic development of the area while at the same time promoting the protection of the natural environment and the preservation of local traditions.

Lesvos has many natural resources, such as olive groves, vineyards, livestock farms, and cultural monuments linked to rural traditions. Hiking and cycling activities are also popular on Lesvos, with many trails crossing the island's mountainous and coastal landscapes. The hot springs of Eftalou and Polihnitos offer unique opportunities for relaxation and wellness, attracting visitors seeking natural healing (https://www.lesvosgeopark.gr/gastronomia/agrotouriistikoi-synetairismoi/).

The history of the island, which stretches from antiquity to modern times, has left indelible marks on its cultural identity (Poulaki, et al, 2021a). Archaeological finds, museums and many historical monuments offer unique experiences to visitors, allowing them to explore the history and cultural heritage of Lesvos. In addition, cultural events organized throughout the year enrich the visitor's experience and highlight the tangible and intangible cultural heritage.

The gastronomy of Lesvos is an integral part of its cultural identity, with traditional dishes based on local products and recipes passed down from generation to generation. The production of local products is worthy of mention and is one of Lesvos' most important assets. The olive oil of Lesvos, with its rich taste and high nutritional value, is recognized worldwide and is a key element of the Mediterranean diet. The cheeses, such as the famous "ladotyri," and the wines of Lesvos offer authentic gastronomic experiences, while honey and traditional sweets complete the variety of local products. Seafood and fish also feature prominently in the local diet, with dishes such as sardines from Kalloni and prawns from Sikamnia standing out. Furthermore, the ouzo of Lesvos is also internationally renowned, with local distilleries producing high-quality ouzo, which is an integral part of local culture and social life (Lesvos Geopark, n.d.).

Cultural tourism is one of the most important forms of tourism in Lesvos due to the rich cultural and historical heritage of the island. Visitors can explore archaeological sites, museums, and traditional villages that retain their picturesqueness and authenticity. Lesvos has a rich history dating back to prehistoric times, with archaeological findings testifying to the presence of man from the Neolithic period. Important ancient cities demonstrate the history and culture of the island (Rachiotis & Poulaki, 2022; Rachiotis & Poulaki, 2024a).

Also, the cultural heritage of the island is reflected in its architecture with traditional stone houses, churches, and monasteries that are important sights. The inhabitants of Lesvos keep alive their traditions and customs through numerous cultural events, festivals, theatrical performances, and exhibitions of various content. The festivals of Lesvos are organized in honor of local saints and are a unique opportunity to get to know the local culture and traditions (Poulaki, Rachiotis & Vasilakis, 2025).

A very important natural monument on this island is the Petrified Forest, which has been characterized as a protected monument of nature and is included in the global list of geoparks of UNESCO. As is known, it includes petrified tree trunks millions of years old and provides a unique experience for visitors (Poulaki, et al, 2021a; Rachiotis & Poulaki, 2024c). Other notable sights include the medieval castles of Mytilene and Mithymna, which are important examples of military architecture and offer spectacular views of the Aegean Sea. The tourist development of Lesvos began to appear in the 1950s, focusing on Molyvos. This development model was based on the belief that Molyvos could become an ideal destination for highly educated visitors, mainly from Europe, offering multiple benefits.

Many residents of the area left their other professional activities and focused exclusively on tourism. Other areas of the island, such as Petra, Eresos, Kalloni, Plomari, etc., have experienced the same tourism policy and development, based on the 3S model.

The town of Mytilene was not initially a popular destination, as visitors preferred other parts of the island. However, many tourists from Turkey choose to stay in the town for one or two nights. Also, the island of Lesvos, with its rich coastline and deep blue beaches, offers significant opportunities for marine tourism. The beaches of Eressos, Petra, and Skala Kalloni are popular destinations for swimming, sunbathing, and water sports. Lesvos also offers fishing opportunities, with visitors having the chance to participate in traditional fishing activities and learn about local techniques and the types of fish caught in the island's seas.

Furthermore, Lesvos' hot springs, known for their therapeutic properties, attract many visitors seeking natural healing and relaxation. The hot springs of Eftalou and Polihnitos offer hot baths known to relieve various ailments (Visit Lesvos, n.d.). Agritourism in Lesvos offers visitors the opportunity to experience life in the countryside and participate in rural activities. Tourists can visit traditional farms, participate in harvesting, and learn about local agricultural practices. This is a unique and authentic experience that promotes the sustainable development of the island.

Many agritourism accommodations in Lesvos also offer cooking classes, where guests can learn how to prepare traditional dishes using local products (Poulaki, et al, 2021b). These activities enhance the visitors' connection with the local culture and tradition and offer unforgettable experiences.

Lesvos, with its rich natural heritage and strong agricultural tradition, has emerged as an important destination for agritourism in recent years. Agritourism, which combines rural life with tourism activities, offers visitors a unique opportunity to experience authentic rural life and participate in various rural activities. There are many olive groves on the island that produce high-quality olive oil. Visitors can tour the olive groves, participate in the olive harvest, and learn about the olive oil production process.

Several agritourism accommodations and farms offer educational programs where visitors can taste different varieties of olive oil and even get involved in the preparation of local dishes (Poulaki et al, 2021a; Rachiotis & Poulaki, 2024d). However, wine production on the island of Lesvos is also an important part of agritourism. Visits to wineries often include tours of the vineyards, demonstrations of the wine production process, and tastings that offer a deeper understanding of the wine tradition of Lesvos. Visitors to Lesvos can also visit traditional farms and learn about the production of local products such as cheese, honey, and herbs. Local cultural events, often accompanied by traditional music, dances, and food, offer visitors the opportunity to participate in authentic cultural experiences. Many traditional buildings and farms have been renovated and converted into agritourism accommodations, offering high-quality hospitality to visitors.

The Municipality of Mytilene participates in the city marketing and CityBranding program under the "Interreg V-A Greece Cyprus" program for smart cities and aims to facilitate the daily life of both the local community and visitors by creating tourism promotion applications and digitizing material of cultural and tourist interest. According to the Discover Greece website, created by the Greek National Tourism Organisation, Lesvos is promoted as the home of ouzo, with an emphasis on the town of Mytilene, the island's picturesque villages (Molyvos, Petra, Agiasos, Plomari, etc.), the petrified forest, beaches, thermal springs, monasteries, and the observation of rare birds. The Visit Greece website highlights the island's gastronomy and its natural environment (https://www.visitgreece.gr/).

4.1.4 Agritourism Cooperatives of Lesvos

The agritourism cooperatives of the regional unit of Lesvos, according to the Ministry of Rural Development and Food, are thirteen. (Indicatively, the following women's agricultural cooperatives of Lesvos are mentioned: Agritourism Women's Cooperative of Agia Paraskevi "Selada," Agritourism Cooperative of Women of Agra "Ta Lefka," Agritourism Cooperative of Women of Gera "Aristea," Agritourism Cooperative of Women of Mesotopos, Agritourism/Agritourism Cooperative of Women of Mithymna, Agritourism Cooperative of Women of Parakoila, Agritourism Cooperative of Women of Petra, Agritourism Women's Processing Cooperative of Plomari, Agritourist/Agri-Industrial Women's Cooperative of Polichnitos, and Women's Agritourism Cooperative of Skalochori.

Specifically, the agritourism women's cooperatives of Gera, Filia, Polichnitos, Mesotopos, Skalochori, Agia Paraskevi, Parakoila, Mithymna (Molyvos), and Agra are engaged in the production of spoon sweets, liqueurs, baking sweets, local sweets (almonds), local pasta ("trahana", noodles, etc.), pastries, and the preservation of olives and cheeses. All products of the cooperatives are based on local goods and local traditional recipes.

The women's agritourism cooperative of Petra, one of the first agritourism cooperatives in the country, apart from the production of local products, offers visitors accommodation through the accommodation owned by the cooperative. Also, in the village of Agiasos, there is the agritourism processing cooperative of Agiasos, which, in addition to producing local dishes, manufactures a variety of traditional textiles. In the village of Asomatos, there is a cooperative that produces exclusively spoon sweets and also engages in basketry art by making traditional baskets and clothes of various sizes. Finally, in the village of Plomari, there is located the agritourism women's processing cooperative of the village, which produces local products as well as soaps and jewelry. The women's agritourism cooperatives of the island reveal the effort of the women of the local community to save and pass on to the next brave women the traditional flavors and arts of the place.

In addition, they are a tourist attraction, as visitors are given the opportunity to taste and acquire authentic local products and get in touch with the traditional gastronomy of Lesvos (Ministry of Rural Development and Food, n.d.).

4.1.5 Methodological Framework of the Research: Conclusions

Qualitative primary research was conducted using interviews with stakeholders on the island of Lesvos during the period August–October 2023. The stakeholders (public and private) who took part in this research were involved in tourism in general and agritourism in particular.

The conclusions obtained from this research are as follows: The development of agritourism in Lesvos promotes economic sustainability and brings many benefits to the local community. Promoting agritourism can protect the natural environment by encouraging the sustainable use of tourism resources.

Agritourism is considered an incentive for the revival of traditional professions, the strengthening of local gastronomy, and the creation of new business opportunities for the inhabitants of the island. The development of agritourism can lead to more balanced tourism activity throughout the year, helping to remove seasonality. Agritourism promotes environmental awareness and sustainable development. However, there are factors that act as inhibitors and relate to the need to improve infrastructure and services, as well as cooperation between tourism sector operators.

The absence of strategic planning and promotion of agritourism at the local, regional, and national levels is one of the main weaknesses of the sector, and appropriate policy measures need to be taken in this regard. Lesvos does not have a single marketing plan for the promotion of tourism. Operators implement different strategies and programs to attract tourists. It is necessary to improve the transport infrastructure and access to agritourism facilities. It is imperative to implement sustainable practices and enhance environmental awareness among both tourists and local communities. There is also an absence of attractive holiday packages that combine the natural beauty of the island with experiential tourism.

It is necessary to promote and strengthen collaborations between local entrepreneurs and tourist agents by creating a network of communication between visitors and the businesses involved, as well as collaborations with international tourism organizations to promote agritourism in Lesvos. Various national and European funding programs that can support the development of agritourism infrastructure and activities must be exploited. It is necessary to use digital technologies to promote agritourism, giving impetus to sustainable tourism development.

Lesvos invests in the creation of quality and differentiated products and services related to agritourism. Agritourism, by promoting contact with nature and local culture, can attract a wide audience interested in environmentally responsible holidays. Visitors participating in agritourism activities contribute to the preservation of local agricultural practices/traditions and the sustainability of local entrepreneurship. Climate change has begun to affect the agricultural production and tourism activities of Lesvos, so this is an area that needs attention.

Achieving true sustainability requires the cooperation and participation of all stakeholders, such as local communities, farmers, tourism businesses, and government authorities. Agritourism successfully combines the island's natural beauty, rich history, and cultural heritage, offering visitors a unique and unforgettable experience. Agritourism encourages cooperation among rural residents and creates a sense of community and solidarity. Women's participation and activity not only strengthen tourism but also strengthen the local community and promote the preservation of its cultural elements.

The role of women is dynamic in agriculture, animal husbandry and the production of local products, and is constantly developing. The creation and development of women's agricultural cooperatives can contribute significantly to the economic strengthening of local communities and the preservation of traditional agricultural practices. Women's participation contributes to the creation of many positive social, cultural, and environmental impacts, and this is strongly relevant to the effort to develop rural tourism (and, in other words, agritourism). Through cooperatives, Lesvos can create new sources of income and strengthen the economy.

Lesvos has the potential to be a leading agritourism destination, capitalizing on the growing trends for sustainable and authentic travel experiences. Access to funding programs, collaborations with international organizations, and the strengthening of local communities are critical factors for the success of this effort. With the proper management and promotion of local products and cultural heritage, the island can emerge as a model agritourism destination in Greece and Europe. However, in order for this to occur, it is necessary to develop and implement a comprehensive marketing plan, increase incentives for investment in agritourism, support the modernization of women's cooperative production, increase funding for agritourism, and improve infrastructure.

REFERENCES

Adams, B. B. (2008). *The New Agritourism: Hosting Community and Tourists on Your Farm*. Carlisle, Cumbria: National Lilac Publishing LLC.

Al-Dajani, H., & Marlow, S. (2013). Empowerment and entrepreneurship: A theoretical framework. International Journal of Entrepreneurial Behavior & Research, 19(5), 503–524. https://doi.org/10.1108/IJEBR-10-2011-0138.

Amaral, N. K. & Edgar L. D. (2010). *Agricultural Communication Students' Perceptions, Knowledge and Identified Sources of Information about Agritourism*. Arkansas: University of Arkansas, Department of Agricultural Extension.

Brown, D. & Reeder, R. (2007). Farm-based recreation: A statistical profile. *United States Department of Agriculture Economic Research Service Report 53*.

Busby, G., & Rendle S., (2000). The tradition from tourism of farms to farm tourism. *Tourism Management*, *21*(6), 635–642.

Camisón, C., Forés, B., & Boronat-Navarro, M. (2017). Cluster and firm-specific antecedents of organizational innovation. Current Issues in Tourism, *20*(6), 617–646. https://doi.org/10.1080/13683500.2016.1177002.

Carpio, E. C., Wohlgenant, K. M., & Boonsaeng, T. (2008). The demand for agritourism in the United States. *Journal of Agricultural and Resource Economics*, *33*(2), 254–269.

Discover Greece. (n.d.). Lesvos, North Aegean Islands. https://www.discovergreece.com/el/north-aegean-islands/lesvos.

Drakopoulou-Dodd S., & Anderson, A. (2007). Mumpsimus and the mything of the individualistic entrepreneur. *International Small Business Journal*, *25*(4), 341–360.

Ecotourism Greece. (n.d.). Hellenic Agrotourism Federation. https://ecotourism-greece.com/providers/hellenic-agrotourism-federation/.

Enagron Ecotourism Village. (n.d.). Enagron. https://www.enagron.gr/.

European Commission. (2023). LEADER Approach for Rural Development. Publications Office of the European Union.

European Commission. (2021, July 29). Partnership Agreement for the Development Framework 2021–2027 (NSRF 2021–2027). https://commission.europa.eu/publications/partnership-agreement-greece-2021-2027_en.

ESPA.io. (n.d.). Invitation to the Action "Green Agrotourism". https://espa.io/en/invitation-to-the-action-green-agrotourism/.

Gao, R., Huang S., & Huang, R. (2008). Rural tourism development in China. *International Journal of Tourism Research,* 11, 439–450.

García, M. C. D., & Welter, F. (2013). Gender identities and practices: Interpreting women entrepreneurs' narratives. *International Small Business Journal*, *31*(4), 384–404.

Hieu, V. M., & Rasovska, I. (2017). Craft villages and tourism development: A case study in Phu Quoc island of Vietnam. Management, 21(1), 223–236. https://doi.org/10.1515/manment-2015-0090.

Knowd, I. (2001). *Rural Tourism: Panacea and Paradox: Exploring the Phenomenon of Rural Tourism and Tourism's Interaction with Host Rural*

Communities. Richmond, Australia: UWS Hawkesbury. Originally produced as a briefing paper on Rural Tourism, 1998.

Lesvos Geopark. (n.d.-b). Agrotourism Cooperatives. https://www.lesvosgeopark.gr/en/gastronomy/agrotourism-cooperatives/.

Milia Mountain Retreat. (n.d.). Milia. https://milia.gr/.

Mills, M., Tsang, F., Präg, P., Ruggeri, K., Miani, C., & Hoorens, S. (2014, October 29). Gender Equality in the Workforce: Reconciling Work, Private and Family Life in Europe (Research Reports No. RR-462-EC). RAND Corporation. https://doi.org/10.2838/54302.

Ministry of Rural Development and Food. (n.d.-b). Agrotourism – Agricultural Association. https://www.minagric.gr/for-farmer-2/agrotourism/agricultural-association.

Ndlovu, N., & Rogerson, C. M. (2004). The local economic impacts of rural community-based tourism in the Eastern Cape. In: C. M. Rogerson & G. Visser (eds.), Tourism and Development Issues in Contemporary South Africa, 436–451. Pretoria: Africa Institute of South Africa.

O'Halloran, M., Cook S., Sbragi, A., & Buchanan I. (2000). Rural tourism in Australia: The visitor's perspective. *BTR Occasional Paper Number 30*. Canberra: Bureau of Tourism Research.

Ollenburg, C. (2006). *Farm Tourism in Australia: A Family Business and Rural Studies Perspective*. Doctorate thesis, Griffith University, Queensland.

Peeters, L. W. J., & Ateljevic, I. (2009). Women empowerment entrepreneurship nexus in tourism: Processes of social innovation. In: Page, S., & Ateljevic, J. (eds.), *Tourism and Entrepreneurship: International Perspectives*. Oxon: Routledge, 75–89.

Perleas Mansion. (n.d.). Perleas, https://www.perleas.gr/.

Pittman, M. H., (2006). *Planting the Seeds for a New Industry in Arkansas: Agritourism*. Arkansas: National Agricultural Law Center Research.

Porcaro, P. (2009). *Agritourism in Italy*. Pretoria, South Africa: ISS Institute/Italy Fellowship.

Poulaki, P., Rachiotis, T., & Vasilakis, N. (2025). Trends and development prospects of gastronomic tourism in Rhodes and its connection to cultural tourism. In: Emerging Trends and Practices in Gastronomy and Culinary Tourism. https://doi.org/10.4018/979-8-3693-7530-3.ch003.

Poulaki, P., Lagou, M., & Valeri, M. (2021a). The contribution of female entrepreneurship to the development of agritourism in Greece. In: Valeri, M., Cusano, N., & Katsoni, V. (eds.), *Gender and Tourism: Challenges and Opportunities*, 219–234. Bingley: Emerald Publishing.

Poulaki, P., Kritikos, A., Vasilakis, N., & Valeri, M. (2021b). The contribution of female creativity to the development of gastronomic tourism in Greece: The case of the island of Naxos in the South Aegean. In: M. Valeri (ed.), New Governance and Management in Touristic Destinations, 246–258. IGI Global. https://doi.org/10.4018/978-1-6684-3889-3.ch015.

Rachiotis, T., & Poulaki, P. (2022). The contribution of cultural routes to the enhancement of urban cultural tourism. *Journal on Hospitality and Tourism*, *20*(2), 31–46, https://doi.org/10.5281/zenodo.8322203.

Rachiotis, T., & Poulaki, P. (2024a). Cultural routes as a factor of sustainable management of cultural reserve and development of cultural tourism. *Sustainable Development, Culture, Traditions*, *4*(A), 50–72. https://doi.org/10.26341/issn.2241-4002-2024-4a-4-T02072.

Rachiotis, T., & Poulaki, P. (2024b). Exploring the sustainability and management of overtourism in globally recognized destinations. *Journal of Regional & Socio-Economic Issues*, *14*(2), 37–45. https://doi.org/10.26215/heal.3n9m-8v15.

Rachiotis, T., & Poulaki, P. (2024c). Innovating cultural tourism in Greece: The strategic role of tourist guides in heritage promotion. *Journal of Regional Socio-Economic Issues*, *14*(2), 14–28. https://doi.org/10.26215/heal.3n9m-8v15.

Rachiotis, T., & Poulaki, P. (2024d). Management of cultural routes as the new status quo in urban cultural tourism. In: Valeri, M. (ed.), (2024). *Innovation Strategies and Organizational Culture in Tourism: Concepts and Case Studies on Knowledge Sharing (1st ed.).* Routledge, 165–181. https://doi.org/10.4324/9781032633374.

Šostar, M., Budić, H., & Škoko, I. (2024). Overcoming administrative obstacles in financing Croatian farmers and entrepreneurs: The policy dimension of the European Union's fund absorption. Scientific Papers Series Management, Economic Engineering in Agriculture and Rural Development, 24(1), 937.

Tucker, H., & Boonabaana, B. (2012). A critical analysis of tourism, gender and poverty reduction. *Journal of Sustainable Tourism*, *20*(3), 437–455.https://doi.org/10.1080/09669582.2011.622769

Ventura, F. (1994). Women in Italian Agriculture: New Roles, New Problems. In: L. van der Plas & M. Fonte (eds.), Rural Gender Studies, 45–60. Rome: KEGME.

Viljoen, J., & Tlabela K., (2007). *Rural Tourism Development in South Africa: Trends and Challenges.* Cape Town: Human Sciences Research Council, HSRC Press.

Visit Lesvos. (n.d.). Eftalou Aghioi Anargyroi, https://www.visitlesvos.gr/pois/eftalou-aghioi-anargyroi/.

Wall, G. (2004). Agrotourism. In: Jafari, J. (ed.), *Encyclopedia of Tourism.* Oxon: Routledge, 14–15.

Welter, F. (2011). Contextualizing entrepreneurship-conceptual challenges and ways forward. *Entrepreneurship Theory and Practice*, *35*(1), 165–184.

Ying T., & Zhou Y. (2007). Community, governments and external capitals in China's rural cultural tourism: A comparative study of two adjacent villages. *Tourism Management*, *28*, 96–107.

5. Intersection of digital technology, social innovation, and female entrepreneurship in tourism: A theoretical review

Michelle Maiurro, Zélia Breda, Filipa Brandão, and Carlos Costa

5.1 INTRODUCTION

Women were severely impacted in terms of job losses during the COVID-19 pandemic. Many of these women (58%) worked informally, with little or no social support and limited access to technology and financing (UN Women, 2020). In 2020, more than 64 million women lost their jobs globally, a 5% decline compared to men at 3.9% (UN Women, 2020). According to the World Economic Forum (2021), because of the pandemic, the period of global disparity between men and women increased from 99.5 to 135.6 years. Before the pandemic, 54% of the global tourism workforce was female, with significant variations between countries.

The Global Report (2019) highlights that for women's economic empowerment and increased participation within the tourism sector, there must be synergy within five areas: employment, entrepreneurship, education and training, leadership and decision-making, community and civil society. From this perspective, there is growing attention being paid to the role of women entrepreneurs in socioeconomic development (Osei & Zhuang, 2020). However, one of the differences, when compared to male entrepreneurs, is linked to access to capital (Alesina et al., 2013; Basiglio et al., 2019; Cole & Mehran, 2009). Particularly in developing countries, women entrepreneurs are generally more vulnerable and face even more resource constraints (Adom, 2015) in addition to a lack of experience and lower risk propensity. This all contributes to women's hesitancy to engage in entrepreneurship (Fairlie & Robb, 2009).

The enhancement and diversification of women entrepreneur networks can significantly contribute to their capacity for social innovation and entrepreneurial performance (Lozano et al., 2019), and social innovation can be achieved through social networks and social dynamics (Osei & Zhuang, 2020). Social innovation and female entrepreneurship in the tourism sector can contribute to female empowerment and greater gender equality, for which digital technologies are an enhancing factor. Indeed, female participation in the tourism market is increasingly growing (Baum, 2013), and its expansion is fueled by various sector-related projects that offer incentives to become more productive (Brush et al., 2009). Progressively, digital development through technologies is changing the business sector and expanding options for future entrepreneurs (Dholakia & Kshetri, 2004; Khajeheian, 2013).

Women can benefit from digital technologies as they provide them with greater work flexibility, mobility (Ughetto et al., 2020), and access to new means of knowledge (Dy et al., 2018), contributing to business and financing opportunities (Ughetto et al., 2020). Digitalization is a means of female empowerment and a way to make the labor market, financing, and entrepreneurship more equal, and tourism is increasingly conceptualized as an important arena enabling development projects which foster gender equality in society (Ferguson, 2007). According to Ughetto et al. (2020), gender issues are understudied in this area, making it important to debate how digital technologies can alleviate existing constraints in this field for women, and research how access and essential conditions for business growth can be different for men and women (Dy et al. 2018).

This chapter aims to analyze existing literature on digital technology and social innovation in female entrepreneurship in tourism, focusing on the interests and synergies between these fields, as well as women entrepreneurs' contributions to sustainable development; identifying emerging trends; and synthesizing information from social innovation processes in tourism. The methodology used involved the analysis of relevant research on the three objects of study. For this, we used the guidelines of a narrative review, where previously published materials on the topic were researched non-exhaustively and without the need for rigid systematization for data collection. To gather relevant literature, databases were consulted, along with some keywords: digital technology, social innovation, and female entrepreneurship.

5.2 FEMALE ENTREPRENEURSHIP

The theory of entrepreneurship began to be thoroughly researched by economist Richard Cantillon in his work "Essai sur la Nature du Commerce en Général", dated 1755, according to Berg (2015). However, the term "entrepreneur" was expanded by the French economist Jean-Baptiste Say in 1964 when he defined the entrepreneur as being responsible for bringing together production factors with administrative guidance and associated risks (Say, 2008). For Schumpeter (1912), entrepreneurial people are associated with the ability to seize or create opportunities and take risks. They are drivers of change and transformation, founding companies, new businesses, or new concepts within an organization or society. Since then, various academics have attributed various concepts to the terms "entrepreneur" and "entrepreneurship". In Hébert and Link's work (2007), the authors attributed 12 terms for entrepreneur according to analysis by different authors on various specific themes: (1) a person who takes risks associated with uncertainties, (2) provides financial capital, (3) innovator, (4) decision-maker, (5) industrial leader, (6) director or superintendent, (7) organizer of economic resources, (8) business owner, (9) employer of production factors, (10) contractor, (11) arbitrator, and (12) resource distributor. Beyond the concepts of entrepreneur and entrepreneurship, Dornelas (2007) argues that there is not a single type of entrepreneur; in his work, he analyzes more than 300 types of entrepreneurs and defines them in eight profiles: (1) born, (2) learner, (3) serial, (4) corporate, (5) social, (6) necessity, (7) heir, and (8) planned.

Female entrepreneurship is linked to gender issues, which most often influence entrepreneurial dynamics. Many studies highlight the importance of female entrepreneurship for society (Vukovic et al., 2021) and how it is fundamental for economic development (Brush & Cooper, 2012; De Vita et al., 2014). Many of these studies associate female entrepreneurship with a way of eliminating social and economic barriers for women (Fang et al., 2018; Anderson & Ojediran, 2021; Bagheri et al., 2022) and empowerment (Zimmerman, 2000). Women and female entrepreneurship can play a vital role in developing economies (Ratten, 2014; Zhu et al., 2019).

According to data from the Global Entrepreneurship Monitor (GEM) 2021, two in five early-stage active entrepreneurs worldwide are women. Previous studies have shown that women entrepreneurs face challenges and cannot participate in entrepreneurial activities in the same way as male entrepreneurs. This is primarily a result of the differences women face regarding access to networks and resources needed to start and manage a business (Yadav et al., 2022). The problem of access to capital intensifies when considering women's access to equity capital. Venture capital funding rates for women-led and men-led companies are clearly different (Brush et al., 2019). According to World Bank indicators (2015), women manage to save less compared to men to start or expand a business.

Studies still reveal the motivations for women to undertake entrepreneurship. According to GEM (2022), women were more likely than men to state that the main reasons for creating a company were to make a difference (52.9% vs. 51.0%) or job scarcity (72.5% vs. 67.2%). In comparison, men are more likely to state that the main aim of creating a company is to accumulate wealth (56% vs. 63,6%) or maintain a family tradition (32,9.% vs. 35,7%). Among the motivations, we can highlight that the main one is entrepreneurship by necessity or opportunity (Monllor & Murphy, 2017). Therefore, due to poverty levels, women in developing countries may have more access to necessity-based entrepreneurship (Kimbu & Ngoasong, 2016). Opportunity-based entrepreneurship is clearly more common among women in developed economies, where more money is available and easily accessible (Correa et al., 2021). Women entrepreneurs' motivation is linked to life's needs and opportunities, including rewards such as earning money and recognition, as well as the desire to contribute to communities. Motivators vary according to the local circumstances in which businesses are run (Filimonau et al., 2022).

It is fundamental to emphasize the role of women entrepreneurs in the tourism field and how this sector can serve as a bridge of empowerment for vulnerable women within communities. For example, using tools such as social innovation can combat gender disparity. The *Global Report on Women in Tourism* (UNWTO, 2010) states that 36.08% of employers in tourism were women, primarily in hospitality and catering. This is significantly higher than the 21.95% relating to the general economy. It's important to highlight that entrepreneurship offers opportunities to empower women and achieve gender equality, although these opportunities require public and private level interventions. Moreover, these women face gender-related issues in entrepreneurship, such as limited financing, access to education and technology, among other things (UNWTO, 2019). Sociodemographic, psychological, and professional characteristics (Huarng et al., 2012) are factors that contribute to success or failure in female entrepreneurship (Savage et al., 2022). Bull and Willard (1993) note that it is difficult to create a universal female entrepreneurship model.

Nevertheless, entrepreneurship is an important business tool for women who need and desire social and economic independence. However, it appears that women in developed economies are more driven by opportunities, while women in less developed economies are more driven by necessity (Anderson & Ojediran, 2021). It is important to note that women's independent work in tourism has been increasing, despite the great difficulties in entrepreneurship. Trends in tourism increasingly highlight the gender inequality that exists in entrepreneurship (UNWTO, 2019). Similarly, the World Bank Group (2015) states that worldwide laws and regulations that perpetuate gender discrimination prevent women from entering the labor market or creating a business. For these and other reasons, studies involving these themes related to gender equality and social innovation should be deepened to find and develop solutions for sustainable development.

5.3 SOCIAL INNOVATION: SUSTAINABLE TRANSFORMATION

Social innovation is gaining ground in solving the social problems that pose challenges to society and the market as a whole (Murray et al., 2010). One of the first to begin studying this concept was Taylor (1970) in his work "Introducing social innovation". The concept of social innovation has been widely studied in its various definitions, including in the context of creating new ideas, processes, products, or services aimed at solving social problems (Mulgan, 2006; Murray et al., 2010; Nicholls & Murdock, 2012). Among the most observed definitions in research is Mulgan's (2006, p. 146) which states that "social innovation consists of innovative activities and services motivated by the goal of meeting a social need". In tourism, this can be observed in various ways; according to Trunfio and Campana (2019), innovation is divided into "social innovations, co-creation of experiences, smart destinations and participatory governance". Social innovations in tourism are still mainly discussed from the perspective of social changes. These changes can be interpreted as organizational changes in tourism businesses (Alkier et al., 2017).

Considering the dynamics and rapid development of tourism (Sharma & Bhat, 2022b), research on sustainability in the area has emerged as a significant challenge (Bangare et al., 2021; Niñerola et al., 2019). For this reason, studies addressing these issues of sustainability and development related to social innovation and social entrepreneurship in the tourism sector have been growing. Even though attention to social innovation has been increasing, the research field is still in its early stages (Pol & Ville, 2009).

Social innovation is directly linked to social entrepreneurship as demonstrated by Harvey et al. (2011), and entrepreneurs create solutions through social innovation (Zahra et al., 2009). However, social innovation demands a set of entrepreneurial competencies due to its complexity (Dwivedi & Weerawardena, 2018). There are still only a few studies on the processes and contributions of social innovation developed by companies (Mahato et al., 2021), just as research in social entrepreneurship in tourism is also limited (Boluk, 2011).

It is important to emphasize the involvement of social innovation beneficiaries; for Font et al. (2016), in the tourism context, social innovations are those that benefit the local community and destination. Tourism as a product and service industry is directly dependent on host communities' cooperation (Cole, 2006). Developing communities, for example, use tourism initiatives as a means to boost the economy and grow, emphasizing the relationship between tourism, social entrepreneurship, and community development (Mahato et al., 2021). In this sense, the combination of social and economic value creation can emerge from social entrepreneurship in tourism (Jørgensen et al., 2021). For this to occur, collaborative networks between various stakeholders such as companies, institutions, and communities are important for the innovative process (Phi, 2017).

Entrepreneurial processes are always built on some form of innovation, which is why innovation is framed as a central concept in entrepreneurship (Shane, 2003). It is notable that much is said about innovation and how it relates to entrepreneurship. When it comes to social innovation, the fundamental pillars are focused on social issues rather than profit. The social innovation process is developed and conducted through continuous interaction between developers and beneficiaries to meet individuals' needs, expectations, and aspirations (Bignetti, 2011). According to Santos (2010), for an action to be considered social innovation, it must provide solutions to people's real problems, be a new idea for a context, and encourage improvement of current conditions, including promoting social justice. Social innovation can significantly improve the distribution of resources, policies, and social institutions to solve major problems of modernity (Sharma & Bhat, 2022b), thus mitigating industry's negative effects and implementing social improvement practices and maximizing benefits (Aquino et al., 2018).

Social innovation in tourism can be related to different dimensions, including process perspective, knowledge, types of innovation (Pikkemaat et al., 2019), technologies (Gomezelj, 2016), stakeholder involvement (Trunfio & Campana, 2019), local community development (Malek & Costa, 2015), new forms of problem solutions (Moulaert et al., 2013), among other paradigms. For Benevides et al. (2018), social innovation in tourism is defined through the implementation of regional policies aiming to create new jobs, promote local culture, increase income, and preserve natural resources. For Wirth et al. (2023), social innovation involves new forms of cooperation between individuals or organizations that direct new ideas.. These innovations in regional development can have a positive impact on society, improving quality of life and altering social relations and power dynamics.

Social innovation practices in the tourism sector need to prioritize the following problems (Eren, 2010; Mulgan, 2006): urbanization, ending poverty, gender equality, migrations, environmental issues, consumer rights, health, support for vulnerable groups, education, and professional-ethical issues. Social innovation does not represent a conceptual novelty but rather an emerging paradigm that proposes structural and systemic solutions to social challenges. This concept has the potential to promote significant changes in how nations structure their resources, regulations, and social institutions with its aim to confront contemporary challenges and foster dynamic research environments (Sharma & Bhat, 2022a).

5.4 DIGITAL TECHNOLOGY: TRANSFORMATIVE TOOL

Women entrepreneurs can benefit from a range of opportunities provided by information and communication technologies, which allow them to adopt digital tools (programming, translation, marketing, content production, process management, sales) for business development (Mivehchi, 2019). Indeed, digitalization opens new perspectives for women who want to increase their participation in the labor market and entrepreneurship. Women can access new markets, work flexibly and remotely, connect with consumers, receive training, and increase their financial autonomy through digital services. Moreover, technologies may help reduce gender disparity (Krieger-Boden & Sorgner, 2018).

It is important to recognize that gender-related disparities encounter these intersections. Gender imbalances, such as the lack of networks for company founders, the lack of female entrepreneurship role models, and lack of networking opportunities, can hinder women's recognition and business opportunities (Krieger-Boden & Sorgner, 2018). Furthermore, another gender aspect that influences entrepreneurship is maintaining a work-life balance (Adkins et al., 2013; Brush et al., 2009; Eddleston & Powell, 2012; Jennings et al., 2016; Shelton, 2006). Due to differences in professional and family commitments between male and female entrepreneurs, women tend to benefit from using digital technologies in their ventures (Pergelova et al., 2018).

Indeed, it is possible to interconnect technologies and innovation in the development of women-led companies, thus contributing to society's efforts in reducing the gender gap (Goyal, 2011). According to Ughetto et al. (2020), there is a gap in this research field (business creation and development in the digital era) and gender issues are poorly explored in this area. Likewise, more study is needed on how women can be empowered by digital technologies (Dy et al., 2018). Nevertheless, it is clear that technological advances are a way of creating opportunities for disadvantaged groups, including women.

According to Krieger-Boden and Sorgner (2018), women tend to possess superior social skills which represent a comparative advantage, especially when combined with education and digital literacy. However, many barriers hinder women's advancement, depriving them of many opportunities and benefits of the digital era, including new entrepreneurial opportunities. Therefore, policy is necessary to facilitate women's successful adoption of new opportunities in the digital era. Digitalization will contribute to entrepreneurship (Krieger-Boden & Sorgner, 2018) and social innovation, and the impact that digital technologies will have on social innovation is crucial. Charalabidis et al. (2014) state that few studies have addressed the importance of digital technology in entrepreneurship. Moreover, Fang et al. (2018) concluded that the understanding of the effects of digital technology on entrepreneurship is still emerging. Thus, it is evident that more studies are needed within these aspects, focusing mainly on sustainable development and women's empowerment.

5.5 DISCUSSION

This research integrates theories about digital technology, female entrepreneurship, and social innovation, demonstrating how tourism entrepreneurship can create value and empower women through innovative initiatives. As noted by Aghazamani and Hunt (2017), gender issues are pertinent to the discourse on empowerment within tourism. However, more research is needed to investigate the challenges faced by women in the field of tourism entrepreneurship (Nomnga, 2017). Studies relating to social innovation and gender are relatively limited (Lindberg et al., 2015), as are digital technology and social innovation studies (Tracey & Stott, 2017). On the other hand, new studies show that women entrepreneurs are important participants in social innovation (Peeters & Ateljevic, 2017).

Although entrepreneurship in tourism is a social process involving women's empowerment, obstacles and barriers are evident (Pécot et al., 2024). Women entrepreneurs, especially in developing countries, are often vulnerable and face a series of resource constraints (Adom, 2015).

Social innovations are defined as the combination of new methods, concepts, opportunities, and social systems designed to solve social problems. Therefore, female entrepreneurship can be driven by social innovation (Osei & Zhuang, 2020). Social innovation and empowerment are evolving practices of social change and resistance that question and modify the systemic structures of gender inequality (Edwards & Cornwall, 2014). Studies such as those by Edwards-Schachter and Wallace (2017) highlight social outcomes, encompassing the empowerment of individuals and communities through social innovation.

The promoting female entrepreneurship is fundamental to reducing inequalities and encouraging community participation and involvement. Some studies demonstrate that women entrepreneurs are more conscious of the impact of their businesses at the local level; as a result, they make more effort to support their community's economy, human resources, and businesses (Al-Qahtani et al., 2022). Thus, social innovation is believed to have transformative power, as it offers creative opportunities to meet a community's needs with its participation (Nyseth & Hamdouch, 2019). In addition, digital technologies can be a powerful tool for realizing innovative ideas, allowing women to find more opportunities and overcome the obstacles usually placed before them.

In the social context, the convergence of these three elements (digital technology, social innovation and female entrepreneurship) can creates positive opportunities for a more inclusive and dynamic society. This allows for a vision of the future where creativity and diversification cooperate to shape the entrepreneurial environment. Moreover, these aspects, especially social innovation, can contribute to improving the well-being of populations in general (Negas et al., 2020).

Based on content analysis and an inductive process, and according to the studies mentioned in this chapter, Figure 5.1 synthesizes the effects of interconnection through dimensions and elements emerging from female entrepreneurship, social innovation, and digital technology. The dimensions highlight the main impacts from these elements, thus indicating the intersection of these areas in contributing to Sustainable Development Goals (SDGs). Through its processes, digital technology, drives social innovation in female entrepreneurship, promoting gender equality, opportunity generation, social and financial autonomy, political participation, inclusion and positive impacts on communities.

The effects of the intersection between these elements can generate transformative impacts, in this case, in the tourism sector. Digital technologies play a facilitating role in the creation, promotion, and development of women's businesses. Moreover, they can minimize the negative impacts and barriers that women entrepreneurs face. Through social innovation, solutions are developed with the purpose of social transformation,

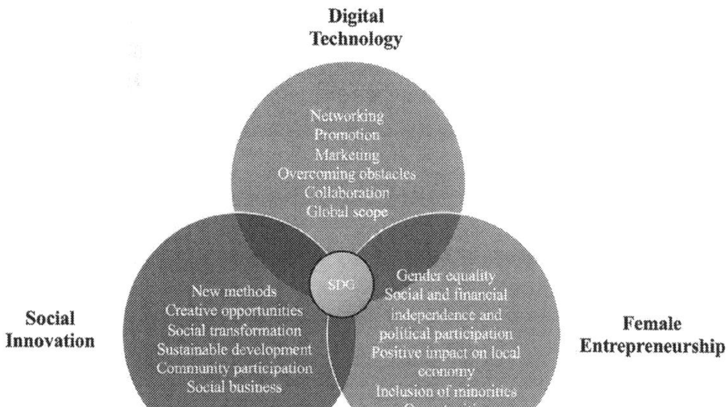

Source: Developed by the authors based on content analysis.

Figure 5.1 The effects of the intersection of digital technology, social innovation, and female entrepreneurship

sustainable development, and active community participation. This process contributes to and strengthens women-led businesses, thus generating effects such as gender equality, social and financial independence, as well as political participation, and consequently, a positive impact in the communities where these women entrepreneurs operate.

5.6 CONCLUSION

The integration of digital technologies as a tool for social innovation in the context of female entrepreneurship in the tourism sector represents a step forward for gender equality and the economic development of communities. Women entrepreneurs can increase their competitive advantages and reduce existing barriers through the possibilities that entrepreneurship and social innovation bring. The tourism sector plays a significant role in increasing the number of self-employment opportunities among women (UNWTO, 2019). Overall, female entrepreneurship is an important component of women's empowerment with its potential for increasing their social and financial independence, as well as their political participation (Khan, 2015).

It is important to emphasize the role of social innovation in female entrepreneurship, which plays a significant factor in sustainable and economic development, as it initially aims to solve a social problem. Social innovation and traditional innovation offer new ways to meet different needs and objectives. However, the main distinction lies in intentionality: social innovation aims to create and develop social value first, and consequently economic value (Mulgan, 2006). Bežovan et al. (2016) and Borges (2017) highlight that social innovation can help unite society and reduce the effects of social problems and social vulnerability.

Tourism entrepreneurship creates opportunities, and new social business models can contribute to local communities through innovations, thus differentiating themselves from traditional entrepreneurship models. Moreover, the use of digital tools in conjunction with social innovation can contribute to the tourism sector's role in developing a fairer and more prosperous society. Technologies, in turn, not only facilitate the promotion of women-led businesses but also contribute to network creation. Women entrepreneurs should invest in digital skills to expand their global reach, create connections, and inspire other women to follow in their footsteps. Indeed, digital technologies are considered a significant part of business environment transformation (Bi et al., 2017; Giones & Brem, 2017).

It is clear that the barriers faced by female entrepreneurs are greater than those faced by males. Regarding this, it was noted how gender inequality affects women in the entrepreneurial sphere, and some of these barriers are highlighted in the Global Entrepreneurship Monitor 2021 report (GEM, 2021). Moreover, motivations for entrepreneurship range from opportunity to necessity, and motivators vary according to local circumstances (Filimonau et al., 2022).

It is noted that social businesses are part of the backbone of social entrepreneurship and impact businesses (Dandolini et al., 2020). Impact businesses driven by sustainable development goals contribute to building the intersection that we discuss here. Besides innovative advantages and social problem-solving, this type of business enables economic development for women entrepreneurs.

Future research is expected to deepen the theme, leading to understanding of how these connections (female entrepreneurship, social innovation, and digital technologies) can contribute to Sustainable Development Goals (SDGs) and creating insights that can boost female entrepreneurship in the tourism sector, as well as demonstrating how the adoption of digital tools promotes social innovation and fosters local community development through female entrepreneurship.

Tourism, being a major driver of entrepreneurship, contributes to women creating business opportunities. The inclusion of minorities in innovative projects is increasingly important, helping to develop actions that contribute to economic and sustainable development. Digital technologies can serve as a tool for social innovation in female entrepreneurship in the tourism sector, allowing for the building of intersections that support the dismantling of social, economic, and political obstacles.

REFERENCES

Adkins, C. L., Samaras, S. A., Gilfillan, S. W., & McWee, W. E. (2013). The relationship between owner characteristics, company size, and the work-family culture and policies of women-owned businesses. *Journal of Small Business Management*, *51*(2), 196–214.

Adom, K. (2015). Recognizing the contribution of female entrepreneurs in economic development in sub-Saharan Africa: Some evidence from Ghana. *Journal of Developmental Entrepreneurship*, *20*(1), 1550003.

Aghazamani, Y., & Hunt, C. (2017). Empowerment in tourism: A review of peer-reviewed literature. *Tourism Review Internationa*, *21*, 333–346. https://doi.org/10.3727/154427217X15094520591321.

Alesina, A. F., Lotti, F., & Mistrulli, P. E. (2013). Do women pay more for credit? Evidence from Italy. *Journal of the European Economic Association, 11*(1), 54–66.

Alkier, R., Milojica, V., & Roblek, V. (2017). Challenges of the social innovation in tourism. In: *Proceedings of the 4th International Scientific Conference ToSEE – "Tourism in Southern and Eastern Europe 2017"*. https://doi.org/10.20867/tosee.04.24.

Al-Qahtani, M., Zguir, M. F., Ari, I., & Koç, M. (2022). Female entrepreneurship for sustainable economy and development: Challenges, drivers, and suggested policies for resource-rich countries. *Sustainability, 14*(20), 13412. https://doi.org/10.3390/su142013412.

Anderson, A., & Ojediran, F. (2021). Perspectives, progress and prospects: Researching women's entrepreneurship in emerging economies. *Journal of Entrepreneurship in Emerging Economies 14*(2), *292–315*. https://doi.org/10.1108/jeee-07-2020-0214.

Aquino, R. S., Lück, M., & Schänzel, H. A. (2018). A conceptual framework of tourism social entrepreneurship for sustainable community development. *Journal of Hospitality and Tourism Management, 37*, 23–32. https://doi.org/10.1016/j.jhtm.2018.09.001.

Bagheri, F., Ghaderi, Z., Abdi, N., & Hall, C. M. (2022). Female entrepreneurship, creating shared value, and empowerment in tourism: The neutralizing effect of gender-based discrimination. *Current Issues in Tourism, 26*(21), 3465–3482. https://doi.org/10.1080/13683500.2022.2126749.

Bangare, M. L., Bangare, P. M., Ramirez-Asis, E., Jamanca-Anaya, R., Phoemchalard, C., & Bhat, D. A. R. (2022). Role of machine learning in improving tourism and education sector. *Materials Today: Proceedings*, 51, 2457–2461. https://doi.org/10.1016/j.matpr.2021.11.615.

Basiglio, S., Devincentiis, P., Isaia, E., & Rossi, M. C. (2019). Credit access and approval. *CeRP Working Papers 189*. Turin, Italy: Center for Research on Pensions and Welfare Policies.

Baum, T. (2013). *International Perspectives on Women and Work in Hotels, Catering and Tourism*. Geneva: ILO.

Benevides, S. L. M., Pedro Filho, F., Madeira, M. J. A., Sakuno, I. Y. T., & Arenhardt, V. (2018). Social innovation for tourism strategy in Western Amazonia. *International Journal of Advanced Engineering Research and Science, 5*, 78–92.

Berg, R. (2015). *Richard Cantillon's Essay on the Nature of Trade in General*. Oxon: Routledge.

Bežovan, G., Matancevic, J., & Baturina, D. (2016). Social innovations as a contribution to strengthening social cohesion and mitigating the social crisis in European urban social programs. *Revista de Sociologia e Política, 23*(1), 61–80.

Bi, R., Davison, R. M., & Smyrnios, K. X. (2017). E-business and fast growth SMEs. *Small Business Economics, 48*(3), 559–576.

Bignetti, L. P. (2011). Social innovations: A foray into ideas, trends and research focuses. *Ciências Sociais Unisinos, 47*(1), 3–14. https://doi.org/10.4013/csu.2011.47.1.01.

Boluk, K. (2011). Revealing the discourses: White entrepreneurial motivation in black South Africa. *Tourism Planning & Development*, *8*(2), 199–213.
Borges, M. A. (2017). Dynamics of intersectoral partnerships in social innovation initiatives: From description to proposal of guidelines. Doctorate thesis (in Engineering and Knowledge Management), Federal University of Santa Catarina (UFSC), Florianópolis, Brazil.
Brush, C. G., De Bruin, A., & Welter, F. (2009). A gender-aware framework for women's entrepreneurship. *International Journal of Gender and Entrepreneurship*, *1*(1), 8–24.
Brush, C., & Cooper, S. (2012). Female entrepreneurship and economic development: An international perspective. *Entrepreneurship and Regional*, *24*. 1–6. https://doi.org/10.1080/08985626.2012.637340.
Brush, C., Edelman, L. F., Manolova, T., & Welter, F. (2019). A gendered look at entrepreneurship ecosystems. *Small Business Economics*, *53*(2), 393–408. https://doi.org/10.1007/s11187-018-9992-9.
Bull, I., & Willard, G. E. (1993). Towards a theory of entrepreneurship. *Journal of Business Venturing*, *8*(3), 183–196. https://doi.org/10.1016/0883-9026(93)90026-2.
Charalabidis, Y., Loukis, E., & Androutsopoulou, A. (2014). Fostering social innovation through multiple social media combinations. *Information Systems Management*, *31*(3), 225–239.
Cole, S. (2006). Information and empowerment: The keys to achieving sustainable tourism. *Journal of Sustainable Tourism*, *14*(6), 629–644.
Cole, R. A., & Mehran, H. (2009). Gender and the availability of credit to privately held firms: Evidence from the surveys of small business finances. *Federal Reserve Bank of New York Staff Report*, No. 383, August.
Correa, V. S., Brito, F., de Lima, R. M., & Queiroz, M. M. (2021). Female entrepreneurship in emerging and developing countries: A systematic literature review. *International Journal of Gender and Entrepreneurship, 14*(3), *300–322* https://doi.org/10.1108/IJGE-08-2021-0142.
Dandolini, G., de Souza, J. A., Pereira, R., Malvestiti, R., de Oliveira Massad, D., Figueiredo, Y., Prim, M., & Zandavalli, C. (2020). Inovação social. *Negócios Sociais e Desenvolvimento Sustentável*. Pantanal Editora ebooks. https://doi.org/10.46420/9786588319123.
De Vita, L., Mari, M., & Poggesi, S. 2014. Women entrepreneurs in and from developing countries: Evidences from the literature. *European Management Journal*, *32*(3), 451–460.
Dholakia, R. R., & Kshetri, N. (2004). Factors impacting the adoption of the Internet among SMEs. *Small Business Economics*, *23*(4), 311–322.
Dornelas, J. C. A. (2007). *Empreendedorismo na prática: Mitos e verdades do empreendedor de sucesso*. Rio de Janeiro: Elsevier.
Dwivedi, A., & Weerawardena, J. (2018). Conceptualizing and operationalizing the social entrepreneurship construct. *Journal of Business Research*, *86*, 32–40. https://doi.org/10.1016/j.jbusres.2018.01.053.
Dy, A. M., Martin, L., & Marlow, S. (2018). Emancipation through digital entrepreneurship: A critical realist analysis. *Organization*, *25*(5), 585–608.

Eddleston, K., & G. Powell (2012). Nurturing entrepreneurs: Work-family balance: A gendered perspective. *Entrepreneurship Theory and Practice, 36*(3), 513–541.

Edwards, J., & Cornwall, A. (eds) (2014). *Feminisms, Empowerment and Development: Changing Women's Lives*. London: Bloomsbury Publishing.

Edwards-Schachter, M., & Wallace, M. L. (2017). "Shaken, but not stirred": Sixty years of defining social innovation. *Technological Forecasting and Social Change, 119*, 64–79.

Eren, H. (2010). *Technological Innovation of University Students' Social Innovation Capabilities: A Model Proposal to Measure the Impact on Trends*. Ankara: Defense Sciences Institute of the Military Academy.

Fairlie, R. W., & Robb, A. M. (2009). Gender differences in business performance: Evidence from the characteristics of business owners survey. *Small Business Economics, 33*, 375–395.

Fang, Y., Henfridsson, O., & Jarvenpaa, S. L. (2018). Editorial on generating business and social value from digital entrepreneurship and innovation. *Journal of Strategic Information Systems, 27*(4), 275–277.

Ferguson, L., 2007. The United Nations World Tourism Organisation. *New Political Economy, 12*, 557–568.

Filimonau, V., Matyakubov, U., Matniyozov, M., Shaken, A., & Mika, M. (2022). Women entrepreneurs in tourism in a time of a life event crisis. *Journal of Sustainable Tourism, 32 (3), 457–479*. https://doi.org/10.1080/09669582.2022.2091142.

Font, X., Garay, L., & Jones, S. (2016). A social cognitive theory of sustainability empathy. *Annals of Tourism Research, 58*, 65–80. https://doi.org/10.1016/j.annals.2016.02.004.

GEM (Global Entrepreneurship Monitor) (2021). *GEM 2020/2021 Global Report*. https://www.gemconsortium.org/report/gem-20202021-global-report.

GEM (Global Entrepreneurship Monitor) (2022). *Global Entrepreneurship Monitor 2021/2022 Women's Entrepreneurship Report: From Crises to Opportunity*. GEM.

Giones, F., & Brem, A. (2017). Digital technology entrepreneurship: A definition and research agenda. *Technology Innovation Management Review, 7*(5), 44–51.

Gomezelj, D. G. (2016). A systematic review of research on innovation in hospitality and tourism. *International Journal of Contemporary Hospitality Management, 28*(3), 516–558. https://doi.org/10.1108/IJCHM-10-2014-0510.

Goyal, A. (2011). Developing women: Why technology can help. *Information Technology for Development, 17*(2), 112–132. https://doi.org/10.1080/02681102.2010.537252.

Harvey, C., Maclean, M., Gordon, J., & Shaw, E. (2011). Andrew Carnegie and the foundations of contemporary entrepreneurial philanthropy. *Business History, 53*(3), 425–450.

Hébert, R. F., & Link, A. N. (2007). Historical perspectives on the entrepreneur. *Foundations and Trends in Entrepreneurship, 2*(4), 261–408. https://doi.org/10.1561/0300000008.

Huarng, K. H., Mas-Tur, A., & Yu, T. H. K. (2012). Factors affecting the success of women entrepreneurs. *International Entrepreneurship and Management Journal*, *8*(4), 487–497. https://doi.org/10.1007/s11365-012-0233-4.

Jennings, J. E., Jennings, P. D., & Sharifian, M. (2016). Living the dream? Assessing the "entrepreneurship as emancipation" perspective in a developed region. *Entrepreneurship Theory and Practice*, *40*(1), 81–110.

Jørgensen,M. T., Hansen, A. V., Sørensen, F., Fuglsang, L., Sundbo, J., & Jensen, J. F. (2021). Collective tourism social entrepreneurship: A means for community mobilization and social transformation. *Annals of Tourism Research*, *88*, 103171. https://doi.org/10.1016/j.annals.2021.103171.

Khajeheian, D. (2013). New venture creation in social media platform: Towards a framework for media entrepreneurship. In: Friedrichsen, M., & Mühl-Benninghaus, W. (eds.), *Handbook of Social Media Management: Value Chain and Business Models in Changing Media Markets*, 125–142. Springer. https://doi.org/10.1007/978-3-642-28897-5_8.

Khan, M. (2015). Women empowerment, entrepreneurship, and capacity development. *Journal for Studies in Management and Planning*, *1*, 43–56.

Kimbu, A. N., & Ngoasong, M. Z. (2016). Women as vectors of social entrepreneurship. *Annals of Tourism Research*, *60*, 63–79. https://doi.org/10.1016/j.annals.2016.06.002.

Krieger-Boden, C., & Sorgner, A. (2018). Labor market opportunities for women in the digital age. *Economics*, *12*(1), 20180028. https://doi.org/10.5018/economics-ejournal.ja.2018-28.

Lindberg, M., Forsberg, L., & Karlberg, H. (2015). Gendered social innovation: A theoretical lens for analysing structural transformation in organisations and society. *International Journal of Social Entrepreneurship and Innovation*, *3*, 472. https://doi.org/10.1504/IJSEI.2015.073540.

Lozano, A. V., Moliner, L. A., Murillo, D., & Buckland, H. (2019). Understanding the effects of social capital on social innovation ecosystems in Latin America through the lens of social network approach. *International Review of Sociology*, *29*(1), 1–35.

Mahato, S. S., Phi, G. T., & Prats, L. (2021). Design thinking for social innovation: Secrets to success for tourism social entrepreneurs. *Journal of Hospitality and Tourism Management*, *49*, 396–406. https://doi.org/10.1016/j.jhtm.2021.10.010.

Malek, A., & Costa, C. (2015). Integrating communities into tourism planning through social innovation. *Tourism Planning & Development*, *12*(3), 281–299. https://doi.org/10.1080/21568316.2014.951125.

Mivehchi, L. (2019). The role of information technology in women entrepreneurship: The case of e-retailing in Iran. *Procedia Computer Science*, *158*, 508–512. https://doi.org/10.1016/j.procs.2019.09.082.

Monllor, J., & Murphy, P. J. (2017). Natural disasters, entrepreneurship, and creation after destruction: A conceptual approach. *International Journal of Entrepreneurial Behavior & Research*, *23*(4), 618–637. https://doi.org/10.1108/IJEBR-02-2016-0050.

Moulaert, F., MacCallum, D., & Hillier, J. (2013). Social innovation: Intuition, precept, concept, theory and practice. In: F. Moulaert, D. MacCallum, A.

Mehmood, & A. Hamdouch (eds.), The International Handbook on Social Innovation: Collective Action, Social Learning and Transdisciplinary Research, 13–24. Cheltenham, UK: Edward Elgar Publishing. https://doi.org/10.4337/9781849809986.00011.

Mulgan, G. (2006). The process of social innovation. *Innovations: Technology, Governance, Globalization*, *1*(2) 145–162. https://doi.org/10.1162/itgg.2006.1.2.145.

Murray, R., Caulier-Grice, J., & Mulgan, G. (2010). *The Open Book of Social Innovation*. London: The Young Foundation.

Negas, M. C., Carvalho, L. C., & Sousa, I. D. (2020). *Inova, ção e Tecnologia: Uma isão Multidisciplinar* (1ª ed.). Lisboa: Sílabo í.

Nicholls, A., & Murdock, A. (2012). The nature of social innovation. In: Nicholls, A., & Murdock, A. (eds.), *Social innovation*. London: Palgrave Macmillan.

Niñerola, A., Sánchez-Rebull, M. V., & Hernández-Lara, A. B. (2019). Tourism research on sustainability: A bibliometric analysis. *Sustainability*, *11*, 1377.

Nomnga, V. (2017). Unlocking the potential of women entrepreneurs in the tourism and hospitality industry in the Eastern Cape Province, South Africa. *Journal of Economics and Behavioral Studies*, *9*, 6–13. https://doi.org/10.22610/jebs.v9i4(J).1817.

Nyseth T., & Hamdouch A. (2019). The transformative power of social innovation in urban planning and local development. *Urban Planning*, *4*(1), 1–6.

Osei, C. D., & Zhuang, J. (2020). Rural poverty alleviation strategies and social capital link: The mediation role of women entrepreneurship and social innovation. *SAGE Open*, *10*(2), 1–11. https://doi.org/10.1177/2158244020925504.

Pécot, M., Ricaurte-Quijano, C., Khoo, C., Alonso Vázquez, M., Barahona-Canales, D., Chiao, E., & Tan, R. (2024). From empowering women to being empowered by women: A gendered social innovation framework for tourism-led development initiatives. *Tourism Management*, *102*, 104883–104883. https://doi.org/10.1016/j.tourman.2024.104883.

Peeters, L. W., & Ateljevic, I. (2017). Women empowerment entrepreneurship nexus in tourism: Processes of social innovation. In: C. Costa, E. Panyik, & D. Buhalis (eds.), *Tourism and Entrepreneurship:* International Perspectives, 94–109. Routledge.

Pergelova, A., Manolova, T., Simeonova-Ganeva, R., & Yordanova, D. (2018). Democratizing entrepreneurship? Digital technologies and the internationalization of female-led SMEs. *Journal of Small Business Management*, *57*(1), 14–39. https://doi.org/10.1111/jsbm.12494.

Phi, G. (2017). *A Critical Analysis of Microfinance Tourism and Poverty Alleviation: Characteristics, Opportunities and Constraints*. Queensland: Griffith University.

Pikkemaat, B., Peters, M., & Bichler, B. F. (2019). Innovation research in tourism: Research streams and actions for the future. *Journal of Hospitality and Tourism Management*, *41*, 184–196. https://doi.org/10.1016/j.jhtm.2019.10.007.

Pol, E., & Ville, S. (2009). Social innovation: Buzz word or enduring term. *The Journal of Socio-Economics*, *38*(6), 878–885.

Ratten, V. (2014). Encouraging collaborative entrepreneurship in developing countries: The current challenges and a research agenda. *Journal of Entrepreneurship in Emerging Economies*, *6*(3), 298–308.

Santos, F. M. (2010). *A Positive Theory of Social Entrepreneurship*. INSEAD Working Paper No. 2009/23/EFE/INSEAD, Social Innovation Centre. https://doi.org/10.2139/ssrn.1553072.

Savage, A. E., Barbieri, C., & Jakes, S. (2022). Cultivating success: Personal, family, and societal attributes affecting women in agritourism. *Journal of Sustainable Tourism*, *30*(7), 1699–1719. https://doi.org/10.1080/09669582.2020.1838528.

Say, J. B. (2008). *A Treatise on Political Economy* (6th ed.). New York: Sentry Press.

Schumpeter, J. A. (1912). *Theorie der wirtschaftlichen Entwicklung*. Leipzig: Duncker & Humblot.

Shane, S. (2003). *A General Theory of Entrepreneurship: The Individual-opportunity Nexus*. Cheltenham, UK: Edward Elgar Publishing.

Sharma, V., & Bhat, D. A. R. (2022a). Co-creation and technological innovation: The predictors of guest satisfaction and revisit intention in hospitality industry. *International Journal of Hospitality & Tourism Systems*, *15*, 91–100.

Sharma, V., & Bhat, D. (2022b). The role of community involvement in sustainable tourism strategies: A social and environmental innovation perspective. *Business Strategy and Development*, *6*(2), 119–127. https://doi.org/10.1002/bsd2.227.

Shelton, L. M. (2006). Female entrepreneurs, work-family conflict, and venture performance: New insights into the work-family interface. *Journal of Small Business Management*, *44*(2), 285–297. https://doi.org/10.1111/j.1540-627X.2006.00168.x.

Taylor, J. B. (1970). Introducing social innovation. *The Journal of Applied Behavioral Science*, *6*(1), 69–77. https://doi.org/10.1177/002188637000600104.

Tracey, P., & Stott, N. (2017). Social innovation: A window on alternative ways of organizing and innovating. *Innovation: Management, Policy and Practice*, *19*(1), 51–60.

Trunfio, M., & Campana, S. (2019). Drivers and emerging innovations in knowledge-based destinations: Towards a research agenda. *Journal of Destination Marketing and Management*, *14*, *100370*. https://doi.org/10.1016/j.jdmm.2019.100370.

Ughetto, E., Rossi, M., Audretsch, D., & Lehmann, E. E. (2020). Female entrepreneurship in the digital era. *Small Business Economics*, *55*(2), 305–312. https://doi.org/10.1007/s11187-019-00298-8.

UN Women (2020). *Addressing the Economic Fallout of COVID-19: Pathways and Policy Options for a Gender-Responsive Recovery*. https://www.unwomen.org/en/digital-library/publications/2020/06/policy-brief-addressing-the-economic-fallout-of-covid-19.

UNWTO (2010). *Global Report on Women in Tourism: Preliminary Findings*. https://www.unwomen.org/sites/default/files/Headquarters/Media/Stories/en/folletoglobarlreportpdf.pdf.

UNWTO (2019). *Global Report on Women in Tourism* (2nd ed.) https://doi.org/10.18111/9789284420384.

Vukovic, D. B., Petrovic, M., Maiti, M., & Vujko, A. (2021). Tourism development, entrepreneurship and women's empowerment: Focus on Serbian countryside. *Journal of Tourism Futures*, 9(3), 417–437. https://doi.org/10.1108/jtf-10-2020-0167.

Wirth, S., Bandi Tanner, M., & Mayer, H. (2023). Social innovations in tourism: Analysing processes, actors, and tipping points. *Tourism Geographies*, *25*(5), 1322–1340. https://doi.org/10.1080/14616688.2022.2155697.

World Bank Group (2015). Women, Business and the Law 2016: Getting to Equal. Washington, DC: World Bank.

World Economic Forum (2021). *Global Gender Gap Report 2021: Insight Report*. Cologny/Geneva, Switzerland: WEF.

Yadav, V., Unni, J., Naik, R., & Dutta, S. (2022). Gender differentials in entrepreneurship: Insights from a multi-method study. *Journal of Entrepreneurship*, *31*(1), 30–64. https://doi.org/10.1177/09713557211069283.

Zahra, S., Gedajlovic, E., Neubaum, D., & Shulman, J. (2009). A typology of social entrepreneurs: Motives, search processes and ethical challenges. *Journal of Business Venturing*, *24*. 519–532. https://doi.org/10.1016/j.jbusvent.2008.04.007.

Zhu, L., Kara, O., & Zhu, X. (2019). A comparative study of women entrepreneurship in transitional economies: The case of China and Vietnam. *Journal of Entrepreneurship in Emerging Economies*, *11*(1), 66–80.

Zimmerman, M. A. (2000). Empowerment theory. In: Rappaport, J., & Seidman, E. (eds.), *Handbook of Community Psychology*. Amsterdam: Kluwer Academic Publishers, 43–63.

6. Rethinking gender bias in China's tourism and hospitality industry: How to improve employees' well-being?

Kexin Yuan

6.1 WHY DO TOURISM PRACTITIONERS NEED TO RETHINK GENDER BIAS?

Traditional gender division ties women to "empathy" (e.g., emotional labour) (Chen et al., 2014) and men to "physical labor" (e.g., luggage handling), resulting in a homogenization trap of service experience under stereotypes (Kogovsek & Kogovsek, 2015). According to "*episteme*", individual social knowledge and understanding of gender were constructed based on the nature of the family. In the context of Chinese culture, before 1978, the ideology of the main relationship between males and females was conservative and mainly centered around marriage. At this time, the dominant form of Chinese marriage was arranged marriage, and was often agreed based on partners' political backgrounds (Qiu, 2013). After 1978, the liberal ideology of Chinese gender relationships started to focus on love and economic conditions, but women still generally had lower educational backgrounds than the men involved in the partnerships (Qiu, 2013). Xu and Pan (2023) found that women's education and socioeconomic status are also important in the marriage exchange. Shifting to the workplace context, influenced by historical culture and family gender structures, individuals bring gender expectations into their jobs, such as mistaken thinking that men should assume more work responsibilities or that women are inherently more patient (i.e., Kogovsek & Kogovsek, 2015). This phenomenon is demonstrated by the core argument of Job Demand-Resources Theory (JD-R Theory)

- when job demands are distorted by gender labels, mismatches between human resources and service needs become inevitable. Additionally, during job applications, it is often mistakenly assumed that women need higher educational qualifications than men to enter the same positions. This requires not only more women to enter decision-making and managerial positions, but also voices from different gender perspectives to discuss work-related topics. China's social evolution in gender cognition has permeated all sectors, including tourism and hospitality. Compared to the traditional workplace stereotype of "male-dominated management and female-oriented service", the gender composition of industry leadership has changed significantly in recent years. Research has found that after more than a decade of continuous growth, the proportion of women employed in the tourism industry has exceeded that of all other industries, with women accounting for 54% of the total workforce (UNWTO, 2023). Diverse gender perspectives have entered the public view through corporate strategy conferences, industry forums, and other channels. For example, the CEO of a leading hotel chain proposed the concept of "gender-neutral service" in a public speech, challenging the traditional single expectation of female employees as "affable" or "patient", and emphasizing the value of cross-gender collaboration in crisis management and customer relationship maintenance. However, it still required more effort in terms of salary and job security during the pandemic (UNWTO, 2023).

Against the backdrop of these existing phenomena and issues, there is a need to rethink gender bias. Gender bias can impede enterprises' efficient utilization of resources and hinder talent development. In this case, based on JD-R Theory (Bakker et al., 2014; Bakker et al., 2023), gender bias may cause two resource mismatches: 1) External resources: The best candidates may lose their job resources because of gender bias. For example, female managers often face an "emotional" stigma, and may lose decision-making power in budget allocation; 2) Internal resources: Under the influence of gender bias, the development of employees' ability is significantly constrained. For example, male employees with empathy and high emotional intelligence cannot fully leverage and develop their unique advantages and are forced into unsuitable positions.

Furthermore, from a corporate management perspective, gender stereotypes may results in unmet gender-related expectation in the workplace. It may induce emotional exhaustion, and erodes employees' organizational identification and commitment to corporate culture in the long run. From a sustainable brand development perspective, tourism and hospitality enterprises gain a competitive edge by co-creating value for customers and society alongside employees (Font et al., 2021). For example, integrating corporate social responsibility (CSR) initiatives can extend beyond employment creation to drive social evolution—specifically by enhancing professional awareness and dismantling stereotypes. This process enables employees to transcend gender-based expectations in the workplace, thereby fostering improved well-being.

6.2 WHAT IS THE CURRENT STATUS IN CHINA?

To date, according to the fifth Sustainable Development Goal (SDG) released by the United Nations, efforts are being made to promote more women to decision-making positions. There is a notable increase in the number of female leaders and employees in tourism and hospitality (Suesz, 2020). For instance, according to a 2024 McKinsey report, women in senior manager/director roles rose from 32% in 2015 to 37% in 2024 (McKinsey & Company, 2024). As of March 2025, female general managers accounted for 26% of Hilton Group's hotels in Greater China, and female members exceeded 60% in hotel management teams. Female executives account for 25% of management in Chinese mainland enterprises, higher than the global average of 21%, influencing the hotel industry to increase female executive appointments (TTG China, 2025). In terms of female employment, since 2018, the Accor Group has upgraded its international gender equality and diversity network from the WAGG (Accor Women of the Times) project to RiiSE. It is open to both men and women, promotes talents (especially female talents) to hold important positions, and opposes all forms of discrimination. In 2023, Ctrip Group and 10 other tourism enterprises jointly launched the "Travel Mulan Plan" aimed at increasing female employment, and simultaneously released the "Survey Report on Female Employment in the Tourism Industry" for the entire travel industry (China Daily, 2023). According to the 2025 Tujia Homestay Female Host Community Report, female hosts account for nearly 60% of the platform (Bakker & Twining-Ward, 2018). As more women advance into managerial roles, the gender gap has gradually narrowed, a shift that relies on internal corporate education and training.

This transformation is rooted in structural social changes: on the one hand, the China Women's Development Outline (2021–2030) incorporates workplace gender equality into policy frameworks, prompting enterprises to establish anti-discrimination systems; on the other hand,

Generation Z practitioners increasingly demand "gender-neutral career development"—data from a recruitment platform shows that 67% of post-1995 candidates in the tourism industry in 2024 prioritized whether enterprises offered "gender-differentiated promotion channels". As the industry transitions from "standardized service" to "personalized experience", the traditional model of dividing roles by gender (e.g., men for outdoor guiding, women for front-desk reception) is facing challenges. For example, a Yunnan cultural tourism group trialed male employees in "butler" roles at parent-child homestays, and their meticulous service achieved a 92% customer satisfaction rate, breaking the stereotype that "women excel in emotional labor".

The study adopts a qualitative research approach to gain in-depth insights in the tourism and hospitality industry. Semi-structured interviews were conducted with managers in the hotel and tourism industry in China. The selection of participants was based on their diverse job roles and levels of experience within the industry. The interview questions were designed to explore the managers' perspectives on job demand and resources, reflecting how they lead and complete their jobs. This study adopts JD-R Theory (Bakker et al., 2014; Bakker et al., 2023) and Social Identity Theory (SIT) (Tajfel & Turner, 1979) to explore how to improve employees' well-being in a gender-biased situation. Job demands are related to their expectations from gender stereotypes. Job resources depend on individual employees' operant and operand resources (Prebensen & Uysal, 2021). However, not all employees are obliged to meet gender-stereotypical expectations beyond the scope of their work—such as the fallacy that men should undertake more physical labor, or that women should be inherently gentle and patient. Based on SIT, it is suggested that the process of developing social identity is from categorization and comparison (Tajfel & Turner, 1979). In the subsequent section, key information and content will be extracted from the dialogues of 15 interviewees for elaboration and summarization. It will explore strategies for enhancing employee well-being from the perspectives of male and female managers, focusing on whether or not gender influences responses to employee management and work-related issues within power dynamics.

6.3 RESULTS

6.3.1 What Do Employees Mean for the Brand/Corporate?

Managers advocate for "familial organizational identity", replacing transactional employment relationships with emotional bonds, which links to reduced gender bias and improved employee well-being. Employees serve as "active brand/corporate ambassadors", translating abstract brand values into tangible experiences. The employees' role in prior discussions helps to dismantle gender stereotypes in service. Science employees act as both "cultural inheritors" and "ecological filters", sustaining brand vitality by attracting like-minded talent, a finding from the analysis of occupational gender segregation. Those managers position "emotional connection" as the core driver of employee-brand relationships, extending the traditional focus on material incentives to include intangible, identity-based motivations.

Manager #4 (female) explained:

> Firstly, let's talk about the *internal relationship*. The internal relationship is the prerequisite for the external development of our brand. Within the brand, our employees are like family members. When new employees join, we also treat them as family. The employees will have regular dinners and enjoy the same treatment as guests in catering. They have a cordial relationship with the boss during breaks. Only in this way can the sense of belonging between employees and the brand be truly cultivated, making employees more than just ordinary employees. This sense of belonging can inspire their loyalty and dedication to the enterprise and actively participate in the development and growth of the enterprise.
>
> Once the internal sense of belonging is established, the foundation for the growth and expansion of the brand is laid. Externally, employees are the representatives of the brand. A brand cannot speak. Without employees, it is just a name. The words and deeds of these employees are closely related to the connotation and value of the brand. Our employees are first and foremost the representatives and conveyors of the brand image, and their service quality directly affects the customer's service experience. Our front-line employees always greet guests with a smile, and our employees will meet any reasonable needs of guests promptly. Therefore, many of our guests are familiar with the employees, and they feel our brand is very friendly.
>
> Secondly, they also determine the quality of the fresh "blood" we attract and have a great impact on the survival of the brand. The good brand image and corporate culture established by employees can attract more excellent talent to join the enterprise, and can also help the enterprise screen out inappropriate people and maintain the high-quality development of the brand. We have recruited a lot of fresh blood since the opening, but only a small number

of people have stayed. The power to decide whether they stay or leave is not only concentrated in me but also in our front-line employees.

Manager #8 (male) & #12 (male) emphasized:

> Currently, employees and enterprises are indeed in a relationship of growing together through our internal and external activities.
>
> It is *not a pure superior-subordinate relationship*, but it is also inseparable. Basically, our company is staffed by young people with artistic inclinations, and they all dislike being constrained. Among them, there are relationships like dream chasers, superiors, and subordinates, *brothers, and family members.*

6.3.2 How Do Managers Contribute to Employees' Well-being?

The interviewed managers unanimously agreed that their leadership styles and personalities had a significant impact on the brand climate within their organizations, not gender.

Manager #5 (female) & #6 (female) stated:

> We will establish loyalty programs for employees similar to those for customers, while providing special care and welfare benefits at every node.
>
> Well, regarding this point, in domestic hotels, I think it depends on the individual leader. This depends more on *leadership*.

Manager #2 (female) & #3 (female) added:

> In the training of our management, it must be about how to *improve* employees' leadership, how to *motivate* subordinates, and how to *delegate authority*. What we talk about is the training of some management concepts. Then, if it is for employees, I think it should focus more on how to *improve personal knowledge and skills*, train them how to control each position in the company, and how to enable us to do better, that is, how to *practice more*. Another point is that most employees lack a sense of security. Most of our positions require service operations, which is very hard. It is necessary to reasonably arrange and coordinate the time of employees. And most employees with families have a lot of concerns, such as having to support the elderly and raise children. As a company manager, as a management layer, you need to relieve the concerns of employees. If they can't even get better guarantees for these concerns, then how can we talk about a sense of belonging, right? For example, providing annual physical health examinations for employees or their families. And for some management cadres who are from other places and we want to retain them, we can provide childcare services for their children.

> It is this kind of welfare. *Employee welfare is probably more important, and [also] very important is salary and compensation and employee benefits. Besides, we also provide an additional care package for our employees with better internal services, such as ice-pack in hot weather.*

By compared with manager #1 (male) & #14 (male), they explained:

> Then it may be to create a certain value in their work. Actually, in our hotel, especially this kind of economy hotel, the requirements for female employees when recruiting are not high. Because this is an industry with a relatively low entry threshold, and their social level may not have reached a certain height, so the entry is relatively easy. For this group, it may be just a process of solving their survival and food and clothing problems. However, if they have work experience in this kind of economy hotel in the early stage, for some relatively junior employees, it may not be too easy for them to find other jobs. But with certain work experience in a chain hotel, it will not be too difficult for them to find a job. In addition, because our hotel is a franchise store, the employees' feelings are not obvious. But for directly-operated hotels, when employees can see a clear promotion path, they will be more motivated to move forward.
>
> In the context of competing with other competitors, we place greater emphasis on achieving unanimous recognition—both externally and internally. Our commitment lies in delivering more meticulous services to enhance the experience of those who engage with our company/brand, thereby fostering a better experience for all stakeholders.

All managers agree that employee loyalty in China's hospitality industry relies on "direct leadership behavior" (e.g., management style, welfare distribution) over top-down brand culture, echoing the document's emphasis on leadership-driven gender equality. Managers prioritize "practical skills" in training, by matching training to operational needs. Regardless of managers' gender, their answers show no significant differences in work content.

6.4 WHAT CAN WE DO NOW AND IN THE FUTURE?

This study finds that both male and female managers demonstrate commonalities in their perspectives and suggestions regarding job demands and resources, including building relationships, creating a family-like work atmosphere (i.e., Kwok et al., 2015), and proposing additional work benefits. The research question explores how to eliminate beyond-job content gender expectations in the workplace and enhance employees' work well-being amid existing gender biases. Based on this, the interviews reveal that a job demand-oriented cross-gender collaboration team helps employees refine their gender cognition, reduce gender-based expectations, and enhance job satisfaction, thereby further promoting employee well-being. Through role comparisons across diverse gender groups, reconstructing the "familial concept" within corporate branding, reshapes employees' gender perceptions. That is, managing employee expectations proves more critical than merely meeting them. This approach enhances gender identification by embedding inclusive values in organizational culture, thereby reducing stereotypes in order to help employees obtain a comprehensive social identity. Furthermore, openness and empathic leadership can motivate employees to be successful, no matter what their race, gender, age, nationality, or disability status (Celestin & Vanitha, 2020; Rahman, 2016). As manager #2 claimed, "Our brand values fuel employees to keep enthusiasm and explore infinite possibilities".

Guided by SIT and the JD-R Theory, we need to coordinate resource allocation with job demands, which involves reducing gender stereotypes among employees (i.e., managing expectations) and satisfying employee expectations. Furthermore, managers should influence employees through leadership modeling, demonstrating equal treatment of different genders without expectations. Gender-neutral service team collaboration is also used to deepen employees' understanding of the organization and help build stable work relationships. When employees' inherent gender stereotypes are challenged, and their implicit expectations are unmet, it can lead to emotional exhaustion. Job-oriented emotional intelligence training can help employees develop rational thinking and empathy (Porath & Boissy, 2023). Namely, employees enhance resource utilization efficiency to address more job demands and think from others' perspectives. Meanwhile, integrating employees' inherent preferences and characteristics into organizational culture fosters familiarity and creates a psychologically safe work environment. By doing so, employees engage in self-categorization and are categorized into cross-gender workgroups. Through intergroup and outgroup comparisons, a comprehensive gender cognition system can be established. Given that most studies emphasize work-family conflict (Byron, 2005), constructing family-friendly workplaces can demonstrate support for employees, regardless of gender. Leaders with a family-oriented approach can encourage employees to bring their family members to participate in company activities. This can not only enhance employees' credibility and authenticity but also provide them with a psychological sense of security and belonging, facilitating better integration into the company culture. For instance, Universal and Disney provide employees' families with seasonal complimentary tickets, while AMECO offers limited free flight tickets for employees and their families to travel.

REFERENCES

Bakker, A. B., Demerouti, E., & Sanz-Vergel, A. (2023). Job demands–resources theory: Ten years later. *Annual Review of Organizational Psychology and Organizational Behavior, 10*(1), 25–53.

Bakker, A. B., Demerouti, E., & Sanz-Vergel, A. I. (2014). Burnout and work engagement: The JD–R approach. *Annual Review of Organizational Psychology and Organizational Behavior, 1*(2014), 389–411.

Bakker, M., & Twining-Ward, L. (2018). Tourism and the sharing economy: policy and potential of sustainable peer-to-peer accommodation.

Byron, K. (2005). A meta-analytic review of work–family conflict and its antecedents. *Journal of Vocational Behavior, 67*(2), 169–198.

ChinaDaily (2023). 2023 旅游行业女性从业报告 发布旅游行业女性从业比例和稳定性高. https://cn.chinadaily.com.cn/a/202303/08/WS64086ad2a3102ada8b232998.html.

Chen, W., Lu, J., Liu, L., Lin, W. (2014). Gender differences of empathy. *Advances in Psychological Science, 22*(9): 1423–1434.

Celestin, M., & Vanitha, N. (2020). The rise of empathetic leadership: Why emotional intelligence is the new power skill. *International Journal of Interdisciplinary Research in Arts and Humanities (IJIRAH), 5*(2), 49–56.

Ctrip (2023) Women's Employment in the Travel Industry. https://mp.weixin.qq.com/s/kNZejmi2OXPLKy7o9u4x4A.

Diaz, T. I. (2024). Uniquely feminine traits of successful female leaders. *Globis Insights.* https://globisinsights.com/career-skills/communication/successful-female-leaders/.

Font, X., English, R., Gkritzali, A., & Tian, W. S. (2021). Value co-creation in sustainable tourism: A service-dominant logic approach. *Tourism Management, 82*, 104200.

Kogovsek, M., & Kogovsek, M. (2015). Hospitality and tourism gender issues remain unsolved: A call for research. *Quaestus*, (6), 194.

Kwok, S. Y. C. L., Cheng, L., & Wong, D. F. K. (2015). Family emotional support, positive psychological capital and job satisfaction among Chinese white-collar workers. *Journal of Happiness Studies, 16*, 561–582. https://doi.org/10.1007/s10902-014-9522-7.

Lin, Y. C., Yu, C., & Yi, C. C. (2014). The effects of positive affect, person-job fit, and well-being on job performance. *Social Behavior and Personality: An International Journal, 42*(9), 1537–1547.

McKinsey & Company (2024). *Women in the Workplace 2024: The 10th-Anniversary Report.* https://www.mckinsey.com/featured-insights/diversity-and-inclusion/women-in-the-workplace.

National Bureau of Statistics (2025). *Statistical Monitoring Report on the Programme for the Development of Chinese Women (2021–2030).* https://www.stats.gov.cn/sj/zxfb/202501/t20250124_1958439.html.

Obrenovic, B., Jianguo, D., Khudaykulov, A., & Aamir Shafique Khan, M. (2020). Work-family conflict impact on psychological safety and psychological well-being: A job performance model. *Frontiers in Psychology, 11*, 475.

Prebensen, N. K., & Uysal, M. S. (2021). Value co-creation in tourism eco-systems: Operant and operand resources. In: *Routledge Handbook of the Tourist Experience* (pp. 564–576). UK: Routledge.

Porath, C., & Boissy, A. (2023). Practice empathy as a team. *Harvard Business Review.*

Qiu, Y. (2013). *Chinese Marriage Traditions: Exploring Contemporary Changes.* Bachelor thesis. Lund University. https://lup.lub.lu.se/student-papers/search/publication/3994741.

Rahman, W. A. (2016). Empathy and trust: Into a better workplace environment. *Journal of Business and Economics, 7*(12), 2025–2034.

Suesz, E. (2020). *Has the Tourism Industry Made Progress on Gender Equality?* Booking.com. https://partner.booking.com/zh-cn/click-magazine/%E8%B6%8B%E5%8A%BF%E4%B8%8E%E8%A7%81%E8%A7%A3/%E6%97%85%E6%B8%B8%E4%B8%9A%E5%9C%A8%E6%80%A7%E5%88%AB%E5%B9%B3%E7%AD%89%E6%96%B9%E9%9D%A2%E5%8F%96%E5%BE%97%E8%BF%9B%E6%AD%A5%E4%BA%86%E5%90%97%EF%BC%9F.

Tajfel, H., Turner, J. C., Austin, W. G., & Worchel, S. (1979). An integrative theory of intergroup conflict. Organizational Identity: A reader, 56–65.

Tajfel, H., & Turner, J. C. (1979). An integrative theory of intergroup conflict. In: W. G. Austin & S. Worchel (eds.), *The Social Psychology of Intergroup Relations* (pp. 33–48). Monterey, CA: Brooks/Cole.

TTG China (2025). The number of female executives in China's hotel industry has increased significantly. *TTG ASIA*. https://ttgchina.com/2025/04/15/%E4%B8%AD%E5%9B%BD%E9%85%92%E5%BA%97%E8%A1%8C%E4%B8%9A%E5%A5%B3%E6%80%A7%E9%AB%98%E7%AE%A1%E6%95%B0%E9%87%8F%E5%A2%9E%E9%95%BF%E6%98%BE%E7%9D%80/.

UNWTO (2023) *Women Take 'Centre Stage' in Tourism Development.* https://www.unwto.org/news/women-take-centre-stage-in-tourism-development.

Xu, Q., & Pan, X. (2023). Beauty and status: Matching and exchange within Chinese marriages. *Chinese Journal of Sociology, 9*(3), 375–407. https://doi.org/10.1177/2057150X231189027.

7. Nexus of cultural heritage sustainability, gender equality, and tourism in Swat

Hassan Ali, Farhad Nazir, and Durre Shehwar

7.1 INTRODUCTION

Tourism helps enhance goodwill among the people and increases the socio-economic growth of countries (Adnan Hye & Ali Khan, 2013). Tourism as an industry boosts a nation's foreign exchange reserves; meanwhile, it provides both direct and indirect employment for the population at every level of society. Furthermore, introducing a country's handicrafts and fine arts contributes to conserving this world's beauty, preserving cultures, promoting people's moral values, and increasing national cohesiveness and global solidarity (Manzoor et al., 2019). Apart from the direct impact on the national economy, tourism also has relationships with other sectors of the economy, such as agriculture, animal husbandry, handicrafts, construction, transport, entertainment, etc. Inbound tourism, which has been presented as a globalized service, has become one of the largest industries in the world (Katircioglu, 2009). For most countries, global tourism is the biggest foreign exchange earner in matters of foreign exchange balance (Ferguson, 2007). Currently, many communities focus on promoting tourism investments rather than considering the consequences related to developing tourism facilities in terms of the impact on the environment and culture of their society. Cultural tourism may also benefit in conserving and promoting people's cultural and historical values and traditions, which may promote the conservation of cultural heritage sites and the revival of forgotten or dying native traditions and arts and crafts (Sarfo-Mensah et al., 2014). Cultural heritage tourism acts as a catalyst in the economic development process through the impact generated by the arrival of foreign visitors. These visitors are attracted by their historical, artistic, scientific, or lifestyle/heritage interest in the products offered by a community, region, group, or institution. Cultural heritage tourists are known to have extended stays with high expenditures, making this typology of tourism a pivotal contributor to economic development (Stipe, 2003).

Gender equality is a key human rights matter that has received much attention from major international organizations and governments worldwide. Across the globe, discrimination against women has been considered a significant offense, and specific legal bindings are provided to ensure gender equality. This focus on gender is reasonably expected since gender inequality affects society and may slow down the progression of an economy. Gender equality promotes employment opportunities, better productivity, and economic progress in general (Kolovich, 2018). Ever since the United Nations developed the 2030 Agenda for Sustainable Development in 2015, the importance of gender equality, particularly in the course of development, cannot be overemphasized (United Nations, 2015). In this framework of the 2030 Agenda, gender equality and empowering all women and girls are presented as the fifth out of 17 Sustainable Development Goals (SDGs); gender equality and women's economic, social, and political empowerment are acknowledged as prerequisites for advancement toward accomplishing all the SDGs. In a similar context, over the past few years, the subject of tourism has come under much discussion concerning whether it is a factor that supports patriarchy, which leads to the oppression of women, or a factor that empowers women. Baum (2013) asserted that women heavily dominate the tourism sector, and in some countries, the female workforce in the tourism sector is almost twice that of male workers. However, according to Ferguson (2011), tourism is a gender-biased business. Moreover, tourism still holds the merits of conventional power dynamics tilted towards the male gender (Genç, 2018). Despite this, the diverse nature of tourism determinants offers numerous chances for the feminization of economies and has the potential to help emancipate women through a range of employment opportunities (Gil Arroyo et al., 2019).

Women's employment in the tourism industry has been reported to be globally higher, at 54% in most countries. Furthermore, Aghazamani and Hunt (2017) highlighted that women's entrepreneurship is promoted in tourism because of its diversity and low limitations for this gender. This is evident in several countries where more women are involved in tourism businesses than in other sectors. For instance, in Latin America, over 50% of tourism firms are managed by women, whereas only a limited number of women are involved in other businesses (World Bank, 2017). Notwithstanding, in case of several other countries, there are ceratin limitations in the course towards ensuring the gender equality in the workforce domain of tourism sector. While analyzing Swat, Pakistan's case, this chapter has ascertained the nexus of gender equality, cultural heritage, and sustainable tourism. Given this, the study has been aimed at unraveling the potential and limitations of gender equality in cultural heritage tourism using a qualitative research strategy.

7.2 LITERATURE REVIEW

7.2.1 Gender Equality and Tourism Employment

Gender equality is a decisive part of the tourism industry, particularly for the labor force, raising comprehensive societies and equitable financial circulation. In the workplace, self-respect is the ability to establish a sense of self-worth and appreciation, a useful trait in the tourism industry, which is strongly influenced by cultural and social norms, and dignity in the form of a decent work agenda (Gil Arroyo et al., 2019; Higgins-Desbiolles, 2006; Hodson, 2001; ILO, 2013). The International Labour Organization (ILO) defines decent work (SDG 8) as productive work performed with freedom, equity, security, and dignity, where rights are protected and adequate remuneration and social protection are ensured. It also promotes sustainable economic growth to support productive employment and equality in decent work (ILO, 2013). The relevance of decent work in tourism lies in the labor intensity of the industry, and opportunities for migrants and young people, especially for women, are higher than in most other industry sectors (Winchenbach et al., 2019).

Tourism, as an economic activity that generates a high percentage of Gross Domestic Product (GDP) and employment in the world economy, has close links with other financial sectors; when these are considered, tourism's total contribution rises to 10.3% of GDP and 27.3 million jobs (11.7% of total employment), with women forming the majority of the global workforce (Jiménez-García et al., 2020). In addition, studies have analysed economic growth in the tourism sector through changes in employment and increases in per capita income across various countries. Suitable employment is assessed through a multi-criteria approach encompassing many dimensions of the tourism industry.

However, when women achieve economic and social gains through tourism, this may lead to conflicts as traditional gender roles and identities change (Cembranel et al., 2022). Studies have shown that both genders face a double workload, domestic negotiations between partners, conflicts, and poor working conditions (Fischer & Holz, 2010; Higgins-Desbiolles, 2017; Jacobson, 2009; Korczynski & Ott, 2006; Paules, 1991).

Furthermore, suboptimal labour conditions and entrenched economic structures often intensify these challenges, limiting tourism's transformative potential for gender equity.(Cembranel et al., 2022). The literature highlights all those concerns, including the double burden, bargaining about family chores with a partner, and job strain. Additionally, working conditions and alternative economic models are crucial in meeting these challenges while restoring the significance of decent work to human employment (Noronha et al., 2018), particularly for those who suffer insecurity at the lowest levels of the organizational hierarchy (Dill et al., 2014; Hodson, 2001; Sayer, 2007; Thomas & Lucas, 2019).

While promising for growth, the tourism sector often has poor working conditions, including exploitation and low wages, and substantial inequalities in regards to the economic growth experienced (Liu, 2003; Stumpf & Cheshire, 2019).

7.2.2 Trilogy of Gender Equivalence, Heritage Tourism, and SDGs 2015–2030

Gender equality is a critical component of sustainability and calls for a combined and rights-based approach to its realization. Tourism grew significantly in the 1990s, accounting for approximately 9% of global GDP and employing one in every 11 people worldwide (Herbert, 2001; Wirawan et al., 2021). This growth, however, has not been all good since it has adopted some existing environmental, economic, and socio-cultural problems (Menchenko & Javed, 2024). There has been a focus on sustainable tourism to address these drawbacks, the primary goal of which is to try to reduce the impacts of imposing sustainable limits on the ecological, economic, and social worlds (Torkington et al., 2020). Combining or integrating gender equality, heritage tourism, and the UN's Sustainable Development Goals (SDGs) is essential for realizing sustainable development that cuts across its key dimensions: economic, social, environmental, and cultural dimensions.

The SDGs emphasize that gender equality (SDG 5), sustainable cities and communities (SDG 11), and decent work and economic growth

(SDG 8) are interlinked with heritage tourism (United Nations, 2024). Sustainable development in heritage tourism necessitates integrating gender perspectives to ensure equitable participation and benefit distribution. This means those who manage tangible and intangible cultural heritage should engage the communities in the management process since the importance of their roles cannot be overemphasized. Public- and tourist-oriented strategies and policies must cover gender equality, social participation, and sustainability of heritage tourism. From the mouthpiece of multiculturalism, social barriers and impediments must be erased from people's perceptions through educating them on different cultures and encouraging respect of those cultures. Compliance with policies of nondiscrimination, the embrace of culture, and education and awareness championing the introduction of gender-related cultural factors in the development of the tourism field for the empowerment of women should also be encouraged (Fleras, 2015; Gil Arroyo et al., 2019; Kato, 2019; Petrucci & Rivera, 2018). This can be made possible by implementing policies and other structures such as education, training, and other encouragement activities aimed at supporting women in the tourism business (Shantika et al., 2021).

7.2.3 Women and Cultural Heritage

There is a growing understanding that women are the primary culture bearers and creators, and have the potential to become a foundation for culture-based development and sustainability. Women's involvement in this realm is vital as they are crucial to heritage and development actors, and their policy guidance demonstrates this (Labadi & Gould, 2015). The use of fine arts has historically been a field in which women have invested their cultural heritage. For instance, Omani women artists utilize their art to conserve and raise awareness about cultural practices. These women have promoted traditional clothes and cultural symbols, thus maintaining a good grip on their culture (Salim Mohammed Al Mardhoof Al Saadi, 2020). Grobar (2017) analyzed women's significant contributions to national cultural identity and handicrafts and highlighted that the participation of women in economic development and heritage management is substantial and pivotal. Moreover, women have been involved in indigenous cultural heritage management and participate directly within their socio-cultural institutions to ensure equitable recognition of preservation practices (Onyemechalu & Ugwuanyi, 2021).

Corporate social responsibility has a positive influence on women's participation in cultural tourism, where women often take on leadership roles that boost rural development and help sustain local culture (Uduji et al., 2020). Regarding the demand determinant, women were involved in more heritage visits than men and were likely to contribute more to conserving these sites (Hafiane Hedahdia & Boukhemis, 2024). In other research, scholars emphasize that women are often responsible for passing down and maintaining traditional skills (Yan & Chiou, 2021).

7.3 METHOD

7.3.1 Study Locale

Swat Valley in Pakistan was selected as the site of this study. As an emerging tourist destination, the valley is known for its rich culture (e.g., local traditions, antique shops, handicrafts) and history (e.g., linked to its Buddhist and Hindu heritage (Iori, 2023; Khan, 2017; Ullah et al., 2019), as well as its "rock art" such as paintings, carvings, and inscriptions (Sardar, 2012). Given tourism's prominence in the area, Swat is deemed an appropriate place to investigate the link between cultural heritage, gender equality, and sustainable tourism.

7.3.2 Research Design

As a research strategy, a qualitative approach has been adopted because this strategy dominates the quantitative approach in social sciences due to its exploratory nature. It allows the researcher to collect real-world data, and the participant has the freedom to express themselves (Anderson, 2010). Kuper et al. (2008) asserted that semi-structured or unstructured interviews, focus groups, observation, and documented material are used for collecting qualitative data. The semi-structured interviews allow the respondents freedom of expression and personal narrative (Kakilla, 2021). Prearranged questions and discourse guide them, giving them the advantage of flexibility that allows them to change direction during the investigation. A semi-structured interview was adopted since the study focuses on obtaining people's opinions. Khan and MacEachen (2022) stated that video calling techniques help save time for both the interviewer and interviewee, and this technique was adopted in the study. These interviews were conducted through Zoom and WhatsApp applications.

7.3.3 Preparation for Data Collection

Open-ended questions were designed to facilitate the interview process. The questions were divided into different pre-prepared categories such as demographics, education, employment and relation to the tourism industry, experiences and challenges faced in the tourism industry, the connection between cultural heritage and gender equality, sustainable tourism development, and, lastly, recommendations and further suggestions.

Before beginning the process, finding the targetted interviewees was crucial. Therefore, the first step in this process was finding potential stakeholders in Swat's tourism industry. According to Byrd (2007), the local community, business providers and employees, and government officials are considered stakeholders in the tourism industry. Following this, 15 stakeholders from Swat's tourism and culture industry were contacted for an interview, and eight were confirmed. These included: two lecturers from the University of Swat's Institute of Cultural Heritage, Tourism and Hospitality Management; one employee from the VGuide Tours company; one employee from Swat Serena Hotel; one employee from PTDC Hotel in Malam Jabba, Swat; an independent local tour guide working for different tour companies; a representative of Swat's local government; and an employee from the Swat Museum.

7.3.4 Demographics of the Interviewees

Five participants were male and only three were female. The original plan was to keep the numbers identical, but due to the minimal number of women involved in the tourism industry, it took time to reach them, so it was not easy to maintain a balance in the sample. Table 7.1 shows a summary of the interviewees and their respective affiliations.

From previous personal experiences of the authors, it was clear that the people in Swat use email sparingly; therefore, all the respondents were contacted directly via telephone and briefed about the interview time and medium. The interviews were conducted between the end of July and mid-August 2024. Each interview lasted from 45 to 60 minutes. Five interviews were conducted via Zoom, and three were via WhatsApp video calls. The interviewee was given a choice to select one of three languages: English, Urdu, or Pashto. All the interviewees selected Pashto as the language for the interviews. Pashto was an easy option for the interviewees as it was their mother tongue, so they could express themselves

Table 7.1 *List of the interviewees*

Respondent	Interviewee	Organization	Date	Professional experience	Gender
R1	Lecturer 1	University of Swat, Institute of Cultural Heritage, Tourism and Hospitality Management	26.07.2024	More than six years	Male
R2	Lecturer 2	University of Swat, Institute of Cultural Heritage, Tourism and Hospitality Management	23.0.7.2024	More than six years	Male
R3	Employee	VGuide Tours Company	31.07.2024	More than six years	Male
R4	Employee	Swat Serena Hotel	01.08.2024	4–6 years	Female
R5	Employee	PTDC Hotel, Malam Jabba, Swat	05.08.2024	4–6 years	Female
R6	Independent local tour guide	Various tour companies, Swat	08.08.2024	More than six years	Male
R7	Representative	Local government	08.08.2024	1–3 years	Female
R8	Employee	Swat Museum	10.08.2024	More than 6 years	Male

Source: Authors' own elaboration.

easily and answer each question correctly. All the interviews were audio recorded with the interviewees' permission. All the answers were carefully listened to and noted by the authors.

The audio was then translated into English, typed up, and saved as Microsoft Word files ready for transcription in Word documents for making code. The transcriptions were rechecked against the recorded audio interviews. This process was in line with Stuckey (2015), who states that it is essential for authors to transcribe the data while keeping the questions in mind to get used to the data and information from the transcript. This helps in the selection of relevant themes and topics for the study. The author further explains that, by using code, researchers might efficiently identify and establish logical relationships between different segments to extract relevant information and organize it based on similarities.

Then it was time to code from the transcriptions. These were created based on research questions. All the codes were noted clearly. The next step was to find information connected to the initial codes. All the data was gathered and divided into groups of themes and sub-themes. The transcriptions were repeatedly checked with these themes to ensure no relevant data was missing. Moreover, every piece of information was valued whether the respondents repeatedly mentioned it or mentioned it just once. This was inspired by Braun and Clarke (2006), who explained that identification of significant themes are not necessarily related to quantity but rather to whether they are helpful information to answer the question. During this phase, unnecessary data was also removed for clarity. In addition, those themes which had similarities were merged.

7.3.5 Ethical Considerations

The respondents were informed that their participation in the study was voluntary, and they had the right to withdraw from the interview at any stage. Before the beginning of the interview, the participants were provided with a clear explanation of the study's objective. All participants who provided consent were told that their feedback would be used solely for research purposes and kept anonymous to avoid power bias. The collection of personal information was avoided, and to protect participant identities during data presentation, names and positions were substituted with codes.

7.4 DATA ANALYSIS

During the data analysis, relevant codes and initial themes were identified. Five prominent themes were then identified as outlined below.

7.4.1 Norms and Gender Discrimination

The respondents' data highlights the pervasive influence of gender discrimination and traditional norms in the tourism sector in Swat. Women face different societal hurdles and experience barriers that limit or stop their involvement and progress in the tourism industry. On the other hand, men's engagement in public and economic activities is prioritized in cultural traditions and longstanding conventions. Women are seen as solely responsible for household tasks, and being employed may be seen as a problem due to this. The following are some of the responses from our respondents.

> When engaging in heritage tourism, women encounter numerous barriers, such as traditional norms in the industry that restrict them to household responsibilities. (R5)

> No matter how hard the women try, it is very difficult to impossible to get a managerial post. That means as a girl you must work in the front office and when over age leave the industry. (R4)

> We are taken as a symbol of showcase. Our opinion does not count but to show the press that the opposite gender is present. (R7)

> There is a lack of gender equality in the tourism business in Swat, as men overwhelmingly occupy most important positions. (R1)

Such limitations imposed by society result in gender bias, which hampers women's ability to move freely, access resources, and pursue professional growth. Although there has been significant advancement, women are still not adequately represented, particularly in leadership positions within the tourism sector. Moreover, women's public engagement and potential contributions to tourism development are limited by cultural conventions that govern their roles.

7.4.2 Lack of Training and Education

The respondents' scarcity of education and proper training is a significant issue. It was argued that in order for women to develop the necessary skills for active participation in tourism, it is mandatory to provide them with specific educational programs and professional training.

> As a woman, there are different hurdles for me in accessing professional training compared to my male colleagues. (R4)

> Women's choice in getting an employment is affected by the societal pressure and norms. (R2)

> Like in every other field, involvement of women is crucial as they bring innovation, which leads to growth, but that is only possible if there is awareness among both sexes. (R2)

Women must have suitable training or education to compete equally with colleagues, especially men. This lack of training and education is also one of the reasons why women are not promoted or hired in managerial roles or any other where training is lacking. This further hampers the innovation and growth of tourism. Specially organized awareness and training programs about women's involvement in tourism and its benefits for individuals and the industry can increase confidence and enhance their capabilities, leading to gender parity in the sector.

7.4.3 Limited Financial Resources

According to the respondents, financial problems are one of the main reasons women's participation in tourism activities is hindered. Women have financial barriers, especially regarding entrepreneurship and new startups in the tourism industry.

> Women are not financially strong as like men to start their businesses, even if one thousand is capable, the society will not allow it. (R6)

> If we [girls and women] wish to start a business or participate in any other means, money is one the main barriers, and unfortunately, girls and women get fewer financial opportunities from society and government. (R7)

> Most of all, we have financial constraints, especially when opening a startup. Even if we want to work for someone, the salary is not enough to work in that specific job for a long time. (R4)

7.4.4 Participation in Cultural Heritage Tourism

Women in Swat play a vital role in cultural heritage tourism, promoting and preserving it despite numerous obstacles. They contribute widely to traditional crafts, especially handicrafts such as shawls from Salampur, and culinary practices involving different local foods. The following are some of the responses shared by the participants.

> Women contribute to cultural heritage, including handicrafts in Salampur, where women work in most house factories. (R8)

> The women also try to promote these handicrafts to portray it by wearing. (R8)

> Food can be something in which women contribute to heritage and tourism. Such as Warjalle and Kakorh. (R5)

As mentioned, women play a crucial part, directly and indirectly, in the cultural heritage of Swat, which is a part of tourism. Women make traditional handicrafts, which are widely known throughout the country. The local food is well-known among tourists, especially when visiting hilly areas in Swat. Local delicacies include *Warjale* (made of rice and different herbs), *Kakorhi*, and *Ghwanzakhi*. Kakorhi and Ghwanzakhi are traditional Pashto delicacies: one a rich, sweet treat made with ghee and flour, the other a hearty, fried snack often enjoyed with tea, both deeply tied to Pashtun hospitality and rural life. Women also help to organize events like cultural festivals. These activities attract tourists and enhance the cultural experience and authenticity of Swat's tourism offerings.

7.4.5 Strategies for Enhancing Gender Equality

During the interview process, different strategies to enhance gender equality and promote sustainable tourism were suggested. These included: providing training programs, scholarships, and mentorship for professional development; financial support to all stakeholders, especially women who are left behind due to cultural and social barriers; changes to the rules and regulations so as to protect everyone's rights at the workplace; providing equal opportunities to all and encouraging awareness to promote social acceptance. Below are some of the responses that the respondents shared:

> Heritage tourism can be promoted by implementing targeted training programs for women. (R2)

> Scholarships and mentorship or professional development programs should be provided at the University of Swat or public sector colleges. (R1)

> Financial government support via loans or subsidiaries for women can be helpful. Also, for the salaried class women, such rules should be implemented so that women are not underpaid. (R2)

Respondents believe that educational development is critical for the involvement of women in heritage tourism. In addition to providing microfinancing, incentives for women-led enterprises and encouraging public-private partnerships could be helpful, or even game changers. Also, rules and regulations should impose salary equality among genders, especially in the hotel and tourism industry, so women are not discouraged and do not search for alternatives.

> Legal frameworks are essential to protect and promote women's rights in the workplace. (R7)

> Equal opportunities in the tourism sector by creating policies that enforce level employment opportunities for both men and women in the tourism sector. (R3)

Respondents are of the opinion that a strong legal framework is crucial for a safe and friendly environment for women in the tourism businesses. It is asked from the government and organizations' internal management to create such policies, rules and regulations that ensure women's rights at the workplace so they can feel as at ease and valuable as men such as a need to enforce equal employment opportunities.

> Without the involvement of stakeholders, it is near to impossible in every sector or business to get the fruits and women hold a large stake in the heritage tourism of Swat, so it is important to keep them on board. (R8)

> More awareness is needed among all the interested parties to involve the women. (R3)

Initiatives should be taken for community engagement by raising awareness about the benefits of gender equality and engaging men in dialogue to foster supportive environments.

7.5 DISCUSSION AND CONCLUSION

In tourism, gender equality is essential in the modern global environment, irrespective of region or social structure. Based on qualitative data analysis, this chapter showed a multidimensional picture of gender dynamics in the tourism of Swat. For instance, gender discrimination and traditional norms act as barriers that prevent women from continuing their involvement in the tourism industry and further limit their participation in public life. Such obstacles are the leading cause of women's under-representation in leadership and decision-making positions in the tourism industry of Swat. Additionally, the lack of proper education and training for women impedes their participation in cultural heritage tourism.

Equally, another obstacle that impedes gender equality is the lack of financial support, especially for women. However, despite these hurdles and limitations, women's contributions remain significant and cannot be ignored. Their role in maintaining and developing cultural heritage tourism is crucial. They contribute to cultural heritage tourism by, for example, making traditional crafts and running culinary activities, giving particular value to Swat tourism. Moreover, women endeavor to contribute equally to men in various ways, such as assisting in handicrafts in Salampur's legacy local textile sector. Salampur is a local name of the union council in Tehsil Baboozai in Swat, officially known as Islampur. This involvement of women in cultural tourism is intrinsically linked to the culture and promotes the authenticity and stability of these traditions, which enhances the overall visitor experience.

The collected data shows that women in Swat, in terms of education and training, are at a severe disadvantage. This gap is a hurdle to individual prospects and discourages potential innovation and development in the tourism industry. According to the Government of Khyber Pakhtunkhwa (2024), the female population in the Swat Valley is 51.53% while the male population is 48.47%, which indicates that women's participation can make a significant change to the industry. Providing them with the necessary basic skills and qualifications can enable them to enter certain professions and work alongside men to improve society. This educational empowerment can be achieved through targeted education programs such as special training, short courses in hotel management, tour guiding, event management, and other vocational training to increase their confidence and ability to contribute more effectively to tourism.

In addition, limited financial resources prevent women from starting or expanding tourism-related businesses. Subsequently, women are underpaid or paid less than men, even in the same positions in the tourism industry. This is why women choose other professions, and their participation in the tourism industry, especially in cultural heritage tourism, is minimal. Moreover, opportunities to start new business ventures are also not encouraged by the private or public sector. These financial hurdles are often based on traditional standards that limit women's economic freedom. To counter these financial obstacles, microfinance and public-private partnerships may help empower women entrepreneurs, allowing and encouraging them to develop new ideas, implement them, and substantially contribute to tourism.

7.5.1 Implications and Limitations

This chapter offers several implications for empowering women and enhancing their participation in cultural tourism based on analysis, findings, and conclusions. Given this, proper strategies, including education, financial support, legal reforms, and community engagement, are necessary to address gender disparities. The norms and traditions in the tourism sector need a prompt alteration to promote acceptance of women's roles. Scholarships, mentorship programs, and professional development opportunities can improve women's qualifications and skills.

Financial support, such as microfinancing and incentives for women-led enterprises, can empower women economically. The government should start such initiatives, especially with private partnerships that financially encourage women to start new ventures or provide them with other means that could help them participate in activities on the supply side of tourism.

Women's rights in the workplace should be protected at any cost to create a harmonious work environment, and equal employment opportunities must be strengthened. For community engagement, bringing all stakeholders in the tourism industry together to raise awareness about the benefits of gender equality is critical. All genders should be involved in dialogues and promoted in supportive environments so as to further challenge traditional norms and open the door to more inclusive practices in Swat's tourism sector.

Like other studies, this study has several limitations. It is limited to the geography and culture of Swat. Being qualitative, it lacks statistical data as well. However, these limitations provide cornerstones for future research to take forward the findings of this study and contribute to theoretical and scientific fronts accordingly.

REFERENCES

Adnan Hye, Q. M., & Ali Khan, R. E. (2013). Tourism-led growth hypothesis: A case study of Pakistan. *Asia Pacific Journal of Tourism Research, 18*(4), 303–313. https://doi.org/10.1080/10941665.2012.658412.

Aghazamani, Y., & Hunt, C. A. (2017). Empowerment in tourism: A review of peer-reviewed literature. *Tourism Review International, 21*(4), 333–346.

Anderson, C. (2010). Presenting and evaluating qualitative research. *American Journal of Pharmaceutical Education*, 74(8). https://doi.org/10.5688/aj7408141.

Baum, T. (2013). International Perspectives on Women and Work in Hotels, Catering and Tourism. Geneva: International Labour Organization.

Braun, V., & Clarke, V. (2006). Using thematic analysis in psychology. *Qualitative Research in Psychology, 3*, 77–101. https://doi.org/10.1191/1478088706qp063oa.

Byrd, E. T. (2007). Stakeholders in sustainable tourism development and their roles: Applying stakeholder theory to sustainable tourism development. *Tourism Review, 62*(2), 6–13. https://doi.org/10.1108/16605370780000309.

Cembranel, P., Rodrigues Soares, J. R., & Costa Perinotto, A. R. (2022). *Promoting Social and Cultural Equity in the Tourism Sector*. Pennsylvania: IGI Global.

Dill, J. S., Morgan, J. C., & Weiner, B. (2014). Frontline health care workers and perceived career mobility: Do high-performance work practices make a difference? *Health Care Management Review, 39*(4), 318. https://doi.org/10.1097/HMR.0b013e31829fcbfd.

Ferguson, L. (2007). The United Nations World Tourism Organization. *New Political Economy, 12*(4), 557–568. https://doi.org/10.1080/13563460701661587.

Ferguson, L. (2011). Promoting gender equality and empowering women? Tourism and the third Millennium Development Goal. *Current Issues in Tourism, 14*(3), 235–249. https://doi.org/10.1080/13683500.2011.555522.

Fischer, A. R., & Holz, K. B. (2010). Testing a model of women's personal sense of justice, control, well-being, and distress in the context of sexist discrimination. *Psychology of Women Quarterly, 34*(3), 297–310. https://doi.org/10.1111/j.1471-6402.2010.01576.x.

Fleras, A. (2015). *The Politics of Multiculturalism: Multicultural Governance in Comparative Perspective*. New York, NY: Springer.

Genç, R. (2018). The impact of tourism in the reduction of gender inequality. *Trakya Üniversitesi İktisadi ve İdari Bilimler Fakültesi E-Dergi, 7*(1), 20–35.

Gil Arroyo, C., Barbieri, C., Sotomayor, S., & Knollenberg, W. (2019). Cultivating women's empowerment through agritourism: Evidence from Andean communities. *Sustainability, 11*(11). https://doi.org/10.3390/su11113058.

Government of Khyber Pakhtunkhwa (2024). *Swat District Demographics*. https://kp.gov.pk/page/swatdistrictdemographics.

Grobar, L. (2017). Policies to promote employment and preserve cultural heritage in the handicraft sector. *International Journal of Cultural Policy, 25*, 1–13. https://doi.org/10.1080/10286632.2017.1330887.

Hafiane Hedahdia, I., & Boukhemis, K. (2024). Appraisal of knowledge and attitudes of local people towards importance of conservation of the archaeological heritage. Case of the Hippone site in Annaba (Algeria). *Journal of Cultural Heritage Management and Sustainable Development*. https://doi.org/10.1108/JCHMSD-08-2023-0132.

Herbert, D. (2001). Literary places, tourism and the heritage experience. *Annals of Tourism Research*, *28*(2), 312–333. https://doi.org/10.1016/S0160-7383(00)00048-7

Higgins-Desbiolles, F. (2006). More than an "industry": The forgotten power of tourism as a social force. *Tourism Management*, *27*(6), 1192–1208. https://doi.org/10.1016/j.tourman.2005.05.020.

Higgins-Desbiolles, F. (2017). Sustainable tourism: Sustaining tourism or something more? *Tourism Management Perspectives 25,* 157–160. https://doi.org/10.1016/j.tmp.2017.11.017.

Hodson, R. (2001). *Dignity at Work*. Cambridge University Press. https://doi.org/10.1017/CBO9780511499333.

International Labor Organization (ILO) (2013, April 1). *International Perspectives on Women and Work in Hotels, Catering and Tourism*. .https://www.ilo.org/publications/international-perspectives-women-and-work-hotels-catering-and-tourism.

Iori, E. (2023). An urban approach to the archaeology of Buddhism in Gandhara: The case of Barikot (Swat, Pakistan). *South Asian Studies*, *39*, 100–125. https://doi.org/10.1080/02666030.2023.2231671.

Jacobson, N. (2009). A taxonomy of dignity: A grounded theory study. *BMC International Health and Human Rights*, *9*(1), 3. https://doi.org/10.1186/1472-698X-9-3.

Jiménez-García, M., Ruiz-Chico, J., Peña-Sánchez, A. R., & López-Sánchez, J. A. (2020). A bibliometric analysis of sports tourism and sustainability (2002–2019). *Sustainability*, *12*(7). https://doi.org/10.3390/su12072840.

Kakilla, C. (2021). Strengths and weaknesses of semi-structured interviews in qualitative research: A critical essay. Preprints, 2021060491. https://doi.org/10.20944/preprints202106.0491.v1.

Katircioglu, S. T. (2009). Revisiting the tourism-led-growth hypothesis for Turkey using the bounds test and Johansen approach for cointegration. *Tourism Management*, *30*(1), 17–20. https://doi.org/10.1016/j.tourman.2008.04.004.

Kato, K. (2019). Gender and sustainability – exploring ways of knowing – an eco-humanities perspective. *Journal of Sustainable Tourism*, *27*, 1–18. https://doi.org/10.1080/09669582.2019.1614189.

Khan, M. (2017). The tradition of Buddhist narrative illustration in the Swat Valley. Ancient Pakistan: Research Bulletin of the Department of Archaeology, University of Peshawar, 28, 119–129.

Khan, T., & MacEachen, E. (2022). An alternative method of interviewing: Critical reflections on videoconference interviews for qualitative data collection. *International Journal of Qualitative Methods*, *21*. https://doi.org/10.1177/16094069221090063.

Kolovich, M. L. L. (2018). *Fiscal Policies and Gender Equality*. Washington, DC: International Monetary Fund.

Korczynski, M., & Ott, U. (2006). The menu in society: Mediating structures of power and enchanting myths of individual sovereignty. *Sociology*, *40*(5), 911–928. https://doi.org/10.1177/0038038506067514.

Kuper, A., Reeves, S., & Levinson, W. (2008). Qualitative research: An introduction to reading and appraising qualitative research. *BMJ*, *337*(7666), 404–407. https://doi.org/10.1136/bmj.a288.

Labadi, S., & Gould, P. G. (2015). Sustainable development. In: L. Meskell (ed.), Global Heritage, 196–216. Chichester, UK: John Wiley & Sons, Ltd.

Liu, Z. (2003). Sustainable tourism development: A critique. *Journal of Sustainable Tourism*, *11*(6), 459–475. https://doi.org/10.1080/09669580308667216.

Manzoor, F., Wei, L., Asif, M., Haq, M. Z., & Rehman, H. (2019). The contribution of sustainable tourism to economic growth and employment in Pakistan. *International Journal of Environmental Research and Public Health*, *16*(19). https://doi.org/10.3390/ijerph16193785.

Menchenko, A., & Javed, M. (2024). A systematic literature review of tourism demand and future research agenda. *Inproforum*, *17*(1), 78–85. https://doi.org/10.32725/978-80-7694-053-6.12.

Noronha, S., Aquinas, P., & Manezes, A. (2018). Is job performance better attributable to performance management system through work engagement? *Indian Journal of Commerce & Management Studies*, *9*, 1–6.

Onyemechalu, S. J., & Ugwuanyi, J. K. (2021). Íhé Ńkètá and Òkè: Concepts and practice of indigenous cultural heritage management in the Igbo cultural area of south-eastern Nigeria. *Journal of Cultural Heritage Management and Sustainable Development*, *12*(4), 609–624. https://doi.org/10.1108/JCHMSD-12-2020-0177.

Paules, G. F. (1991). *Dishing it Out: Power and Resistance Among Waitresses in a New Jersey Restaurant*. Pennsylvania: Temple University Press.

Petrucci, T., & Rivera, M. (2018). Leading growth through the digital leader. *Journal of Leadership Studies*, *12*. https://doi.org/10.1002/jls.21595.

Al Saadi, N. S. M. A. (2020). The importance of fine art to sustain the cultural heritage in Oman. Journal of Arts and Humanities, 9(4), 62–67.

Salim Mohammed Al Mardhoof Al Saadi, N. (2020). The Importance of Fine Art to Sustain the Cultural Heritage in Oman. *Journal of Arts and Humanities*, 62–67.

Sardar, B. (2012). Rock art in the Swat Valley, Pakistan. *Ancient Asia*, *3*, 66–78.

Sarfo-Mensah, P., Owusu-Bi, A., Awuah-Nyamekye, S., & Amisah, S. (2014). Environmental conservation and preservation of cultural heritage: Assets for tourism development in Ghana's Akyem Abuakwa traditional area. *Worldviews: Global Religions, Culture, and Ecology*, *18*(1), 30–53. .https://doi.org/10.1163/15685357-01801003.

Sayer, A. (2007). Dignity at work: Broadening the agenda. *Organization*, *14*(4), 565–581. https://doi.org/10.1177/1350508407078053.

Shantika, B., Ernawati, N. M., & Sarja, N. L. A. K. Y. (2021). Balinese women's role and gender gap in the sustainable tourism development. *International*

Journal of Green Tourism Research and Applications, *3*(2). https://doi.org/10.31940/ijogtra.v3i2.49-57.

Stipe, R. E. (2003). *A Richer Heritage: Historic Preservation in the Twenty-first Century*. Chapel Hill: University of North Carolina Press.

Stuckey, H. (2015). The second step in data analysis is coding qualitative research data. *Journal of Social Health and Diabetes*, *3*(1), 7–10. https://doi.org/10.4103/2321-0656.140875.

Stumpf, T. S., & Cheshire, C. L. (2019). The land has voice: Understanding the land tenure – sustainable tourism development nexus in Micronesia. *Journal of Sustainable Tourism*, *27*(7), 957–973. https://doi.org/10.1080/09669582.2018.1538228.

Thomas, B., & Lucas, K. (2019). Development and validation of the workplace dignity scale. *Group & Organization Management*, *44*(1), 72–111. https://doi.org/10.1177/1059601118807784.

Torkington, K., Stanford, D., & Guiver, J. (2020). Discourse(s) of growth and sustainability in national tourism policy documents. *Journal of Sustainable Tourism*, *28*(7), 1041–1062. https://doi.org/10.1080/09669582.2020.1720695.

Uduji, J. I., Okolo-Obasi, E. N., & Asongu, S. A. (2020). Sustaining cultural tourism through higher female participation in Nigeria: The role of corporate social responsibility in oil host communities. *International Journal of Tourism Research*, *22*(1), 120–143. https://doi.org/10.1002/jtr.2323.

Ullah, F., Aziz, M., & Rehman, A. (2019). Assessment of interfaith harmony between Muslims and Hindus in socio-cultural activities in Swat. *Journal of Interreligious Studies*, *6*, 75–84.

United Nations (2015). *Transforming Our World: The 2030 Agenda for Sustainable Development*. New York: United Nations.

United Nations. (2024). *United Nations | Peace, Dignity and Equality on a Healthy Planet*. New York: United Nations.

Winchenbach, A., Hanna, P., & Miller, G. (2019). Rethinking decent work: The value of dignity in tourism employment. *Journal of Sustainable Tourism*, *27*(7), 1026–1043. https://doi.org/10.1080/09669582.2019.1566346.

Wirawan, G. B. S., Mahardani, P. N. T. Y., Cahyani, M. R. K., Laksmi, N. L. P. S. P., & Januraga, P. P. (2021). Conspiracy beliefs and trust as determinants of COVID-19 vaccine acceptance in Bali, Indonesia: Cross-sectional study. *Personality and Individual Differences*, *180*, 110995. https://doi.org/10.1016/j.paid.2021.110995.

World Bank (2017). *Women and Tourism: Designing for Inclusion*. https://www.thefias.info/sites/fias/files/2019-06/Women%20and%20Tourism.pdf.

Yan, W.-J., & Chiou, S.-C. (2021). The safeguarding of intangible cultural heritage from the perspective of civic participation: The informal education of Chinese embroidery handicrafts. *Sustainability*, *13*(9), https://doi.org/10.3390/su13094958.

8. Gender equality as a catalyst for sustainable development in tourism and hospitality

Bapon Chandra Kuri, Tanmay Barman, Shadia Sharmin, and Marco Valeri

8.1 INTRODUCTION

The economic condition of a nation largely depends on its tourism and hospitality sector. Therefore, contribution to social, financial, and sustainable development is indispensable for a country's economy.[1] To leverage this possibility, it is necessary to integrate gender equality as a crucial factor in sustainable development strategies. As noted by the United Nations' Sustainable Development Goals (SDGs), gender equality is not only a single goal but also a turning point that overlaps and promotes other development goals that influence the tourism and hospitality industry.[2] Moreover, the tourism industry has traditionally been characterized by considerable gender inequalities with women confined to lower-salaried positions, denied executive positions, and often limited to precarious roles (Costa et al., 2011). A significant obstacle to

[1] BSBI: The role of tourism and hospitality in a country's economy. https://www.berlinsbi.com/blog/the-role-of-tourism-and-hospitality-in-a-country-s-economy.

[2] OHCHR: Gender equality and women's rights. https://www.ohchr.org/en/topic/gender-equality-and-womens-rights?gad_source=1&gclid=Cj0KCQjwsoe5BhDiARIsAOXVoUva1wHW2bAy5CV2_7mvsewaa5olJo2ZNMPnYHLfBjqihTTZQSNGCTkaAuHmEALw_wcB.

sustainable development is gender disparities[3] that impede the complete use of human potential and undermine the social foundation of sustainability (Menton et al., 2020).

A considerable number of women are employed in the tourism and hospitality industry, but, despite its enormous growth, the industry continues to be affected by substantial gender disparities (Segovia-Pérez et al., 2019a). The United Nations World Tourism Organization (UNWTO) reported that women comprise approximately 54% of the tourism labor force yet their visibility in executive roles is minimal (Sobaih & Elnasr, 2024). Predominantly, women are disproportionately embodied in low-wage and low-skilled jobs, including reception work, waitressing, and housekeeping. Meanwhile, managerial and decision-making positions are mainly populated by men. Moreover, women frequently receive lower salaries than their male colleagues in low-income and middle-income countries (Segovia-Pérez et al., 2019b). Therefore, the organizational sector's overall creativity and productivity are hampered due to the lack of equity for women, which extends to social injustice.

There is a deep connection between stabilizing present demands with fair distribution across generations and the influence on social, economic, and environmental leads to sustainable development (Richardson, 2021). Meanwhile, gender equality is an essential factor of socioeconomic sustainability that plays a pivotal role in attaining comprehensive development in the industry. Regardless of the clear advantages of gender equality for sustainable development, several challenges continue to obstruct its progress in the tourism and hospitality industry (Carrasco-Santos et al., 2024). A primary impediment to gender equality in this sector is the persistence of closely ingrained stereotypes and gender norms within the industry (Tabassum & Nayak, 2021). For instance, women are seen as more suited to care-oriented and frontline roles while men are perceived as more qualified for technical and management positions (Silva & Couto, 2023). These prejudices restrict women's career progression as well as perpetuate unequal power structures in the work environment.

Tourism is considered a driver for promoting gender equality and participation of women in the labor market. Previously, myriad studies on gender equality and women's entrepreneurial leadership in tourism

---

[3] SEI: Gender inequality is a significant barrier to sustainable development. https://www.sei.org/perspectives/gender-inequality-sustainable-development/.

have been accessed through systematic review (Kourtesopoulou & Chatzigianni, 2021). For example, a case study of the domestic tourism industry in Cox's Bazar, Bangladesh (Gomes & Blake, 2020) found tourism as a driver for promoting gender equality. Another case study of the participation of women in the tourism labor market in Cox's Bazar, Bangladesh (Gomes & Blake, 2020), in line with the UNWTO Global Report on Women in Tourism, reported that tourism has a significant impact on gender equality. Moreover, systematic bibliometric reviews on empowerment (Araújo-Vila et al., 2021), gender equality (De Jong & Figueroa-Domecq, 2022), and sustainability in the tourism industry (Kaunda & Shereni, 2023) have been conducted to identify the interplay between gender equality and tourism. However, there is a lack of research on how gender equity can catalyze sustainability in the tourism and hospitality industry. Therefore, this chapter emphasizes how the sustainability and enduring prosperity of the tourism industry can be addressed through gender equality.

8.2 LITERATURE REVIEW

The tourism and hospitality industry comprises various components (accommodation, transportation, tour operators, travel agencies, entertainment) that offer and produce tourism products and services for travelers. Organizations can achieve better business performance with an emphasis on gender equality. According to Sukalova and Ceniga (2021), the terms "gender equality" and "equal opportunities" are correlated in terms of the work and field of labor protection. Moreover, gender equality can also be considered a tool to foster sustainable development goals by ensuring economic, social, cultural, and environmental resilience and viability. Being a coordination-intensive and labor-intensive industry, tourism has enormous employment opportunities, particularly for women (Singh et al., 2024, Samad & Alharthi, 2022). As a result, tourism plays a substantial role in gender equality, offering economic empowerment and generating employment opportunities. In Table 8.1, 15 articles have been analyzed regarding gender equality and its role in promoting sustainable development. Within the context of the tourism and hospitality sector, this chapter provides an essential linkage between gender equality and sustainable development, which has received little attention in previous literature.

A study by Cejas et al. (2021) stated that, despite women having entrance in business activities such as decision making, managerial

Table 8.1 *Literature review*

Authors and year	Context	Country	Independent variable	Dependent variable	Findings
Gomes & Blake, 2020	Promoting gender equality	Bangladesh	Perceived lack of skills or qualifications, social norms, gendered workplace, gender segregation	Women's participation in the hotel industry	Perceived lack of skills or qualifications, social norms, gendered workplace, and gender segregation limit women's participation in the hotel industry (+ & sig)
Cejas et al., 2021	Gender equality during the COVID-19 situation	Ecuador	COVID-19 public policies and responses	Gender equality and women's status in the tourism sector	COVID-19 public policies and responses affect gender equality in the tourism sector (+ & sig)
Latjuba, 2024	Sustainable tourism development and women	Bulukumba, Indonesia	Experience, education, age	Choice of words and speech style	Experience, education, and age influence the linguistic behavior of women working in tourism at Bira Beach (+ & sig)

Authors and year	Context	Country	Independent variable	Dependent variable	Findings
Zhang et al., 2022	Tourism and gender equality	Asia	Economy, employment, and education	Gender equality	Economy, employment, and education promote gender equality in tourism (+ & sig)
Radović-Marković & Živanović, 2019	Women's empowerment and green entrepreneurship	Serbia	Practical work and experience, formal education and training, informal education, special programs	Position of women in tourism	Practical work and experience influence the position of women in tourism (+ & sig)
Samad & Alharthi, 2022	Tourism and women entrepreneurs	Saudi Arabia	Perception of women's works, self-efficacy, empowering leadership, psychological empowerment	Tourism involvement, sustainable development	Sustainable development is influenced by Perception of women's works,self-efficacy, empowering leadership, psychological empowerment, (+ & sig)

Authors and year	Context	Country	Independent variable	Dependent variable	Findings
Costa et al., 2011	Gender inequalities in tourism	Portugal	Vertical segregation, low levels of education, regional differences, part-time work, gender pay gap, challenging work schedules	Gender inequalities	Vertical segregation, education levels, and gender pay gap influence gender inequalities (+& sig)
Segovia-Pérez et al., 2018	Gender and hospitality	Spain	Self-perceptions and self-imposed barriers, gender norms, stereotyping, dichotomy in leadership expectations, long working hours, gender roles and work-life balance, support from partners, and organizational culture	Women's representation in decision-making positions	Self-perceptions, gender norms, stereotyping, leadership expectations, working hours, gender roles, and organizational culture have a direct impact on women's representation in decision-making positions (+& sig)
Lawal et al., 2016	Women's empowerment	Africa	Gender equality, women's empowerment	Sustainable development	Women's empowerment influences sustainable development (+& sig)

Authors and year	Context	Country	Independent variable	Dependent variable	Findings
Nwachukwu & Asuelime, 2018	Sustainable development and women	Africa	Gender-balanced participation	Eco-entrepreneurial performance	Gender-balanced participation and eco-entrepreneurial performance (+& sig)
Medupin, 2020	Women and sustainable future	UK	Strong female mentorship, gender-inclusive approach	Sustainable development	Gender-inclusive approach influences sustainable development (+& sig)
Miles, 2011	Gender in sustainability	–	Gender performance	Organizations' financial strength	Gender performance has a positive impact on organizations' financial strength (+& sig)
Núñez et al., 2020	Social economy and gender equality	Spain	Social economy entities	Gender inequalities	Social economy entities contribute to gender inequalities (+& sig)

Authors and year	Context	Country	Independent variable	Dependent variable	Findings
Escamilla-Solano et al., 2022	Gender policies	–	Gender policies	Business performance	Gender policies have a positive influence on business performance (+& sig)
Faugoo, 2024	Women's leadership	–	Women's leadership	Sustainable outcomes	Women's leadership has a positive impact on sustainable outcomes (+& sig)

Note: sig = Significant, + = Has positive relationship.
Source: Google Scholar.

roles, and leadership at a larger percentage than men, they face greater challenges that obstruct their career paths in the business sector. For example, women lag behind in labor market participation due to complicated social norms (Radović-Marković & Živanović, 2019), gender-based roles, workplace mistreatment, and lack of access to vocational training (Gomes & Blake, 2020).

8.3 THE CONCEPT OF GENDER EQUALITY

Over time, social movements, modifications in laws, and shifting cultural attitudes have all affected the concept of gender equality. Abendroth (2014) argues that gender equality encompasses the idea that both genders should have equal opportunities, rights, and comprehensive care across all aspects of life, including economic, social, political, and cultural. Conventionally, gender responsibilities have been uncompromisingly prescribed to men, who dominate positions in decision-making in business and social matters (Chang & Milkman, 2020). Therefore, a male-dominated society has reinforced these traditional gender responsibilities, which obstruct women's access to political engagement, education, and employment. However, a significant crossroads was reached during the feminist movement of the 19th and 20th centuries. The main focus of this movement centered on women's right to vote (Burkett, 2024). Additionally, feminist movements that followed called for broadened equal rights in education, employment, protection from violence, and reproductive health. In line with this, international organizations such as the United Nations began to focus on advancing women and supporting equity for all genders. As a result, gender equality is now seen as a universal need where international law enforcing agencies should provide health and occupational safety for women (see Figure 8.1).

Figure 8.1 depicts an array of core elements that constitute gender equity, since all of them have a direct association with macro environmental factors, ranging from socio-cultural, economic, political, and other fundamental subjects. These factors involve recognizing and addressing gender equality in terms of education, employment, policy formulation, laws, human rights, and social support. In addition, the key components of gender equality span various aspects focused on disparities between men and women, safeguarding equal rights, and treatment across all aspects of existence. For example, economic equality encompasses guaranteeing equal pay for career advancement and employment and advancing women's financial independence by enabling access to

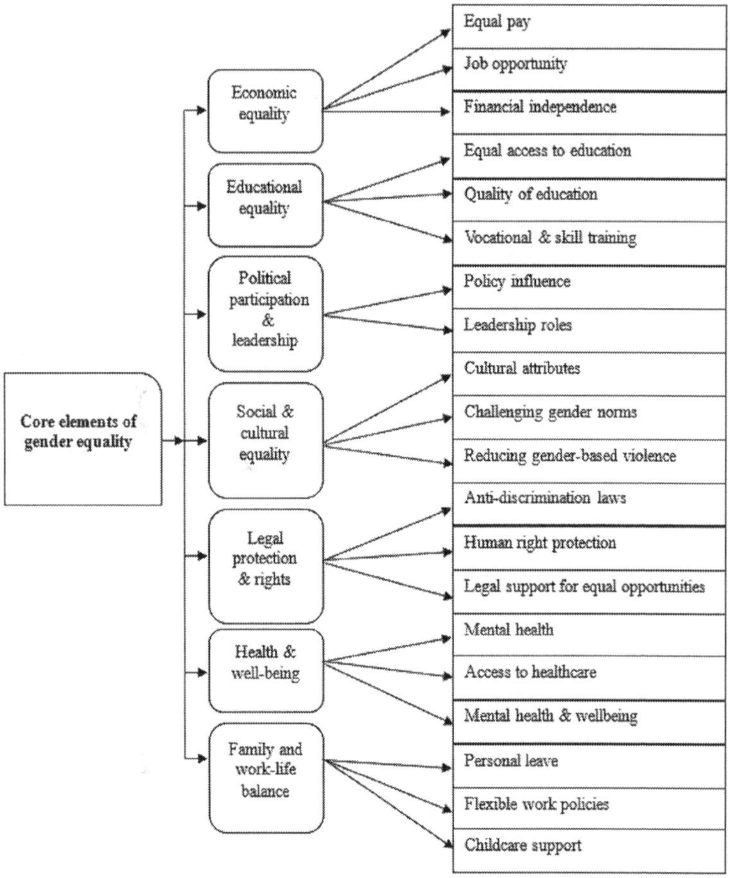

Source: Authors' compilations.

Figure 8.1 Core elements of gender equality

credit, financial resources, and entrepreneurship (Chen, 2004). Moreover, unrestricted parity diminishes gender biases in educational materials and opportunities for vocational training to capitalize on employment opportunities for all (Subrahmanian, 2005). Equal representation of men and women in leadership roles is another aspect of political engagement that guarantees women have an impact on policies that address gender equity

(Pande & Ford, 2012). In addition, legal protection guarantees human rights, equality of opportunities, and inclusivity, while social and cultural equality disputes gender stereotypes. In addition, family and work-life balance facilitates women to enjoy flexible work schedules, parental leave, and childcare support that can lead to higher job satisfaction and improved performance in their working environment.

8.4 ROLE OF GENDER EQUALITY IN ECONOMIC GROWTH

A thriving society must emphasize gender equality, which is a basic human right. Numerous studies have demonstrated that promoting gender equality has a positive influence on economic expansion (Kabeer & Natali, 2013). In particular, gender parity has a significant impact across diverse economic sectors, improving sustainable development, societal results, and productivity. It helps organizations to create positive work environments, mitigate poverty, promote diversity in ideas, and fortify the overall social tapestry of a nation. Incorporating women into the labor force has been an instrumental driver of the economic expansion of both developed and developing nations. In this context, women's incorporation in the workforce leads to productivity growth and subsequently spurs general development (Mitra et al., 2014). Since women make up about half of the global population, their inclusion in the economy potentially elevates skills, talent, and ideas.

According to the World Economic Forum's Gender Gap Report (2022), increasing women's employment has the potential to boost global GDP by $12 trillion and enhance economic output in some countries by up to 35%. For example, in countries such as the United States, women's labor force inclusion has consistently risen since the mid-20th century, which has resulted in notably strong economic growth (Stone, 2015). The OECD also predicts that attaining gender equality in employment could foster overall economic growth in its member countries by an estimated 10% by 2030.[4] Despite various obstacles that continue to limit women's participation in the labor market, including limited access to education, cultural norms and discrimination, unpaid work, and informal labor

[4] OECD: Gender equality. https://www.oecd.org/en/topics/policy-issues/gender-equality.html.

markets,[5] gender equality can improve economic expansion. In some regions, such as Sub-Saharan Africa and South Asia, many women are deprived of educational attainment because of poverty, gender-based violence, and child marriage (McCleary-Sills et al., 2015). Additionally, traditional gender roles in certain countries often limit women to domestic chores, and their scope for vocational advancement is reduced (Jayachandran, 2020). Furthermore, In developing countries, women's incorporation into the workforce is also affected by gender discrimination in pay and promotion, and they often work in the informal sectors where wages are low and job sicurity is unstable. As a result, economic growth is assumed to depend on gender inclusivity in decision-making and leadership. Meanwhile, female leaders often prioritize ethical decision-making, collaboration, and long-lasting sustainability, leading to the enhancement of economic development (Thelma & Ngulube, 2024). For instance, women encourage innovation, offer diverse perspectives, and foster inclusion in the workplace.

8.5 IMPACT OF GENDER EQUALITY ON SOCIAL DEVELOPMENT

Any nation's social development is highly affected by gender equality, which has a considerable impact on critical areas including health, education, and poverty alleviation (Ogbari et al., 2024). In addition, to being a social justice issue, gender equality is a catalyst for broader human advancement. Societies that are more cohesive and resilient participate in the equitable inclusion of both men and women, which can improve their social and economic upliftment (Kuteesa et al., 2024; see Figure 8.2).

Additionally, gender equality highlights shared values through the tailoring of inclusive societies. For instance, democratic institutions are strengthened and better governance is reinforced if women and men are equally engaged in strategic planning processes. The role of gender inclusivity in attaining Sustainable Development Goals (SDGs) has been highlighted by the United Nations, who emphasize that gender equality is not just a human right, it is a strategic instrument for achieving

[5] ILO: The gender gap in employment: What's holding women back? https://webapps.ilo.org/infostories/en-GB/Stories/Employment/barriers-women.

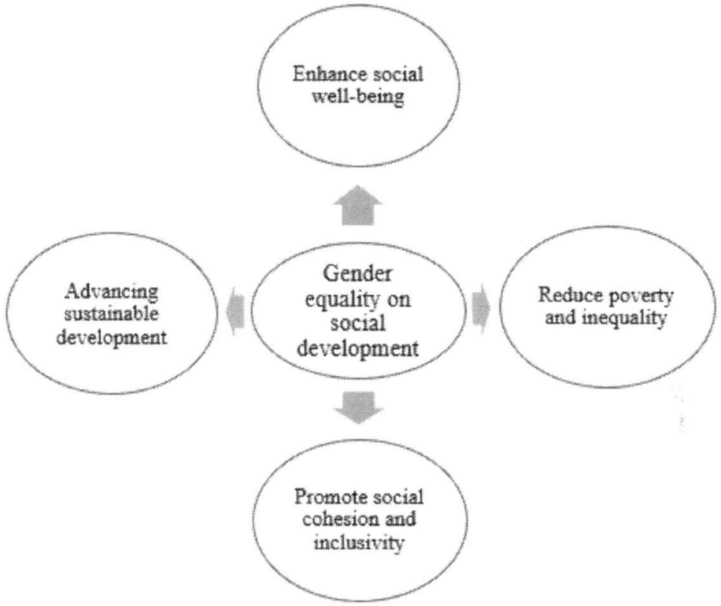

Source: Rasool, 2016.

Figure 8.2 The impact of gender equality on social development

quality education, reducing poverty, and promoting decent work for all. Furthermore, gender equality is associated with sustainable economic growth as it encourages creativity, entrepreneurship, and resource efficacy, which builds cohesiveness in the community and raises social well-being. (Ogbari et al., 2024). Similarly, it provides society with more balanced inclusive growth, and an array of advantages in the fields of health, government, and education. Ultimately, gender equality is a purposeful investment for a country that ensures long-term prosperity (Nanni, 2023).

8.6 SUSTAINABLE BUSINESS PRACTICES IN THE TOURISM AND HOSPITALITY INDUSTRY

The trait of "sustainability" involves fulfilling the requirements of present generations without risking future generations' abilities to consume the same resources. The key components of sustainable practices involve social, economic, cultural, and environmental preservation and conservation. In this context, the tourism industry ensures sustainability by generating new income sources, promoting local culture and heritage, empowering community involvement in tourism projects, and implementing low-impact tourism (ecotourism, responsible tourism, sustainable tourism) to avoid exploitation of natural resources (Manuel-Navarrete, 2015). As the concept of sustainable tourism becomes more universal, therefore, these traits are necessary for long-lasting feasibility and durability in an ever-evolving market (Iddawala et al., 2024).

Sustainable Development Goals (SDGs) promote inclusive workforce participation and decision-making roles where men and women have equal access to employment, career growth, and executive positions in the workplace (Segovia-Pérez et al., 2019a). The sustainable initiatives in tourism and hospitality foster diversity irrespective of gender. Moreover, sustainable local businesses emphasize economic prosperity, growth in society, and respect for cultural heritage. Additionally, sustainable initiatives require a strong partnership between private, public, and non-profit organizations to offer reciprocal appreciation and positive aspects (Li et al., 2021). However, challenges (wage inequalities, male-dominated work environment,and ethnocultural hurdles) require a concerted, strategic effort from every sector in order to create inclusive work environments for people of all backgrounds (Ringblom & Johansson, 2020).

8.7 THE INCORPORATION OF GENDER EQUALITY IN THE TOURISM AND HOSPITALITY SECTOR

As an international economic catalyst, tourism has immense revenue creation potential, promoting cross-cultural exchange and gender equality. By incorporating equitable policies and adopting sustainable business initiatives, tourism can offer a transformative role in mitigating gender inequalities worldwide (see Figure 8.3).

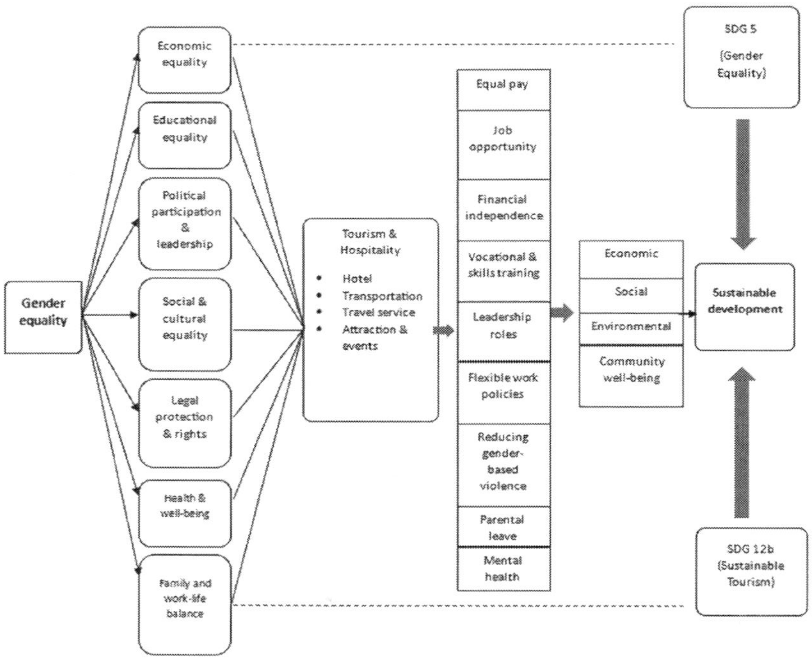

Source: Authors' compilation.

Figure 8.3 *The incorporation of gender equality in the tourism and hospitality sector*

Women make up a large part of the hotel workforce and commonly take up roles such as catering, front desk management, and housekeeping (Gomes & Blake, 2020). However, most of these jobs are not highly paid and have little or no chance for career growth. Economic evolution means providing detailed education and a route to career advancement for women in hospitality. For instance, equipping women with comprehensive hotel management degrees (front office, housekeeping, food and beverage service) as well as entrepreneurial training in culinary arts and tour operations can enable them to develop their careers in the tourism and hospitality sectors. On the other hand, targeted recruitment and skills development programs can provide women with opportunities for higher-paying positions, paving the way to close these hiring gaps. For example, in travel services (like tour operators and travel agencies), an appropriate number of women are recruited, but ownership or decision-making remains largely a male preserve. In addition, many aesthetic and historical venues are managed by women employees. These positions enable them to be close to the residents and engage in the conservation of native culture while ensuring gender inclusivity. The role of tourism in advancing gender equality is dependent upon the government policies and legal frameworks that shape its capacity. Many countries are increasingly mainstreaming gender-based interventions into national tourism development. The UNWTO, for instance, has campaigned for gender equality as a key part of its global tourism framework, asking that member countries incorporate it into their overall tourism development strategies. Given its potential to support gender equality by providing women with economic participation, professional empowerment, and leadership (Zhang et al., 2022), tourism is an area for further exploration. This chapter demonstrates how the tourism and hospitality sector can engage in gender inclusivity while pursuing sustainability—a key agenda for the industry going forward—by focusing on specific determinants like policy reformation and uplifting cultural norms to promote women's empowerment.

8.8 THE ALIGNMENT OF THE SUSTAINABLE DEVELOPMENT GOALS (SDGs) WITH GENDER EQUALITY IN TOURISM AND HOSPITALITY

Sustainable Development Goals (SDGs) have a clear alignment with gender equality in the tourism and hospitality industry as tools for identifying the transformative role of these industries in driving equitable and inclusive growth (see Figure 8.4).

To define a brighter and more equitable future for everyone by 2030, the United Nations initiated the Sustainable Development Goals (SDGs) in 2015. A crucial goal is SDG 5, which focuses on gender equality and aims to empower women and girls and eradicate gender disparities. The tourism and hospitality industry fills a specialized market to contribute to this target by providing a worldwide presence. No matter how many women work in this sector, challenges such as unequal pay, underrepresentation in leadership, and restricted access to vocational training opportunities continue to impede the realization of true gender equality.[6] The tourism and hospitality industry is one of the most female-dominated industries. However, men excessively hold managerial positions while women are often occupied in entry-level positions, such as customer service, food and beverage service, and housekeeping staff (Silva & Couto, 2023). By guaranteeing that women have equal access to managerial positions and leadership roles, SDG 5 focuses on the significance of equal opportunities for both men and women. The need for the tourism sector to cultivate fairness in workplaces by providing environments for women with security and fair pay is emphasized by SDG 8.[7] In many regions of the world, women are susceptible to labor exploitation, involving long working shifts, low wages, and job insecurity.[8] Establishing an atmosphere where women have access to well-compensated jobs that promote economic objectives (SDG 8) and emphasize on gender equality (SDG 5) is imperative for the tourism sector. Meanwhile, SDG 10 is centered on mitigating inequalities that support gender equality in tourism and hospitality by promoting equal job opportunities and reducing unequal pay within the industry.[9] Furthermore, SDG 12 focuses on the

---

[6] UNESCO: Education for Sustainable Development Goals: Learning objectives. https://unesdoc.unesco.org/ark:/48223/pf0000247444.

[7] The Global Goals: Decent work and economic growth. https://www.globalgoals.org/goals/8-decent-work-and-economic-growth/.

[8] ILO: Eliminating the vulnerability of female workers to exploitation in the palm oil and fisheries sectors. https://www.ilo.org/resource/news/eliminating-vulnerability-female-workers-exploitation-palm-oil-and.

[9] Tourism for SDGs: Reduced inequalities. https://tourism4sdgs.org/tips_indicators/toolkit-of-indicators-for-projects-tips-for-sdg-10-reduced-inequalities/.

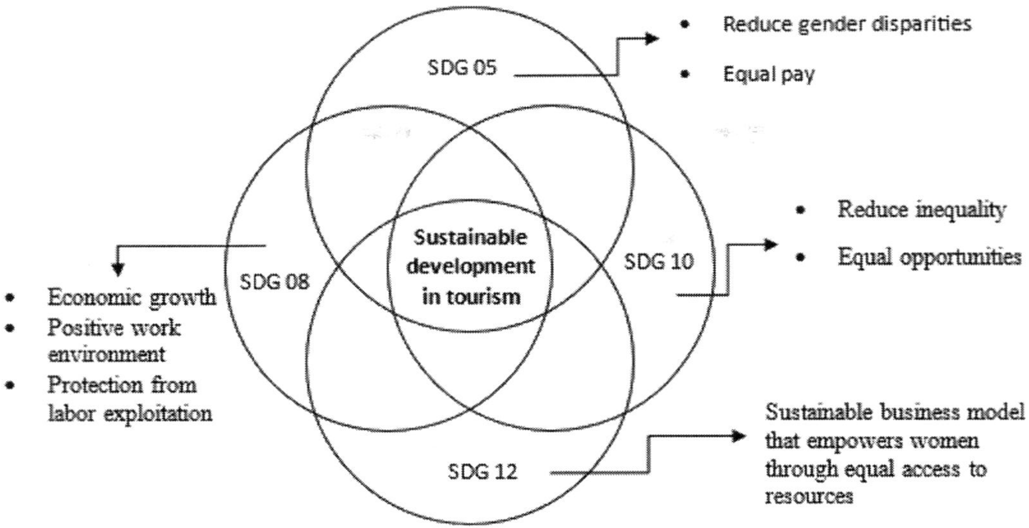

Source: Authors' compilation.

Figure 8.4 Sustainable development in tourism

impact on the consumption and production of tourism products and services regarding gender equality within the tourism and hospitality sector. Therefore, equitable and inclusive operations enable the industry to recruit a skilled labor force from within communities rather than importing staff to carry out its functions.

8.9 CASE STUDY

Chittagong is the second largest city in Bangladesh and has enormous potential for tourism development. It has many beautiful natural landscapes, and there are many possibilities in the cultural and historical tourism, marine and coastal tourism, as well as pilgrimage tourism sectors. Its areas of natural beauty include Cox's Bazar and Patenga Beach, Kaptai Lake, Sitakunda Park, and Chittagong Hill Tracts. Therefore, Chittagong is considered a premier tourist destination, attracting both domestic and international tourists, resulting in infrastructural development in the tourist sector, such as hotels, resorts, and transport facilities. In the beach areas, many women are seen participating in small businesses (homestays, food stalls, or craft shops). However, their participation in hotels that are 0–2, 3, and 4–5 star rated is insignificant compared to men. For example, there are two or three women involved in each 0–2-star hotel who are employed as cleaners or laundry workers. On the other hand, ethnic people who live in Rangamati and Bandarban of the Chittagong Division mostly rely on agriculture to maintain their livelihood. With the emergence of tourism, most locals engage in seasonal tourism businesses, such as tour guiding, homestays, selling food and beverages, and handicrafts. Nevertheless, the involvement of women in these businesses is lower compared to men in various contexts, since they are frequently focused on household work rather than public-facing businesses. In remote areas, women face safety and security concerns that limit them from engaging in entrepreneurial activity. Moreover, the lack of infrastructural development in those areas, as well as vocational training and education, is also restricting ethnic women from engaging in tourism-related businesses.

The involvement of ethnic women in tourism-related businesses could provide them with economic empowerment (income generation, financial independence, reduced poverty). Examples of how they could engage in various tourism ventures include: telling stories about their communities to tourists; guiding tours; selling fruits, handmade traditional dresses, and ornaments; and providing homestay services and unique culinary experiences. Women's participation could foster authentic cultural experiences by preserving and conserving actual traditions. However, a specific problem is that women's engagement in the hotel industry is lower compared to other sectors. Many cases have been reported detailing how women are reluctant to work in the hotel sector due to safety and security, and lack of congenial working environments in the Chittagong Division. Moreover, women who work in hotels are viewed negatively within the social context because this sort of work is seen as unacceptable according to the religious structure in Bangladesh. Women may also face impediments in the case of marriage proposals due to their working status in the hotel sector. However, in Chittagong Division, more than 52 ethnic community people are now engaged in family businesses, by which they can develop improved standards of living. Academicians and policymakers of Chittagong Division have begun taking necessary steps to empower women from economic, social, and technological perspectives. For instance, they organize seminars, conventions, and meetings to encourage women to get engaged in hospitality sectors in the hope that they will be motivated by the potential for social recognition and status.

8.9.1 Questions

1. How can women contribute to expanding the tourism sector in Chittagong Division, Bangladesh?
2. Examine the types of challenges women face in the hotel industry. How can we mitigate these challenges? Explain.
3. How do policymakers and academicians help in developing women's skills in Chittagong Division?

8.10 CONCLUSION

Gender equality in the tourism and hospitality industry fosters the overall economic development of a country's GDP. Meanwhile, women's empowerment in this job sector leads to a better future for all, where both men and women have equal contributions to capitalizing on a country's social, economic, and technological development. Women's engagement in the hospitality sector also builds a congenial environment to generate more revenue by ensuring customer satisfaction. The Sustainable Development Goals (SDGs), in particular SDG 5 (gender equality), SDG 8 (decent work and economic growth), SDG 10 (reduce inequalities), and SDG 12 (responsible tourism) have been demonstrated with several figures, providing an overall overview of how women's participation and gender equality in the hotel sector can draw radical changes in the tourism and hospitality sector. Therefore, sustainable development goals can be achieved by 2030 only if women are equally valued as crucial economic and social contributors in the tourism industry.

REFERENCES

Abendroth, A. (2014). Gender equality. In: Michalos, A. C. (ed.) *Encyclopedia of Quality of Life and Well-Being Research*. Dordrecht: Springer, 2427–2430.

Araújo-Vila, N., Otegui-Carles, A., & Fraiz-Brea, J. A. (2021). Seeking gender equality in the tourism sector: A systematic bibliometric review. *Knowledge*, *1*(1), 12–24. https://doi.org/10.3390/knowledge1010003.

Burkett, E. (2024, September 10). Women's rights movement | Definition, leaders, overview, history, & facts. *Encyclopedia Britannica*. https://www.britannica.com/event/womens-movement.

Carrasco-Santos, M. J., Seyfi, S., Hosseini, S., Hall, C. M., Mohajer, B., Almeida-García, F., & Macías, R. C. (2024). Breaking boundaries: Exploring gendered challenges and advancing equality for Iranian women careers in tourism. *Tourism Management*, *103*, 104913.

Cejas, M. N., Martinez, M. F. C., Aldáz, S. H. M., & Velazco, D. J. M. (2021). The right to gender equality in tourism in the context of pandemic COVID-19 in the canton Riobamba, Ecuador. *Journal of Environmental Management and Tourism*, *12*(6), 1495.

Chang, E. H., & Milkman, K. L. (2020). Improving decisions that affect gender equality in the workplace. *Organizational Dynamics*, *49*(1), 100709.

Chen, D. H. (2004). Gender equality and economic development: The role for information and communication technologies. https://ssrn.com/abstract=610329.

Costa, C., Carvalho, I., & Breda, Z. (2011). Gender inequalities in tourism employment: The Portuguese case. *Revista Turismo & Desenvolvimento*, *15*, 39–54. https://dialnet.unirioja.es/servlet/articulo?codigo=5259520.

De Jong, A., & Figueroa-Domecq, C. (2022). Assessing the UNWTOs Global Report on Women in Tourism: tourism's impact on gender equality. In: Stoffelen, A., & Ioannides, D. (eds) *Handbook of Tourism Impacts*. Cheltenham, UK: Edward Elgar Publishing, 151–165.

Escamilla-Solano, S., Paule-Vianez, J., & Blanco-González, A. (2022). Disclosure of gender policies: Do they affect business performance? *Heliyon*, *8*(1), e08791. https://doi.org/10.1016/j.heliyon.2022.e08791.

Faugoo, D. (2024). Pioneering women's leadership for achieving gender equality and advancing sustainable outcomes: An essential prerequisite for a better tomorrow. *5th International Conference on Management, Education, Social Sciences and Innovation 2024*.

Gomes, T., & Blake, A. (2020). Tourism as a driver for promoting gender equality and participation of women in the labour market? A case study of the domestic tourism industry in Cox's Bazar, Bangladesh. *Journal of Hospitality and Tourism Issues*, *2*(2), 178–189.

Iddawala, J., Welengoda, B. M., & Rathnayaka, B. T. (2024). Sustainability practices in the hospitality industry: Evidence from chain hotels in Kandy. *International Conference on Tourism Research*, *7*(1), 130–139. https://doi.org/10.34190/ictr.7.1.2038.

Jayachandran, S. (2020). Social norms as a barrier to women's employment in developing countries (no. w27449). *National Bureau of Economic Research, 1050 Massachusetts Avenue, Cambridge.*

Kabeer, N., & Natali, L. (2013). Gender equality and economic growth: Is there a win-win? *IDS Working Papers*, *2013*(417), 1–58.

Kaunda, B. E. L., & Shereni, N. C. (2023). Gender equality and sustainability in the tourism industry: Feminist perspectives. *Journal of Human Resources in Hospitality & Tourism*, *23*(1), 149–169. https://doi.org/10.1080/15332845.2023.2253685.

Kourtesopoulou, A., & Chatzigianni, E. (2021). Gender equality and women's entrepreneurial leadership in tourism: A systematic review. In Valeri, M. & Katsoni, V. (eds), *Gender and Tourism*, Bingley, UK: Emerald Publishing, 11–36.

Kuteesa, N. K. N., Akpuokwe, N. C. U., & Udeh, N. C. A. (2024). Gender equity in education: Addressing challenges and promoting opportunities for social empowerment. *International Journal of Applied Research in Social Sciences*, *6*(4), 631–641. https://doi.org/10.51594/ijarss.v6i4.1034.

Latjuba, A. Y. (2024). Women in sustainable tourism development: A case study of the empowerment of women workers in bulukumba tourism destinations. *Journal of Law and Sustainable Development*, *12*(4), e3623. https://doi.org/10.55908/sdgs.v12i4.3623.

Lawal, F. A., Ayoade, O. E., & Taiwo, A. A. (2016). Promoting gender equality and women's empowerment for sustainable development in Africa. In *3rd International Conference on African Development Issues,* Covenant University, Ota, Nigeria.

Li, X., Kim, J. S., & Lee, T. J. (2021). Collaboration for community-based cultural sustainability in island tourism development: A case in Korea. *Sustainability*, *13*(13), 7306. https://doi.org/10.3390/su13137306.

Manuel-Navarrete, D. (2015). Tourism and sustainability. In: Heinrichs, H., Martens, P., Michelsen, G., & Wiek, A. (eds), *Sustainability Science.* Dordrecht: Springer, 283–291.

McCleary-Sills, J., Hanmer, L., Parsons, J., & Klugman, J. (2015). Child marriage: A critical barrier to girls' schooling and gender equality in education. *The Review of Faith & International Affairs*, *13*(3), 69–80. https://doi.org/10.1080/15570274.2015.1075755.

Medupin, C. (2020). Women in environmental sciences (WIES) and the UN SDGs: A catalyst for achieving a sustainable future for all. *Sustainability*, *12*(17), 7116. https://doi.org/10.3390/su12177116.

Menton, M., Larrea, C., Latorre, S., Martinez-Alier, J., Peck, M., Temper, L., & Walter, M. (2020). Environmental justice and the SDGs: From synergies to gaps and contradictions. *Sustainability Science*, *15*(6), 1621–1636.

Miles, K. (2011). Embedding gender in sustainability reports. *Sustainability Accounting Management and Policy Journal*, *2*(1), 139–146. https://doi.org/10.1108/20408021111162164.

Mitra, A., Bang, J. T., & Biswas, A. (2014). Gender equality and economic growth: Is it equality of opportunity or equality of outcomes? *Feminist Economics*, *21*(1), 110–135. https://doi.org/10.1080/13545701.2014.930163.

Nanni, G. (2023). Gender equality, equity, and equal opportunities. In: di Bella, E., Fachelli, S., López-Roldán, P., & Suter, C. (eds), *Measuring Gender Equality*. Cham: Springer, 1–30.

Núñez, R. C., Bandeira, P., & Santero-Sánchez, R. (2020). Social economy, gender equality at work and the 2030 agenda: Theory and evidence from Spain. *Sustainability*, *12*(12), 5192. https://doi.org/10.3390/su12125192.

Nwachukwu, P. T. T., & Asuelime, R. A. (2018). Shaping capabilities for gender-balanced participation in eco-entrepreneurship for sustainable development in Africa. *Gender and Behaviour*, *16*(2), 11308–11323. https://www.ajol.info/index.php/gab/article/download/180793/170138.

Ogbari, M. E., Folorunso, F., Simon-Ilogho, B., Adebayo, O., Olanrewaju, K., Efegbudu, J., & Omoregbe, M. (2024). Social empowerment and its effect on poverty alleviation for sustainable development among women entrepreneurs in the Nigerian agricultural sector. *Sustainability*, *16*(6), 2225. https://doi.org/10.3390/su16062225.

Pande, R., & Ford, D. (2012). *Gender Quotas and Female Leadership*. Washington, DC: World Bank.

Radović-Marković, M., & Živanović, B. (2019). Fostering green entrepreneurship and women's empowerment through education and banks' investments in tourism: Evidence from Serbia. *Sustainability*, *11*(23), 6826. https://doi.org/10.3390/su11236826.

Rasool, S. (2016). Gender equality and social development. In: Midgley, J., & Pawar, M. (eds) *Future Directions in Social Development*. New York: Palgrave Macmillan, 119–139.

Richardson, R. B. (2021). The role of tourism in sustainable development. In: Shugart et al. (ed), *Oxford Research Encyclopedia of Environmental Science*. Oxford, UK: Oxford University Press, article ID. 387.

Rinaldi, A., & Salerno, I. (2019). The tourism gender gap and its potential impact on the development of the emerging countries. *Quality & Quantity*, *54*(5–6), 1465–1477. https://doi.org/10.1007/s11135-019-00881-x.

Ringblom, L., & Johansson, M. (2020). Who needs to be "more equal" and why? Doing gender equality in male-dominated industries. *Equality, Diversity and Inclusion: An International Journal*, *39*(4), 337–353.

Samad, S., & Alharthi, A. (2022). Untangling factors influencing women entrepreneurs' involvement in tourism and its impact on sustainable tourism development. *Administrative Sciences*, *12*(2), 52. https://doi.org/10.3390/admsci12020052.

Segovia-Pérez, M., Figueroa-Domecq, C., Fuentes-Moraleda, L., & Muñoz-Mazón, A. (2018). Incorporating a gender approach in the hospitality industry: Female executives' perceptions. *International Journal of Hospitality Management*, *76*, 184–193. https://doi.org/10.1016/j.ijhm.2018.05.008.

Segovia-Pérez, M., Figueroa-Domecq, C., Fuentes-Moraleda, L., & Muñoz-Mazón, A. (2019a). Incorporating a gender approach in the hospitality industry: Female executives' perceptions. *International Journal of Hospitality Management*, *76*, 184–193.

Segovia-Pérez, M., Laguna-Sánchez, P., & De La Fuente-Cabrero, C. (2019b). Education for sustainable leadership: Fostering women's empowerment at the university level. *Sustainability*, 11(20), 5555. https://doi.org/10.3390/su11205555.

Silva, S., & Couto, M. J. (2023). Gender bias in the hospitality sector: Female and male jobs. *International Conference on Tourism Research*, *6*(1), 292–297. https://doi.org/10.34190/ictr.6.1.1095.

Singh, P., Seal, M., & Sharma, D. (2024). Analyzing the role and contribution of tourism in achieving sustainable development goals. In: Gölçek, A. G., & Güdek-Gölçek, S. (eds), *Harmonizing Global Efforts in Meeting Sustainable Development Goals*. Pennsylvania: IGI Global, 182–195.

Sobaih, A. E. E., & Elnasr, A. E. A. (2024). Challenges to cracking the glass ceiling among Saudi women in the tourism industry. *Tourism and Hospitality*, *5*(1), 203–224. https://doi.org/10.3390/tourhosp5010014.

Stone, R. I. (2015). Factors affecting the future of family caregiving in the United States. In: Gaugler, J. E., & Kane, R. L. (eds), *Family Caregiving in the New Normal*. Oxford: Academic Press, 57–77.

Subrahmanian, R. (2005). Gender equality in education: Definitions and measurements. *International Journal of Educational Development*, *25*(4), 395–407.

Sukalova, V., & Ceniga, P. (2021). Gender equality management in modern company management in era of globalization. *SHS Web of Conferences*, *92*, 07060. https://doi.org/10.1051/shsconf/20219207060.

Tabassum, N., & Nayak, B. S. (2021). Gender stereotypes and their impact on women's career progressions from a managerial perspective. *IIM Kozhikode Society & Management Review*, *10*(2), 192–208. https://doi.org/10.1177/2277975220975513.

Thelma, C. C., & Ngulube, L. (2024). Women in leadership: Examining barriers to women's advancement in leadership positions. *Asian Journal of Advanced Research and Reports*, *18*(6), 273–290. https://doi.org/10.9734/ajarr/2024/v18i6671.

Zhang, Y., Xu, S., & Zhang, J. (2022). Examining the relationship between tourism and gender equality: Evidence from Asia. *Sustainability*, *14*(19), 12156. https://doi.org/10.3390/su141912156.

9. Driving sustainable tourism: Female entrepreneurs' motivations within the value chain

Nishita Chatradhi

9.1 INTRODUCTION

Sustainable tourism is a multifaceted concept that integrates economic, environmental, and sociocultural dimensions to ensure that tourism development is beneficial for local communities, economies, and the environment, while preserving cultural heritage and biodiversity for future generations (Sofronov, 2017; Chirila et al., 2018; Chatradhi, 2024). This form of tourism seeks to minimize negative impacts and maximize positive contributions to the visited areas, aligning with the broader goals of sustainable development (Niedziółka, 2022; Ivanović & Mitić, 2017; Bricker, 2018). Beyond environmental conservation, sustainable tourism fosters social inclusiveness, employment, and poverty reduction, contributing to a more equitable distribution of tourism benefits among local stakeholders (Manuel-Navarrete, 2016; Valeri, 2024). Various regions, such as the Mediterranean, exemplify the need for careful tourism management to balance benefits with potential negative impacts like resource depletion and pollution (Pirlone & Spadaro, 2017). Additionally, engaging local communities in tourism planning promotes new governance structures and challenges existing power dynamics, ensuring that tourism development aligns with community values and sustainability objectives (Manuel-Navarrete, 2016; Valeri, 2024). The International Year of Sustainable Tourism for Development (2017) highlighted tourism's potential to reduce poverty through employment opportunities, provided that appropriate mechanisms support livelihoods and enhance quality of life (Bricker, 2018).

Entrepreneurship, especially within the tourism sector, is pivotal in driving sustainable practices by acting as a catalyst for innovation and positive change. Entrepreneurs are recognized as key instigators of development, with the potential to alleviate sociocultural consequences, environmental degradation, and economic inequalities through their engagement with sustainability (Kensbock & Jennings, 2011). Sustainable entrepreneurship, which combines the principles of sustainability and entrepreneurship, addresses social and environmental issues while considering long-term economic consequences, offering a transformative approach to current unsustainable business practices (Muñoz, 2013; Rajasekaran, 2013). In the context of sustainable tourism, entrepreneurs influence tourist behavior and implement best practices to limit social and environmental impacts, contributing to sustainable development (Battaglia, 2017). The role of female entrepreneurs in promoting sustainable tourism is increasingly recognized. Research suggests that gender differences in entrepreneurial motivations and decision-making significantly impact the sustainability and success of ventures (Slepian & Jones, 2013). Female entrepreneurs tend to prioritize sustainability-related concerns and values more than their male counterparts, which can influence the types of businesses they start and how they operate them (Winter, 2002). This gendered perspective brings diverse values and approaches to entrepreneurship, potentially leading to more innovative and effective solutions to environmental challenges (Winter, 2002; Bohnsack & DiVito, 2019). Furthermore, women entrepreneurs often intuitively integrate ecological considerations into their business practices, making them well-suited to drive sustainable economic growth (Krasavac et al., 2019).

Despite these advantages, female entrepreneurs face unique challenges, including disparities in access to financial resources and perceived risks associated with adopting sustainable technologies (Bendell et al., 2020). These barriers highlight the need for targeted support and resources to empower women in sustainable entrepreneurship. Addressing these challenges is crucial not only for gender equality but also for promoting social justice and equitable development, as women's involvement in sustainable entrepreneurship can lead to more inclusive and diverse economic systems (Marshall, 2011). Additionally, the role of gender-specific support systems, such as women-focused networks and mentorship programs, is vital in enhancing the success and impact of female entrepreneurs (Kanayo et al., 2021; Bichurova & Yordanova-Dinova, 2019).

Given the significance of sustainable entrepreneurship and the unique contributions of female entrepreneurs, this chapter explores the impact of gender on sustainable entrepreneurship in the tourism sector. It seeks to understand how gender influences the motivations, challenges, and successes of sustainable entrepreneurs and how these factors contribute to sustainable development. The focus on gendered perspectives in sustainable entrepreneurship provides valuable insights for policymakers and stakeholders to create more supportive environments that foster sustainable entrepreneurship across genders, ultimately contributing to a more sustainable and equitable global economy.

The research aims to address key questions, such as: *What are the primary motivations driving female entrepreneurs towards sustainable tourism? How do gender-related challenges impact their business practices and success?*, and *What role do gender-specific support systems play in promoting sustainable entrepreneurship in tourism?* By answering these questions, the study seeks to contribute to the literature on sustainable entrepreneurship, gender studies, and tourism, offering evidence-based recommendations to support female entrepreneurs in achieving Sustainable Development Goals. Sustainable tourism and sustainable entrepreneurship are intricately linked concepts that can mutually reinforce positive outcomes for the environment, society, and economy. Female entrepreneurs, in particular, bring unique perspectives and values that align closely with the goals of sustainable development, making their contributions to sustainable tourism crucial. Understanding the gendered dimensions of sustainable entrepreneurship is essential for designing policies and support mechanisms that promote gender equality and sustainable development within the tourism sector.

9.2 LITERATURE REVIEW

9.2.1 Sustainable Entrepreneurship in Tourism

Sustainable tourism practices are fundamental in advancing environmental and social responsibility by mitigating negative impacts and fostering a balanced approach to development. Environmentally, these practices help reduce tourism's ecological footprint through initiatives such as carbon offset programs, eco-friendly transportation, water conservation, and waste management strategies (Daneshwar & Revaty, 2024). For example, sustainable tourism management in Belgrade has successfully integrated green practices to minimize resource use and promote environmental conservation while enhancing the tourist experience (Šimičević et al., 2024). Socially, sustainable tourism contributes to community well-being and cultural preservation by engaging local stakeholders, ensuring equitable economic benefits, and promoting respect for local heritage (Daneshwar & Revaty, 2024). Initiatives like Sadhana Forest in Tamil Nadu illustrate the dual benefits of sustainable tourism by involving visitors in reforestation projects and community development, thereby fostering environmental education and stewardship (Popp et al., 2024). Moreover, sustainable tourism promotes inclusive growth by addressing socioeconomic disparities through responsible tourism, social tourism, and fair employment practices (Talukder et al., 2024; Yadav & Kestwal, 2024). Consequently, the tourism and hospitality industry plays a pivotal role in balancing economic growth with social and environmental considerations, contributing to a more sustainable future for the industry and the communities it serves.

Existing literature reveals its transformative impact through various approaches and strategies. For example, Tourism Social Entrepreneurship (TSE) has been effective in preserving traditional knowledge and enhancing rural community well-being, despite ongoing challenges like limited government support (Mabaso, 2024). Gender-specific contributions, as seen in Turkey, demonstrate how women entrepreneurs drive sustainable tourism by leveraging economic and cultural capital to foster community cohesion (Karatas-Ozkan et al., 2024). Similarly, green entrepreneurship in Indonesia has focused on eco-friendly technologies and conservation efforts, although the implementation of these strategies remains inconsistent (Aryaningtyas et al., 2023). The literature suggests that sustainable entrepreneurship in tourism requires a comprehensive stakeholder-driven approach to address the complexities of sustainable growth and development.

9.2.2 Gender Differences in Entrepreneurship

Research on gender differences in entrepreneurship highlights that women entrepreneurs often encounter unique barriers stemming from societal expectations, cultural norms, and limited support networks, which can inhibit their entrepreneurial aspirations and success, particularly in regions like India (Mishra et al., 2024). While women are often driven by the need for financial independence, self-employment, and personal fulfillment, they tend to be influenced more by push factors, such as necessity, rather than opportunity-based motivations, which are more common among men (Nayak et al., 2023; Yadav et al., 2024). Moreover, the male-dominated sociocultural landscape exacerbates gender disparities, resulting in limited access to education, financial resources, and entrepreneurial opportunities for women (Jaiswal et al., 2024; Sharif et al., 2017). Research also suggests that these disparities start early. For instance, while middle school girls exhibit strong entrepreneurial competencies such as collaboration and creativity, they often report lower levels of self-efficacy compared to boys, which diminishes their entrepreneurial ambitions (Rotnitsky et al., 2023). Gender differences are further evident in entrepreneurial exit patterns, where women are more likely to retire earlier than men due to factors such as inadequate pension policies and the interplay between career aspirations and family responsibilities (Komp, 2024). Targeted interventions, such as confidence-building programs, access to financial resources, and mentorship opportunities, are critical to empowering women entrepreneurs and ensuring equitable participation in the entrepreneurial ecosystem. Understanding these gender-specific dynamics enables the development of strategies that foster inclusivity and gender equity, ultimately contributing to a more balanced and sustainable entrepreneurial landscape (Mishra et al., 2024; Jaiswal et al., 2024; Rotnitsky et al., 2023; Komp, 2024; Nayak et al., 2023).

9.2.3 Motivations for Sustainable Entrepreneurship

The Entrepreneurial Motivation Scale (EMS) is an essential framework for evaluating the motivations that drive individuals toward entrepreneurship, with a particular focus on female entrepreneurs in the tourism sector. This scale encompasses diverse motivational dimensions, such as emotional resilience, adversity management, and strategic learning, which are critical for both personal and entrepreneurial success (Martínez et al., 2024; Wight 1995). Female entrepreneurs in tourism often exhibit motivations that are categorized into intrinsic and extrinsic factors. Intrinsic motivations, including entrepreneurial passion and self-efficacy, are particularly influential in sustaining entrepreneurial persistence and performance, as women in this sector frequently encounter distinct challenges in balancing personal and professional commitments (Guo et al., 2024; Madawala et al., 2023).

The EMS is uniquely suited to capture the psycho-social motivations that are often more significant than economic drivers for women in tourism. These include the need for self-actualization, social impact, and the influence of role models, which are pivotal for sustaining entrepreneurial engagement (Avci & Gümüş, 2022; Agarwal & Agrawal, 2023). For instance, female entrepreneurs in Bangladesh's smart tourism sector are motivated by a desire to innovate and surmount obstacles, motivations that are effectively captured through the EMS (Akter et al., 2024). Similarly, in rural tourism, the EMS provides insights into path-dependent challenges faced by women, offering a nuanced understanding of their motivational dynamics (Nordbø, 2022). The EMS also considers the role of external factors such as governmental support and social networks, which are crucial for the success of female entrepreneurs in tourism. For example, research on Chinese female entrepreneurs illustrates how strong and weak ties, along with supportive policies, significantly influence entrepreneurial outcomes (Jiang & Cui, 2023; Usman et al., 2024). Additionally, the scale helps elucidate the intricate balance between family and business responsibilities, a prominent concern for women entrepreneurs in countries like Indonesia and other developing regions (Heriberta et al., 2024; Agarwal & Agrawal, 2023).

By applying the EMS, policymakers and stakeholders can better tailor support mechanisms to address the specific motivational needs and challenges faced by female entrepreneurs in tourism, thereby enhancing their contributions to economic development and promoting gender equity in entrepreneurship. This holistic approach not only supports individual and business growth but also enriches the broader understanding of women's entrepreneurship across diverse cultural and economic contexts (Liñeiro et al., 2024). Consequently, the EMS serves as a valuable tool for identifying and nurturing the motivations of female entrepreneurs, ensuring their sustainability and success in an increasingly competitive tourism market.

Thus, the study proposes the following hypotheses:

H1: Sustainability Passion positively influences Success in Sustainable Entrepreneurship.

H2: Self-efficacy in Sustainability positively influences Success in Sustainable Entrepreneurship.

H3: Autonomy in Decision-Making positively influences Success in Sustainable Entrepreneurship.

H4: Innovative Sustainability Practices positively influence Success in Sustainable Entrepreneurship.

H5: Recognition for Sustainable Contributions positively influences Success in Sustainable Entrepreneurship.

H6: Challenges and Support Systems positively influence Success in Sustainable Entrepreneurship.

H7: Gender Awareness in Sustainability positively influences Success in Sustainable Entrepreneurship.

9.3 RESEARCH METHODOLOGY

The study employs a quantitative research design, utilizing a structured survey instrument to collect data from female entrepreneurs engaged in the tourism value chain across various geographical regions. The choice of a quantitative approach allows for the collection of numerical data that can be statistically analyzed, providing a clear and objective assessment of the relationships between the identified variables.

9.3.1 Sample and Sampling Technique

The sample consists of 250 female entrepreneurs, selected through a purposive sampling strategy. This technique was chosen to ensure that the respondents possess specific characteristics relevant to the study—namely, their involvement in the tourism industry as entrepreneurs. Purposive sampling allows researchers to target a specific population likely to provide rich and relevant information, facilitating a more focused analysis of the research questions. By selecting individuals who are actively engaged in the tourism value chain, the study aims to gather insights that reflect the unique experiences, motivations, and challenges faced by female entrepreneurs in this sector. Data collection occurred from January to March 2024, ensuring that the information reflects the current landscape of female entrepreneurship in tourism. This timing is critical as it captures recent developments and trends within the industry, particularly in the context of sustainable practices and the evolving dynamics of entrepreneurship.

9.3.2 Questionnaire Development

The survey instrument was developed based on the Entrepreneurial Motivation Scale (EMS), which is a well-established framework for understanding the motivations of entrepreneurs. The EMS facilitated the identification of key motivational factors pertinent to female entrepreneurs in tourism. Through an iterative process, the EMS was adapted to include eight distinct variables, encompassing various dimensions of entrepreneurial motivation, and resulted in a total of 27 items (see Table 9.1). The questionnaire was structured to include both closed-ended and Likert-scale items, allowing respondents to express their level of agreement or frequency related to specific statements about their motivations and experiences. This format enhances the reliability and validity of the data collected by enabling participants to respond consistently across various constructs. To maximize accessibility and convenience, the questionnaire was developed into a Google Form. The digital format allowed for easy distribution and data collection, and the survey link was circulated through various online platforms, including Facebook groups and LinkedIn. These channels were strategically chosen to reach a diverse group of female entrepreneurs, facilitating a broader representation of responses across different regions and business types.

9.3.3 Data Analysis

The collected data were analyzed using SmartPLS software for Structural Equation Modeling (SEM). SEM was selected as the analytical technique due to its ability to assess complex relationships between multiple variables simultaneously. The method is particularly useful in exploring the intricate interdependencies among the variables identified in the study. SEM allows for the examination of both direct and indirect effects, providing a comprehensive understanding of how various motivational factors contribute to the success of sustainable entrepreneurship among female entrepreneurs. Additionally, SEM is advantageous for its capacity to handle measurement error and test the theoretical models developed from the EMS framework (Hair et al., 2014). It provides robust insights into the causal relationships between constructs, enhancing the study's ability to draw meaningful conclusions regarding the influences of motivations on sustainable entrepreneurial success.

9.3.4 Limitations

Despite the strengths of this methodology, there are potential limitations that should be acknowledged. One concern is sampling bias, as purposive sampling may not capture the full diversity of female entrepreneurs

Table 9.1 Questionnaire and item loadings

Construct	Item	Statement	Loadings
Sustainable passion	SP1	As a female entrepreneur, I am deeply passionate about promoting sustainability in my tourism venture.	0.782
-	SP2	I enjoy creating initiatives that enhance the environmental impact of my business.	0.824
-	SP3	My commitment to sustainable practices is a significant source of fulfillment in my work.	0.785
-	SP4	I feel a personal connection to the sustainable goals of my tourism business.	0.805
Self-efficacy in sustainability	SES1	I believe I can successfully implement sustainable practices in my business.	0.799
-	SES2	I am confident in my ability to overcome challenges related to sustainability in tourism.	0.617
-	SES3	I trust my skills to make informed decisions that support sustainability in my venture.	0.675
Autonomy in decision-making	ADM1	I value the freedom to make independent decisions that align with sustainable development.	0.832
-	ADM2	I prefer to have control over the direction of my business to enhance its sustainability.	0.770
-	ADM3	My ability to make autonomous choices is crucial for my venture's success in sustainability.	0.696
Innovative sustainability practices	ISP1	I actively seek innovative solutions to improve sustainability in my tourism operations.	0.792
-	ISP2	I enjoy experimenting with new ideas that contribute to eco-friendly practices.	0.852
-	ISP3	My business often adopts creative approaches to address sustainability challenges.	0.822

Construct	Item	Statement	Loadings
Recognition for sustainable contributions	RSC1	I strive for recognition as a female entrepreneur for my efforts in promoting sustainable tourism.	0.879
-	RSC2	Being acknowledged for my sustainable initiatives motivates me to achieve more.	0.835
-	RSC3	Recognition from peers in the industry reinforces my commitment to sustainability.	0.724
Challenges and support systems	CSS1	I encounter unique challenges in my business due to my gender.	0.821
-	CSS2	Gender biases affect my opportunities for growth in sustainable tourism.	0.721
-	CSS3	I have access to support networks that empower women in sustainable tourism.	0.837
-	CSS4	Mentorship from other women in the industry has positively impacted my business.	0.678
Gender awareness in sustainability	GAS1	I consciously incorporate gender considerations into my sustainable business practices.	0.798
-	GAS2	Understanding gender dynamics is essential for developing effective sustainability strategies in tourism.	0.813
-	GAS3	I actively seek to promote gender equality through my business initiatives.	0.810
Success in sustainable entrepreneurship	SSE1	My business has made a positive impact on environmental sustainability in tourism.	0.781
-	SSE2	I have achieved significant recognition for my sustainable tourism initiatives.	0.836
-	SSE3	My venture has successfully balanced financial performance with sustainable practices.	0.801
-	SSE4	I regularly assess the sustainability outcomes of my business activities.	0.805

Source: Author's own research.

within the tourism sector. It could lead to an overrepresentation of certain demographics or perspectives, limiting the generalizability of the findings (Etikan et al., 2016). The survey achieved a response rate of approximately 70%, which is considered strong for online surveys and strengthens the validity of the findings. A higher response rate indicates the effectiveness of the data collection strategy and enhances confidence in the representativeness of the sample.

9.4 FINDINGS

9.4.1 Demographic Information of Respondents

The sample consisted of 250 female entrepreneurs in the tourism sector. The majority of respondents were aged between 25–34 years (38.4%), followed by 35–44 years (29.2%), and 45–54 years (16.4%). The representation of younger entrepreneurs aged 18–24 years was relatively low at 4.4%, while those aged 55 and above accounted for 11.6%. The distribution suggests that the sample predominantly consists of mid-career professionals actively engaged in entrepreneurship. Most respondents had attained higher education, with 43.2% holding a Bachelor's degree, 32.8% holding a Master's degree, and 13.2% having a Doctorate. Only 10.8% of the respondents had completed high school as their highest level of education. The high educational attainment level indicates that the participants possess substantial academic qualifications, which could influence their entrepreneurial capabilities and decision-making processes. A considerable portion of the sample reported having significant experience in the tourism industry. The largest group had 6–10 years of experience (36.4%), followed by those with 1–5 years (33.2%) and 11–20 years (17.6%). A smaller percentage had less than one year of experience (3.6%) or over 20 years (9.2%), reflecting a diverse range of professional backgrounds among the respondents. The majority of respondents managed small enterprises, with 40.8% reporting having 1–5 employees, and 23.6% indicating 6–10 employees. Sole proprietors comprised 10.0% of the sample, while 15.2% had 11–50 employees. Only 10.4% of businesses had over 50 employees, signifying that the respondents primarily operate within the small and medium-sized enterprise (SME) segment of the tourism industry (see Table 9.2).

The demographic analysis reveals a diverse sample of well-educated and experienced female entrepreneurs operating predominantly in small to medium-sized businesses across various tourism sectors. The respondents are largely driven by non-financial motivations, with a particular emphasis on achieving a better work-life balance and promoting sustainable tourism practices. The demographic profile highlights the importance of values-based entrepreneurship in the tourism sector and suggests that female entrepreneurs are likely to prioritize sustainability and personal well-being in their business decisions.

The primary motivation for starting a business among respondents was seeking a better work-life balance (26.0%), followed by a desire to promote sustainability (20.0%) and independence (19.6%). Passion for travel was also a notable motivator (19.6%), while a smaller group was driven by financial reasons, such as looking for a better income (14.8%). These findings suggest that non-financial motivations, such as personal fulfillment and values alignment, play a crucial role in driving female entrepreneurship in tourism (see Figure 9.1).

Table 9.3 presents the reliability and validity metrics for the constructs utilized in the study. All constructs exhibit satisfactory internal consistency, as indicated by Cronbach's alpha values ranging from 0.649 to 0.821, surpassing the commonly accepted threshold of 0.70. The composite reliability values further affirm this consistency, with rho_c ranging from 0.811 to 0.881, indicating strong inter-item correlations. The AVE values also demonstrate adequate convergent validity, with all constructs exceeding the recommended cutoff of 0.50, suggesting that a significant proportion of the variance in the observed variables is captured by the constructs. Notably, the constructs of Innovative Sustainability Practices (ISP) and Sustainable Success in Entrepreneurship (SSE) show the highest reliability and validity, with Cronbach's alpha of 0.763 and 0.821, respectively, highlighting their robustness in measuring their intended concepts.

The results of the path analysis, presented in Table 9.4, reveals significant positive coefficients for the paths from Autonomy in Decision-Making (ADM), Community Support Systems (CSS), Gender Awareness (GA), and Role Recognition for Sustainable Contributions (RSC) to SSE, with coefficients of 0.175, 0.225, 0.433, and 0.037, respectively, all yielding p-values of 0.000, which confirms their statistical significance. Additionally, the paths demonstrate medium to large effect sizes, particularly for GA, with an f^2 value of 0.40. The path from Innovative Sustainability Practices (ISP) to SSE shows a minimal effect ($f^2 = 0.02$) but remains statistically significant, leading to an acceptance of the hypothesis. However, the path from Socioeconomic Environment (SE) to SSE presents a negative coefficient of -0.106, indicating a detrimental impact, which resulted in the rejection of the corresponding hypothesis. Lastly, the path from Sustainable Passion (SP) to SSE, despite its negative coefficient of -0.019, is accepted due to its significance, indicating a nuanced understanding of its role in influencing sustainable success.

The R-squared value for Sustainable Success in Entrepreneurship (SSE) is 0.546, indicating that approximately 54.6% of the variance in SSE can be explained by the independent variables included in the model (see Table 9.5). The adjusted R-squared value of 0.532 accounts for the number of predictors in the model, suggesting that even after adjusting for the complexity of the model, about 53.2% of the variance in SSE is still explained. These results indicate a moderate explanatory power of the model, suggesting that while the identified constructs contribute significantly to understanding sustainable entrepreneurship, there are likely other factors not captured in this analysis that also influence SSE.

The SEM illustrates that Sustainable Passion (SP) is a pivotal driver of Self-Efficacy in Sustainability (SES). With a positive and statistically significant path coefficient (0.446), the results indicate that female entrepreneurs who are passionate about sustainability tend to exhibit higher levels of confidence in their ability to achieve sustainable outcomes. It suggests that fostering a genuine passion for sustainability can be an essential motivational force that enhances female entrepreneurs' capabilities and drives successful business practices (see Figure 9.2).

Self-Efficacy in Sustainability (SES) is directly influenced by several factors, with varying degrees of impact. Notably, Gender Awareness in Sustainability (GAS) and Challenges and Support Systems (CSS) demonstrate a positive and significant influence on SES, with coefficients of 0.433 and 0.225, respectively. The finding suggests that when female entrepreneurs integrate gender perspectives into their sustainability practices, and when they have effective support systems in place, they are more likely to feel capable of achieving their sustainability goals. These factors are crucial for enhancing self-efficacy, thereby indicating the need for gender-sensitive approaches and supportive environments that empower women in entrepreneurship.

The impact of Recognition for Sustainable Contributions (RSC), Innovative Sustainability Practices (ISP), and Autonomy in Decision-Making (ADM) on SES was found to be relatively minor and non-significant in this model. While these factors are valuable in the broader context of sustainability, they do not appear to directly influence female entrepreneurs' confidence in their sustainability abilities. This may indicate that, while innovation and autonomy are beneficial attributes, they

Table 9.2 Demographic information of respondents

Demographic	Respondents	%
Age group: 18–24	11	4.4%
Age group: 25–34	96	38.4%
Age group: 35–44	73	29.2%
Age group: 45–54	41	16.4%
Age group: 55+	29	11.6%
Education level: High School	27	10.8%
Education level: Bachelor's degree	108	43.2%
Education level: Master's degree	82	32.8%
Education level: Doctorate	33	13.2%
Years of experience: Less than 1 year	9	3.6%
Years of experience: 1–5 years	83	33.2%
Years of experience: 6–10 years	91	36.4%
Years of experience: 11–20 years	44	17.6%
Years of experience: 20+ years	23	9.2%
Type of business: Hotel/accommodation	71	28.4%
Type of business: Tour operator	50	20.0%
Type of business: Travel agency	35	14.0%
Type of business: Eco-tourism	25	10.0%
Type of business: Event planning	24	9.6%
Type of business: Other	45	18.0%
Business size: Sole proprietor	25	10.0%
Business size: 1–5 employees	102	40.8%
Business size: 6–10 employees	59	23.6%
Business size: 11–50 employees	38	15.2%
Business size: 50+ employees	26	10.4%

Source: Author's own research.

may not suffice to enhance self-efficacy unless accompanied by more targeted interventions such as gender awareness and supportive systems.

The outcome variable in the model, Success in Sustainable Entrepreneurship (SSE), is strongly influenced by Self-Efficacy in

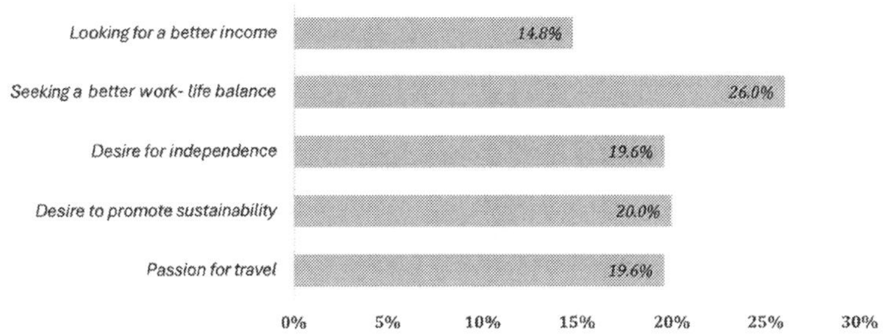

Source: Author's own research.

Figure 9.1 *Motivations for female travel entrepreneurs*

Table 9.3 *Construct validity and reliability*

Constructs	Cronbach's alpha	rho_a	rho_c	AVE
ADM	0.712	0.712	0.839	0.635
CSS	0.702	0.727	0.817	0.531
GA	0.649	0.657	0.811	0.590
ISP	0.763	0.780	0.862	0.676
RSC	0.744	0.761	0.855	0.664
SE	0.719	0.753	0.837	0.631
SP	0.779	0.788	0.858	0.603
SSE	0.821	0.826	0.881	0.650

Source: Author's own research.

Sustainability (SES), with a path coefficient of 0.446. This finding reinforces the critical role that self-efficacy plays in determining the success of sustainable entrepreneurial ventures. When female entrepreneurs believe in their capacity to implement sustainable practices effectively, they are more likely to experience higher levels of business success. This indicates the importance of cultivating self-efficacy as a strategic approach to enhance outcomes in sustainable entrepreneurship.

Table 9.4 Path analysis results and hypothesis outcomes

Paths	Coefficients	P-value	f^2	VIF	Decision
ADM → SSE	0.175	0.000	0.15	2.902	Accepted
CSS → SSE	0.225	0.000	0.20	2.123	Accepted
GA → SSE	0.433	0.000	0.40	1.784	Accepted
ISP → SSE	0.012	0.000	0.02	3.109	Accepted
RSC → SSE	0.037	0.000	0.05	2.422	Accepted
SE → SSE	-0.106	0.000	0.10	3.396	Rejected
SP → SSE	-0.019	0.000	0.02	2.509	Accepted

Source: Author's own research.

Table 9.5 R-squared values

Metric	Value
R-squared	0.546
R-squared Adjusted	0.532

Source: Author's own research.

9.4.2 Discussion of Findings

The findings from this study reveals a sample predominantly comprising mid-career professionals with substantial academic qualifications and extensive industry experience, shaping their business strategies and entrepreneurial outcomes. The respondents' strong educational background and industry experience suggest a level of expertise and confidence that likely facilitates the adoption of innovative and sustainable business practices. The model highlights Sustainable Passion (SP) as a foundational driver of Self-Efficacy in Sustainability (SES), significantly influencing Success in Sustainable Entrepreneurship (SSE). It aligns with the demographic insight that a considerable proportion of respondents were motivated by non-financial reasons, such as promoting sustainability and achieving a better work-life balance. These non-financial motivations suggest that passion, values, and personal fulfillment are paramount for these female entrepreneurs, emphasizing that the drive for social and environmental concerns is a critical component of their entrepreneurial identity.

The findings reveal significant gender differences in motivations for sustainable entrepreneurship. Female entrepreneurs are more likely to be driven by social and environmental concerns compared to their male counterparts, underscoring the importance of values-based entrepreneurship in the tourism sector. This focus on sustainability not only reflects personal passions but also highlights a broader commitment to

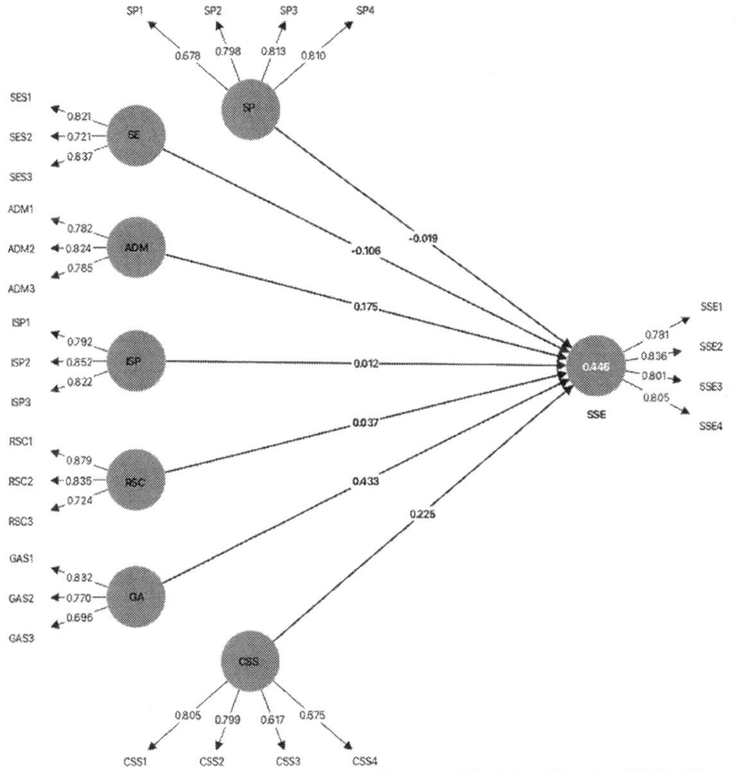

Source: Author's own research.

Figure 9.2 *SEM – summary*

contributing to social good and environmental stewardship. The alignment with global Sustainable Development Goals (SDGs) showcases how sustainable tourism businesses led by women often demonstrate higher social and environmental impacts, further contributing to community well-being and sustainable practices within the industry.

Despite these positive motivations, female entrepreneurs face unique challenges compared to their male counterparts, particularly concerning access to funding and prevailing social norms. The model underscores the role of Challenges and Support Systems (CSS) in influencing self-efficacy, indicating that supportive structures are vital for navigating obstacles. Gender-specific challenges, such as securing funding, can hinder the growth and sustainability of women-led businesses. The difficulties in accessing capital may limit their ability to innovate or expand, thereby impacting their overall success in sustainable entrepreneurship. These barriers reflect systemic issues within the entrepreneurial ecosystem that need addressing to level the playing field.

The findings also emphasize the critical importance of gender-specific support systems, such as women-focused networks and mentorship programs. Such initiatives can significantly enhance the success of female entrepreneurs by providing tailored resources, guidance, and community support. These networks not only help women entrepreneurs build confidence but also facilitate knowledge sharing and collaboration, enabling them to navigate the unique challenges they face. The presence of these support systems fosters a sense of belonging and empowerment, which can be pivotal in promoting innovative sustainability practices and recognizing sustainable contributions.

The model also indicates that while Recognition for Sustainable Contributions (RSC) and Innovative Sustainability Practices (ISP) are valuable attributes, they do not directly influence self-efficacy in the current context. This may suggest that younger and mid-career female entrepreneurs prioritize establishing their self-belief and capabilities before seeking external validation or focusing on innovation. These entrepreneurs might concentrate on building a robust foundation of sustainable practices, influenced by passion and gender awareness, before leveraging recognition or innovation as drivers of business success.

In conclusion, the study reveals that female entrepreneurs in tourism are not solely motivated by financial success but are driven by a strong desire to create positive social and environmental impacts through their businesses. The values-based approach is reflected in the significant role of Sustainable Passion and Gender Awareness in shaping their self-efficacy and, ultimately, their entrepreneurial success. The findings underscore the necessity for a supportive environment that addresses gender-specific challenges and aligns with the values and motivations of female entrepreneurs. Policymakers, educators, and support organizations seeking to empower female entrepreneurship in the tourism industry should prioritize the development of targeted support mechanisms and foster a culture that values sustainability and personal fulfillment. By addressing the challenges faced by female entrepreneurs and enhancing support systems, we can create a more equitable and impactful landscape for women in sustainable entrepreneurship, ultimately contributing to broader social and environmental goals.

9.5 IMPLICATIONS OF THE STUDY

The study advances the theoretical framework surrounding sustainable entrepreneurship by incorporating a gendered perspective that underscores the unique experiences and motivations of female entrepreneurs in the tourism sector. By integrating the Entrepreneurial Motivation Scale (EMS) into the analysis, the research enriches existing literature, offering a nuanced understanding of how motivations—particularly non-financial ones—shape entrepreneurial behaviors and outcomes. The findings emphasize the need for further exploration of the interplay between gender dynamics and sustainable practices in entrepreneurship, thereby providing a foundation for future research in this domain. Practically, the insights gleaned from the study serve as a vital resource for policymakers and support organizations aiming to foster female entrepreneurship in tourism. Tailoring support programs to address the specific challenges that women face—such as access to resources, recognition of contributions, and the establishment of supportive networks—can enhance their ability to navigate the complexities of the industry. Furthermore, the emphasis on sustainability aligns with global priorities, positioning female entrepreneurs as key players in advancing sustainable tourism practices. Collectively, these implications highlight the importance of understanding gender-specific factors in entrepreneurship, thereby facilitating a more inclusive and sustainable entrepreneurial landscape.

9.6 CONCLUSION AND FUTURE RESEARCH AGENDA

The study in this chapter has illuminated the critical dynamics of sustainable entrepreneurship within the tourism sector, particularly among female entrepreneurs. Our findings reveal that while intrinsic and extrinsic motivations drive female entrepreneurs, external factors such as support systems and community engagement play pivotal roles in shaping their entrepreneurial journeys. Notably, the data indicates that self-efficacy and passion are crucial yet underrepresented motivators, necessitating further exploration into their transformative potential. As exemplified by the quote, "In the world of travel, women are not just explorers; they are pathmakers, showing the world that every journey begins with courage, vision, and the drive to make a difference", it is evident that female entrepreneurs embody the spirit of innovation and commitment necessary for creating sustainable tourism landscapes.

Future research should delve deeper into the psychological dimensions of female entrepreneurship, particularly in regards to how self-efficacy and passion can be harnessed to mitigate challenges. Longitudinal studies examining the impact of supportive ecosystems on female entrepreneurs' success in sustainable tourism could provide invaluable insights. Additionally, comparative analyses across different cultural contexts would enrich our understanding of gender dynamics in sustainable entrepreneurship, revealing how various socioeconomic factors influence women's entrepreneurial motivations and outcomes. Finally, exploring the intersection of technology and sustainable entrepreneurship presents an exciting frontier, particularly in regards to examining how digital tools can enhance female entrepreneurs' capacities for innovation and environmental stewardship. By pursuing these avenues, researchers can contribute to a more nuanced understanding of sustainable entrepreneurship and inform strategies that empower women in the tourism sector.

As the tourism industry grapples with escalating environmental concerns and social responsibility imperatives, it is paramount for stakeholders—policymakers, educators, and industry leaders—to foster an environment that supports female entrepreneurs. This chapter underscores the importance of tailored interventions that enhance access to resources, promote gender equity, and cultivate a culture of recognition for sustainable practices. By addressing the unique challenges faced by women in tourism, we can leverage their potential to drive sustainable development in the industry.

DECLARATIONS

- The author affirms that no artificial intelligence (AI) or large language model (LLM) tools were used to generate the content of this chapter.
- The author acknowledges the use of artificial intelligence tools for language improvement and grammar checks during the development of the chapter. Specifically, Grammarly AI was utilized solely for enhancing linguistic clarity and correctness and not for content creation.

REFERENCES

Agarwal, S., & Agrawal, V. (2023). Female entrepreneurship motivational factors: Analyzing effect through the conceptual competency-based framework. *International Journal of Entrepreneurship and Small Business, 49*(3). https://doi.org/10.1504/ijesb.2023.132525.

Akter, M., Gafur, I., & Hossien, Md. A. (2024). Motivations and issues for women entrepreneurs in enhancing business performance in the smart tourism sector of Bangladesh: A case study. *European Journal of Theoretical and Applied Sciences, 2*(1). https://doi.org/10.59324/ejtas.2024.2(1).50.

Aryaningtyas, A. T., Denik, Y., & Helyanan, P. S. (2023). Towards sustainable tourism: An in-depth study of green entrepreneurship strategies in Indonesia. *International Conference On Digital Advanced Tourism Management And Technology, 1*(2), 300–331. https://doi.org/10.56910/ictmt.v1i2.44.

Avci, N., & Gümüş, S. (2022). The motivations of women entrepreneurs in the tourism industry. *Istanbul Business Research, 51*(1), 279–290. https://doi.org/10.26650/ibr.2022.51.910006.

Battaglia, M. (2017). Sustainability in the tourism business. *Symphonya, 3*, 122–134. https://hdl.handle.net/11573/1318951.

Bendell, B. L., Sullivan, D. M., & Hanek, K. J. (2020). Gender, technology and decision-making: Insights from an experimental conjoint analysis. *International Journal of Entrepreneurial Behavior & Research, 26*(4).

Bichurova, I., & Yordanova-Dinova, P. (2019). The green idea in the context of sustainable development of tourism. *Knowledge International Journal 34*(5), 1553–1558.

Bohnsack, R., & DiVito, L. (2019). Motivations and entrepreneurial orientation of sustainable entrepreneurs: An exploratory study of sustainable entrepreneurship archetypes in the fashion industry. In: Lindgreen, A., Vallaster, C., Maon, F., Yousafzai, S., & Palacios Florencio, B. (eds), *Sustainable Entrepreneurship*. Oxon, UK: Routledge.

Bricker, K. (2018). Positioning sustainable tourism: Humble placement of a complex enterprise. *Journal of Park and Recreation Administration, 36*(1).
Chatradhi, N. (2024). Empowering ambitions: The role of public policy in nurturing female entrepreneurial aspirations. *Journal of Social Policy, Social Change and Development*, *2*(2), 22–38. https://so10.tci-thaijo.org/index.php/journalspsd/article/view/1473.
Chirilă, D., Chirilă, M., & Sîrbulescu, C. (2018). Study regarding manifestation forms of sustainable tourism. Scientific Papers: Animal Science and Biotechnologies, 51(1), 191.
Daneshwar, D., & Revaty, E. V. (2024). A paradigm shift towards environmental responsibility in sustainable green tourism and hospitality. *International Journal of Social Science and Human Research*, *7*(5). https://doi.org/10.47191/ijsshr/v7-i05-33.
Etikan, I., Alkassim, R., & Abubakar, S. (2016). Comparision of snowball sampling and sequential sampling technique. *Biometrics and Biostatistics International Journal*, *3*(1), 55.
Guo, F., Sun, X., Zhou, A., Tan, Q., & Lai, K. (2024). Entrepreneurial motivations, entrepreneurial persistence and academic entrepreneurship performance: Moderating effects of innovation and entrepreneurship support institutions and female entrepreneurs. *IEEE Transactions on Engineering Management*, *71*. https://doi.org/10.1109/tem.2024.3407093.
F. Hair Jr, J., Sarstedt, M., Hopkins, L., & G. Kuppelwieser, V. (2014). Partial least squares structural equation modeling (PLS-SEM) An emerging tool in business research. *European Business Review*, *26*(2), 106–121.
Heriberta, H., Gaus, N., Ridwansyah, M., Hastuti, D., & Octavia, A. (2024). Entrepreneurial motivation as a determinant of women success in micro small and medium enterprises: A case of Jambi City of Indonesia. *Human Resources Managament and Services*, *6*(1). https://doi.org/10.18282/hrms.v6i1.3388.
Ivanović, O. M., & Mitić, P. (2017). *Sustainable Tourism and Ecotourism: An Inquiry into Theoretic Ties with Sustainable Development, 2*, 290–305.
Jaiswal, R., Singh, A., & Rai, P. (2024). An investigation of challenges and opportunities for Indian women entrepreneur. *Management Insight*. https://doi.org/10.21844/mijia.19.2.8.
Jiang, Y., & Cui, Y. (2023). Female tourism entrepreneurs in China: Contributing factors to their entrepreneurial journey. In: Ramkissoon, H., & and Mavondo, F. (eds), *Gender and Entrepreneurship in Tourism*. Cheltenham, UK: Edward Elgar Publishing, 90–109.
Kanayo, O., Olamide, E., Agholor, I., & Boshoff, E. (2021). Are there gender differences in sustainable entrepreneurship indicators amongst SMEs in South Africa? Application of MANOVA. *International Journal of Financial Research*, *12*(5). https://doi.org/10.5430/IJFR.V12N5P151.
Karatas-Ozkan, M., Tunalioglu, R., Ibrahim, S., Ozeren, E., Grinevich, V., & Kimaro, J. M. (2024). Actioning sustainability through tourism entrepreneurship: Women entrepreneurs as change agents navigating through the field of stakeholders. *Central European Management Journal*, *32*(1), 31–56.

Kensbock, S. L., & Jennings, G. R. (2011). Pursuing: A grounded theory of tourism entrepreneurs' understanding and praxis of sustainable tourism. *Asia Pacific Journal of Tourism Research, 16(5),* 489–504. https://doi.org/10.1080/10941665.2011.597574.

Komp, K. (2024). Gender-differences in retirement from entrepreneurship: The influence of pension policies across Europe. *International Journal of Gender and Entrepreneurship, 16*(4), 446–464.

Krasavac, B. C., Karamata, E., & Djordjevic, V. (2019). Innovative potential of environmentally motivated female entrepreneurship for sustainable development in the republic of Serbia. *Ekonomika Poljoprivrede, 66*(3), 721–735. https://doi.org/10.5937/EKOPOLJ1903721C.

Liñeiro, A. B., Ochoa, J. A. R., & Barrera, J. M. de la. (2024). Exploring entrepreneurial intentions and motivations: A comparative analysis of opportunity-driven and necessity-driven entrepreneurs. *Journal of Innovation and Entrepreneurship, 13*(11).

Mabaso, S. L. (2024). A Framework to Facilitate Social Entrepreneurship As a Tool for Sustainable Tourism Economies in Bergville, Okhahlamba Municipality (Doctoral dissertation). https://doi.org/10.51415/10321/5337.

Madawala, K., Foroudi, P., & Palazzo, M. (2023). Exploring the role played by entrepreneurial self-efficacy among women entrepreneurs in tourism sector. *Journal of Retailing and Consumer Services, 74.* https://doi.org/10.1016/j.jretconser.2023.103395.

Manuel-Navarrete, D. (2016). Tourism and sustainability. In: Heinrichs, H., Martens, P., Michelsen, G., & Wiek, A. (eds), *Sustainability Science: An Introduction.* New York: Springer.

Marshall, J. (2011). En-gendering notions of leadership for sustainability. *Gender, Work and Organization, 18*(3), 263–281.

Martínez, E. A., Gómez, J. J. R., Martín, D. L. S., & Muiña, F. E. G. (2024). Psychometric properties and factor structure of a motivation scale for higher education students to graduate and stimulate their entrepreneurship. *International Entrepreneurship and Management Journal, 20*, 1879–1906.

Mishra, D., Mangla, G., & Maheshwari, N. (2024). Gendered pathways to entrepreneurial success: A study on women's career choices in India. *International Journal of Sociology and Social Policy, 44*(11/12), 1000–1023.

Muñoz, P. (2013). The distinctive importance of sustainable entrepreneurship. *Current Opinion in Creativity, Innovation and Entrepreneurship, 2*(1). https://doi.org/10.11565/CUOCIENT.V2I1.26.

Nayak, M., Nayak, P. M., Birau, R., Wanke, P., & Tan, Y. (2023). Exploring women entrepreneurs' push–pull motives and challenges: Empirical evidence in an emerging economy. *International Journal of Sociology and Social Policy, 44*(1/2), 188–207.

Niedziółka, I. (2022). Sustainable tourism development. *Regional Formation and Development Studies, 8*(3), 157–166. https://doi.org/10.15181/rfds.v7i2.2371.

Nordbø, I. (2022). Female entrepreneurs and path-dependency in rural tourism. *Journal of Rural Studies, 96*, 198–206. https://doi.org/10.1016/j.jrurstud.2022.09.032.

Pirlone, F., & Spadaro, I. (2017). Sustainable tourism action plan in the Mediterranean coastal areas. *International Journal of Sustainable Development and Planning, 12*(6), 995–1005.
Popp, J. R., Lochhead, B., & Martínez, E. H. (2024). *Sustainable Tourism and Ecotourism.*
Rajasekaran, B. (2013). Sustainable entrepreneurship: Past researches and future directions. *Journal of Entrepreneurship and Management*, *2*(1), 20.
Ribeiro, G. K. A., & Leitão, J. (2024). Sustainable leadership and sustainable entrepreneurship: A systematic literature review. *Discover Sustainability, 5*(188).
Rotnitsky, I., Ukrop, S., Yavich, R., & Davidovich, N. (2023). Gender differences in entrepreneurship studies. *The European Educational Researcher*, *7*(1), 31–52. https://doi.org/10.31757/euer.712.
Samkange, F., Ramkissoon, H., & Amponsah, M. (2024). Tourism entrepreneurship and leadership. In: Hallak, R., & Lee, C. (eds), *Handbook of Tourism Entrepreneurship.* Cheltenham, UK: Edward Elgar Publishing, 69–86.
Sharif, N. M., & Lonik, K. A. T. (2017). Sustaining the entrepreneurship in rural tourism development. *International Journal of Multicultural and Multireligious Understanding*, *4*(6). https://doi.org/10.18415/IJMMU.V4I6.122.
Šimičević, D., Leković, J., & Ilić, M. (2024). Green practices in management of sustainable tourist destinations: The case of Belgrade, *Tourism International Scientific Conference Vrnjačka Banja – TISC*, *8*(1). https://doi.org/10.52370/tisc2487ds.
Slepian, J. L., & Jones, G. E. (2013). Gender and corporate sustainability: On values, vision, and voice. *Organization Management Journal*, *10*(4), 215–226. https://doi.org/10.1080/15416518.2013.859056.
Sofronov, B. (2017). Impact of sustainable tourism in the travel industry. *Annals of Spiru Haret University Economic Series*, *17*(4). https://doi.org/10.26458/1747.
Talukder, M. B., Khan, M. S., & Kumar, S. (2024). Socioeconomic gaps and foster inclusive growth. In: Hassan, V., Staszewska, A., & and Bhartiya, S. (Eds), *Building Community Resiliency and Sustainability With Tourism Development*, 56–82. Pennsylvania: IGI Global.
Trip, D. T., Fagadar, C. F., Badulescu, D., Badulescu, A., & Business, R. (2021). Entrepreneurship and tourism through the lens of sustainability. Charting the knowledge base through bibliometric analysis. *Geojournal of Tourism and Geosites*, *34*(1), 140–146.
Usman, M., Usman, M., Wasim, M., & Habib, A. S. (2024). Determinants for sustainable entrepreneurial intentions: A systematic literature review. *iRASD Journal of Economics*, *6*(2). https://doi.org/10.52131/joe.2024.0602.0220.
Valeri, M. (ed.) (2024). *Entrepreneurial Motivations: Strategies, Opportunities and Decisions* (1st ed.). Cham: Springer.
Wight, P. (1995). Sustainable ecotourism: balancing economic, environmental and social goals within an ethical framework. *Tourism Recreation Research*, *20*(1), 5-13 https://doi.org/10.1080/02508281.1995.11014727.

Winter, D. D. N. (2002). (En)Gendering sustainable development. In: Schmuck, P., & Schultz, W. P. (eds), Psychology of Sustainable Development. Amsterdam: Kluwer Academic Publishers, 79–95.

Yadav, N. & Kestwal, A. K. (2024). Principals, Practices, and Challenges of Social Sustainability in the Tourism and Hospitality Industry. In: P. Kumar, S. Gupta, M. Korstanje, P. Rout, & Madhurima (Eds.), *Managing Tourism and Hospitality Sectors for Sustainable Global Transformation* (pp. 238–248). IGI Global Scientific Publishing. https://doi.org/10.4018/979-8-3693-6260-0.ch018.

10. Corporate sustainability and board gender diversity in the European hotel sector: Implications for financial performance and distress risk

Panagiotis E. Dimitropoulos

10.1 INTRODUCTION

The hospitality industry is among the most flourishing and vibrant economic sectors of the EU region, contributing significantly to employment and GDP growth, as well as providing social and economic benefits to entrepreneurs, employees, and entire countries (Su and Chen, 2020). However, several critical voices have echoed out over the years regarding the negative impact of tourism investments and activities on the natural environment and local societies, taking the form of biodiversity loss, environmental degradation, pollution, and waste generation (Uyar et al., 2020). The economic contribution of hospitality businesses has an intense influence on economic development, creating an expectation among customers and other stakeholders that companies devote resources and efforts to address sustainability-related concerns. These concerns have been embraced by the World Tourism Organization (UN Tourism) and other formal institutions within the EU, who are now urging hotels and hospitality businesses to consider sustainability goals and strategies for reducing reputational costs and even avoiding punitive damages. This fact has motivated hotels to behave sustainably and undertake sustainability policies and practices in order to ease regulator and stakeholder concern regarding their operations.

Under this framework, several researchers have considered the association (or impact) of sustainability activities and performance on various facets of corporate performance, including, among others, firm reputation and employee attractiveness (Turban and Greening, 1996), customer satisfaction (Luo and Bhattacharya, 2006), and higher profitability and credit ratings (Singal, 2014; Rodríguez-Fernández et al., 2019; Su and Chen, 2020). The main arguments in favor of sustainability activities are based on the premise that sustainability performance helps hospitality businesses build good relationships with their key stakeholders, which later improves firms' profitability (Dimitropoulos and Koronios, 2021a). To this end, several studies have examined the relationship between sustainability performance and corporate profitability, and most of them document a positive association (Orlitzky et al., 2003; Singal, 2014).

Furthermore, corporate board gender diversity (BGD) has evolved as an important governance feature of modern businesses and corporations, mainly as an outcome of the Sustainability Development Goals (SDGs) set forth by the UN in 2015—thus, it is closely connected to corporate sustainability performance. BGD has been under scrutiny from researchers, policymakers, and businesses as an important resource for firms, allowing them to improve financial decision-making and ultimately financial performance and viability. According to Lee and Thong (2023) and Yeh and Trejos (2015), the diversity in the board of directors can increase board effectiveness, transparency, innovation, and even financial reporting quality, while reducing incidences of fraud (Adams and Ferreira, 2009; Gupta et al., 2020). Moreover, BGD is extensively connected to corporate financial performance but with contradictory findings. Some studies document a positive impact of BGD on profitability (Liu et al., 2014; Lee and Thong, 2023), while other studies document a negative (Adams and Ferreira, 2009) or no association between BGD and financial performance (Yeh and Trejos, 2015).

The goal of this chapter is to thoroughly examine the impact of sustainability performance and gender diversity as two important features of corporate activity with repercussions on financial performance and distress risk. These issues are even more significant within the hospitality sector for the following reasons. Firstly, hospitality firms have a significant influence on social and economic environments and operate with increased capital intensity, leverage, and competitive rivalry compared to other sectors (Uyar et al., 2020). Secondly, hospitality businesses have a substantial environmental footprint because their service provision involves the support and reliance on various physical components and natural resources, which motivates them to incorporate sustainability policies, practices, and strategies on addressing various social and environmental issues related to their daily operation and development. This issue will have crucial repercussions for their market share and their ability to develop competitive advantages, given stakeholders' demand for sustainability (Singal, 2014). Thirdly, hospitality firms' governance is distinct from the governance of other sectors because hospitality firms have increased interaction with the external environment and face diverse customers. According to Yeh and Trejos (2015), board gender diversity can improve managerial ability to meet rapidly changing customer preferences and needs, as well as manage external interactions efficiently. Also, it should be acknowledged that women represent over 60% of tourism firms' workforce but only a quarter of them are represented within executive positions (International Labour Organization, 2024; World Tourism Organization, 2019). These reports suggest that gender diversity in boards has improved over the last decade but there is still a lot more room for improvement (Dimitropoulos and Koronios, 2021b).

The chapter adds to the growing literature on the financial repercussions of sustainability performance and board gender diversity on the profitability and financial distress of European hotel firms on the basis of several merits. Firstly, we analyze a multi-country sample from 32 countries over a period of 12 years. Thus, we extend the studies of Rodríguez-Fernández et al. (2019) and Yeh and Trejos (2015), which considered only one year of data and only one country, and therefore provide more concrete evidence for the examined association. Secondly, we respond to the call for more research made by Russen et al. (2021) on the resource dependence theory and its implications for the association between sustainability, board gender diversity and financial performance within the hospitality sector. This theory has not been tested within the hospitality and tourism industry, leaving a significant gap in the literature. Even though Yeh and Trejos (2015) utilized this theory for their analysis within the Taiwanese market, their results were inconclusive, highlighting the need for more research on this issue.

10.2 LITERATURE REVIEW AND TESTABLE HYPOTHESES

The impact of sustainability performance on corporate risk and profitability has been examined by several researchers internationally. The resource-based view of the firm (RBV) is one of the most prominent theories used for the examination of the aforementioned relationship and suggests that sustainability impacts positively on financial performance based on the premise that people provide the firm's unique resources and competitive advantages via their experiences and training (Russen et al., 2021). Also, firms can gain competitive advantages by utilizing internal and external resources. Sustainability activities create such resources; beyond that they provide the firm the ability to deal with risks or hazardous events (Russo and Fouts, 1997). Under this framework, sustainability performance has been considered a strategic investment, and sustainability strategies have been utilized for achieving strategic advantages (Dimitropoulos and Koronios, 2021a). Environmental protection and social responsibility activities have been proven to impact positively on corporate value.

Most of the empirical evidence on the association between corporate sustainability and financial performance documents a positive association. Jiang et al. (2018) examined the association between environmental responsibility and profitability in the Chinese market and documented a positive association, arguing that sustainability performance generates competitive resources (internal and external), leading to competitive advantages and enhanced accounting and market-based performance. Corroborative evidence has been provided by Dimitropoulos and Koronios (2021a) using large European samples, with the finding that green and social initiatives impact positively on financial performance. Moreover, meta-analytical studies have verified the above-mentioned arguments on the positive association between sustainability and financial performance since social and environmental investments lead to higher financial returns, improving profitability and firm growth potential (Revelli and Viviani, 2015).

Fewer studies on this issue have been conducted in the hospitality industry, with the overwhelming percentage of results supporting the main arguments in international literature. Environmental performance is crucial in the hospitality sector because several environmental aspects (waste management, water consumption, energy use, etc.) are directly connected to the quality of the tourism product (Uyar et al., 2020). Also, several social issues are pertinent in the hospitality industry, including the implementation of non-discriminatory hiring processes, health and safety issues in the workplace, adapting facilities for disabled customers, and even the protection of the cultural characteristics of local communities. Consequently, sustainability performance, and its association with financial performance, has been examined by Singal (2014), Ghaderi et al. (2019), Uyar et al. (2020), Su and Chen (2020), Rodríguez-Fernández et al. (2019), among others, and all provide strong support for the premise that improved sustainability performance of hospitality firms results in better financial outcomes. So, based on the above discussion and the overwhelming evidence for the positive association between sustainability and financial performance, we state the first research hypothesis as follows:

H1: Sustainability performance will have a positive impact on financial performance.

In addition, sustainability performance is closely related to corporate risk and the probability of distress. Chabowski et al. (2019) documented that corporate environmental efficiency enhances firms' creditworthiness (in the form of bond credit ratings) for two main reasons. Firstly, pollution reduction can reduce operational costs, leading to improved operational performance and profitability. Secondly, the inability of firms to address stakeholders' environmental concerns may signal to the public the inability or indisposition of managers to deal with other important social and environmental issues. Thus, those firms that are poor sustainability performers are perceived as poorly managed and less trustworthy, leading to higher credit spreads and lower ratings, which in turn can increase the probability of financial distress. Additionally, sustainability-related risks could be considered by banks and investors as a source of credit risk, and underestimating such risks and their impact on firms' survivorship could lead to flaws in risk assessment and thus limited capacity of firms to attract necessary funds from financial and capital markets (Dimitropoulos and Koronios, 2023). Put differently, sustainability performance can improve firms' reputational capital, yielding an "insurance-type of protection", thus mitigating stakeholders' perception of firm risk.

Stellner et al. (2015) documented that superior corporate social performance is considered a risk-reducing activity by lenders, leading to improved bond credit ratings and yield spreads. Also, Migliorelli and Marini (2020) suggest that improved understanding of sustainability risks can contribute to a lower cost of capital and even improved credit ratings. It is also evident that banking institutions and other financial firms are already considering sustainability risks in their credit assessments. Empirical evidence by Oikonomou et al. (2014) and Dimitropoulos and Koronios (2023) document that sustainable firms are associated with lower costs of debt capital, lower bond spreads, and improved credit ratings. Schröder (2014) suggests that the positive impact of sustainability performance on risk assessment is attributed to the lower susceptibility of sustainable firms to extreme risks, a fact that leads to lower borrowing costs and improved creditworthiness and lending ability. Thus, following the above discussion, we assess that hospitality firms with improved sustainability performance will be associated with lower distress risk. So, the second research hypothesis is stated as follows:

H2: Sustainability performance will have a negative impact on financial distress risk.

Furthermore, the resource-based view of the firm echoes the board gender diversity, as female directors can improve board monitoring and efficiency by bringing different perspectives, knowledge, experiences, and skills to the table (Adams and Ferreira, 2009; Uyar et al., 2020). This perspective suggests that female directors provide human and relational capital to the firm, allowing the build-up of relations with stakeholders (customers, local society, suppliers etc.), and in conjunction with their diverse skills and experiences, they can influence corporate strategic decisions and even improve financial performance and corporate risk by reducing external uncertainty (Yeh and Trejos, 2015). Moreover, heterogeneous boards can generate (or take advantage of) a broader range of views and thinking, allowing the board to reach more informed decisions or come up with solutions in a complex environment (Fatma and Chouaibi, 2023). Thus, corporate boards with increased gender diversity will have a better understanding of market conditions and customers' needs, which can bring competitive advantages (Lee and Thong, 2023).

Several studies on the service industries, especially on the tourism sector, suggest that firms in these industries are characterized by a higher proportion of females on boards and a closer connection with customers (Lee and Thong, 2023; Dimitropoulos and Koronios, 2021b). Since tourism firms operate in a diverse market where customers come from different world regions and cultures, board gender diversity allows firms to better understand customers and establish efficient connections with them, improving customer loyalty and satisfaction (Yeh and Trejos, 2015). This will have direct implications for tourism firms' market share and eventually financial performance. Empirical evidence by Gröschl and Arcot (2014) indicated that gender diversity in hotels' management teams contributed positively to financial performance proxied via ROA (Return On Assets) and Tobin's Q. Also, Li and Singal (2017) and Singal (2014) concluded that listed hotel firms with increased board gender diversity were positively associated with stock returns (as hotels with female CEOs outperformed hotels with male CEOs) and with improved credit ratings. Thus, following the above discussion, we state the third research hypothesis as follows:

H3: Board gender diversity will have a positive impact on financial performance.

In addition, there are a number of studies regarding the behavioral, psychological, and biological differences between men and women, which almost unanimously suggest that men behave differently than women (Dimitropoulos and Koronios, 2021b). Empirical evidence by Loukil and Yousfi (2016) indicates that corporations with women as board directors experience higher risk avoidance. Similar conclusions are provided by Powell and Ansic (1997), suggesting that women are more risk-averse when making financial decisions. These gender differences seem to impact various dimensions of firms' performance, leading in some cases to reduced cash flows, inefficient resource allocation, and profitability, but, on the contrary, reducing the probability of financial distress compared to firms with male CEOs or board members. Bernile et al. (2018) have documented that female executives carry out less risky investment projects and tend to hold higher levels of liquidity to avoid potential negative outcomes of their decisions and to protect the survivorship of the firm when unexpected situations come along (Dimitropoulos and Koronios, 2021b).

Recent evidence by García and Herrero (2021) indicates that board gender diversity is negatively associated with corporate leverage, cost of debt, and ultimately distress risk. Similar conclusions are drawn by Lee and Thong (2023) who studied an international sample of hospitality firms from 30 countries and concluded that corporate financial distress risk is lower in firms with a higher proportion of female directors on the board. Consequently, if board gender diversity is associated with lower corporate risk-taking, financial distress risk will be significantly reduced for firms with more diverse boards. So, the fourth and final research hypothesis is stated as follows:

H4: Board gender diversity will have a negative impact on financial distress risk.

10.2.1 Data Selection and Research Design

We collected a sample of listed corporations operating within the hospitality services sector, originating from 32 countries of the European continent over the period 2008–2019. Accounting, corporate governance, and sustainability (ESG) data were collected from the Eikon Datastream database. Following previous studies by Dimitropoulos and Koronios (2021a, 2021b), we first selected firms included in the discretionary consumer group of firms from Datastream and focused on firms providing hospitality services as their main activity (hotels, motels, and cruises). The second phase of the data selection process included hospitality firms with full coverage of ESG data provided by Datastream as well as available financial data. This procedure produced a sample of 6,847 firm-year observations from which we had to exclude firms without sufficient data on board gender diversity and ESG scores. All remaining firms were closing their fiscal year in December and had at least five consecutive years of full data to be included in the sample. Finally, we winsorized the upper and lower 1% of the data distribution to reduce any potential impact of outliers on the empirical analysis. Overall, we ended up with a final unbalanced sample of 3,335 firm-year observations and 579 unique hospitality firms from the Isle of Man, Austria, Bulgaria, Croatia, Cyprus, Denmark, Finland, France, Germany, Gibraltar, Greece, Hungary, Ireland, Italy, Lithuania, Luxembourg, Malta, Monaco, the Netherlands, Norway, Poland, Portugal, Romania, Russia, Slovakia, Slovenia, Spain, Sweden, Switzerland, Turkey, Ukraine, and the United Kingdom.

To test the research hypotheses, we followed previous studies by Uyar et al. (2020) Lee and Thong (2023), and Fatma and Chouaibi (2023) and estimated a panel random-effects linear regression model, where the dependent variables were earnings before interest and taxes (EBIT) to total assets (capturing financial performance); and the Altman Z-score for measuring financial distress risk, where higher values suggest lower distress risk. The main independent variables were the percentage of women serving on the board (relative to the total number of directors) and the weighted average of the ESG score from the Datastream database. To deal with potential problems of omitted correlated variables, we utilized a panel random-effects regression analysis as in Dimitropoulos and Koronios (2021a), including year and country fixed effects. To select between the fixed and random effects specifications, we performed the Hausman test. The test was statistically insignificant (producing a p-value of 0.244), leading to the conclusion that random effects are the proper design for our data. The functional form of the models is provided below, where i denotes the firm, t denotes the year, and e is the error term:

$$EBIT_{it} = a_0 + a_1 SUST_{it} + a_2 BDG_{it} + \beta CONTROLS_{it} + Country_i \,\&\, Year_t FixedEffects + e_{it} \tag{10.1}$$

$$Z - SCORE_{it} = a_0 + a_1 SUST_{it} + a_2 BDG_{it} + \beta CONTROLS_{it} + Country_i \,\&\, Year_t FixedEffects + e_{it} \tag{10.2}$$

SUST indicates companies' annual average sustainability performance score and is estimated by the weighted average of nine social and environmental performance scores from Datastream ESG data, including firms' CSR strategy, workforce, human rights protection, community involvement, shareholders' protection, product responsibility, resource utilization, emission reduction, and environmental innovation (Refinitiv, 2021). This database collects over 500 measures at the company level from publicly available data sources and weights each ESG category using a different weight in each sector to capture any differential impact on the overall score. The pillar weights are transformed to percentage so as the overall score ranges between zero (0) and 100, with a higher score signifying higher sustainability performance. BGD (board gender diversity) is the percentage of female directors serving on the board. If our first and second research hypotheses are valid, coefficients a_1 in models (1) and (2) are expected to have a positive sign, suggesting that hospitality firms with higher sustainability performance are associated with higher profitability and lower financial distress risk (higher Z-score). In addition, if the third and fourth research hypotheses are valid, coefficients a_2 in models (1) and (2) are expected to have a positive sign, suggesting that hospitality firms with higher board gender diversity are associated with higher profitability and lower financial distress risk (higher Z-score).

CONTROLS signifies a vector of control variables that previous research proved to be significant determinants of financial performance and distress risk (Uyar et al., 2020; Lee and Thong, 2023; Dimitropoulos and Koronios, 2021a). These include LEV, which is financial leverage measured as the ratio of total debt to total equity. Fatma and Chouaibi (2023) argue that highly leveraged firms face reduced investment opportunities, which may have a negative impact on financial performance, which further exacerbates distress risk. Therefore, we expect a negative impact of LEV on EBIT and Z-score. We also include SIZE as the natural logarithm of total assets, which captures firm size; CFO estimated as operating cash flows to total assets; and GROWTH, which captures firms' growth opportunities and is estimated as the annual percentage change in sales revenues. Lee and Thong (2023) and Dimitropoulos and Koronios (2021a) document that firm size, operating cash flows, and growth opportunities are positively related to firm performance because larger, more liquid, and growing firms can take advantage of economies of scale in their operations. Thus, they can exert greater control on their external stakeholders and resources, leading to enhanced financial performance. Additionally, this feature will have a positive effect on financial survivorship, so a positive impact of SIZE, CFO, and GROWTH is expected on the Z-score, signifying a lower probability of financial distress.

10.2.2 Empirical Results

Table 10.1 presents the descriptive statistics of the sample variables. EBIT comprises 1.4% of the firms' assets, which is somewhat lower compared to other studies in Taiwan (Yeh and Trejos, 2015) and international sample studies such as Uyar et al. (2020) and Lee and Thong (2023). The Z-Score has an average value of 2.02, indicating that the sampled hospitality firms are not facing significant distress risk. However, there is a large range between minimum and maximum values, indicating an increased diversity of distress risk among the sampled hospitality firms. SUST has an average value of 83.375, indicating that European hospitality firms have incorporated significant sustainability strategies and practices, as they score higher compared to other world regions and sectors (Dimitropoulos and Koronios, 2021b; Singal, 2014; Lee and Thong, 2023). Board gender diversity (BGD) has an average of 22.1%, indicating that, on average, one fifth of board members within European hospitality firms are women, with a maximum value of 54.5%. This number is high compared to the percentages in the studies by Uyar et al. (2020), Lee and Thong (2023), and Fatma and Chouaibi (2023), indicating that European hospitality firms exercise board gender diversity to a higher

Table 10.1 *Descriptive statistics of sample variables (full period 2008–2019)*

Variables	Mean	Stand. deviation	Minimum	Maximum
EBIT	0.014	0.636	– 15.912	6.555
Z-SCORE	2.020	23.527	– 1233.56	772.711
SUST	83.375	30.897	1.36	100
BGD	0.221	0.132	0.000	0.545
SIZE	20.342	2.304	9.042	24.910
LEV	0.235	0.231	0.021	2.371
GROWTH	6.613	48.443	– 1.023	522.18
CFO	0.794	0.428	– 12.149	1.954

Source: Author's own work.

extent compared to firms in other sectors. Moreover, hospitality firms in Europe are characterized by acceptable leverage levels (average debt comprises 24% of total equity), while they present growth opportunities (6.613) and adequate liquidity as operating cash flow levels cover almost 80% of total assets, indicating that European hospitality firms are able to create increased cash flows and revenues

Table 10.2 presents the Pearson correlation coefficients of the sample variables. EBIT is positively and statistically significantly correlated with SUST and Z-Score, indicating that profitability is positively associated with sustainability performance and lower distress risk. The correlation coefficients between BGD and EBIT, SUST, and Z-Score are positive and significant, indicating that hospitality firms with higher board gender diversity are associated with higher sustainability performance, viability, and profitability. Also, firms with higher cash flows are positively correlated with sustainability performance, Z-Score (lower distress risk), and lower BGD. Finally, larger hospitality firms are characterized by higher profitability, Z-Score, and BGD, yet they present lower sustainability performance. All correlation coefficients are below the threshold of 0.60, and the variance inflation factors (VIFs) for the sample variables were below the threshold of five, verifying that multicollinearity is not present in the data.

Table 10.3 presents the empirical results from the estimation of models (1) and (2) using panel random-effects estimation. The regression

Table 10.2 *Correlation coefficients of sample variables*

Variables	1	2	3	4	5	6	7	8
1.EBIT	1	–	–	–	–	–	–	–
2.Z-SCORE	0.531*	1	–	–	–	–	–	–
3.SUST	0.191*	0.245*	1	–	–	–	–	–
4.BGD	0.068*	0.103*	0.064*	1	–	–	–	–
5.SIZE	0.234*	0.065*	−0.334*	0.241*	1	–	–	–
6.LEV	−0.017	−0.109*	0.103*	0.167*	0.233*	1	–	–
7.GROWTH	0.012	0.001	−0.001	−0.015	−0.004	−0.009	1	–
8.CFO	0.505*	0.561*	0.210*	−0.157*	0.217*	0.010	0.010	1

Note: Pearson correlation coefficients are below the diagonal. * Denotes correlation coefficients which are statistically significant at the 5% level.
Source: Author's own work.

Wald Chi^2 is highly significant, and the overall R^2 (0.561 for model 1 and 0.342 for model 2) is more than satisfactory for this type of analysis, considering the variability in our sample firms within several countries and fiscal years. Referring to the first two hypotheses, the coefficient on SUST is positive and significant at least at the 5% level in both models (0.018 for model 1 and 0.014 for model 2). These results verify the first two research hypotheses suggesting that hospitality firms with enhanced sustainability performance are producing more profits and are facing lower distress risk (higher Z-score). Consequently, our evidence corroborates arguments by Singal (2014), Ghaderi et al. (2019), Uyar et al. (2020), Su and Chen (2020), Rodríguez-Fernández et al. (2019), among others, yielding support for the premise that improved sustainability performance results in better financial outcomes and viability.

Table 10.3 Panel random effect regression results of SUST and BGD on profitability and the probability of distress

Variables	EBIT	Z-SCORE
SUST	0.018*** (4.33)	0.014** (2.25)
BGD	0.022** (2.19)	0.007*** (3.20)
SIZE	0.006*** (5.55)	0.098** (2.17)
LEV	− 0.023*** (− 2.95)	− 5.249*** (− 15.09)
GROWTH	0.009** (2.11)	− 0.045 (− 0.53)
CFO	1.023*** (52.42)	9.515*** (10.97)
Constant	− 0.203*** (− 7.09)	0.139 (0.14)
Overall R^2	0.561	0.342
Wald Chi^2 (p-value)	3393.89** (0.001)	571.17*** (0.001)

Note: Dependent variables are EBIT and Z-SCORE respectively. Z-stats in parentheses. ***, ** indicate statistical significance at the 1% and 5% significance levels, respectively.
Source: Author's own work.

Moving to the third and fourth research hypotheses, the variable BGD produced positive and highly significant coefficients (0.022 for model 1 and 0.007 for model 2), suggesting that firms with an increased number of female directors on the board are again more profitable and viable. This result supports H3 and H4, suggesting that female executives within hospitality firms carry out less risky investment projects, achieve higher profitability and avoid potentially negative outcomes of their decisions, and protect the survivorship of the firm. Consequently, female directors provide human and relational capital to the firm, allowing the improvement of relations with stakeholders (customers, local society, suppliers etc.), and, in conjunction with their diverse skills and experiences, they can influence corporate strategic decisions and even improve financial performance and corporate risk by reducing external uncertainty (Yeh and Trejos, 2015). These conclusions verify evidence by Lee and Thong (2023) who also concluded that corporate financial distress risk is lower in firms with a higher proportion of female directors on the board.

Regarding the control variables, SIZE and CFO produced positive and significant coefficients as expected, suggesting that larger and more liquid firms are more profitable and viable since they can take advantage of economies of scale in their operations, exerting greater control on their external stakeholders and resources, leading to enhanced financial performance and viability (Fatma and Chouaibi, 2023). Additionally, LEV was found to impact negatively on EBIT and Z-score, indicating that highly leveraged firms face reduced investment opportunities, leading to a negative impact on financial performance, which further exacerbates distress risk. Finally, GROWTH produced a positive and significant coefficient only in model (1), yielding support to our initial intuition and previous evidence by Dimitropoulos and Koronios (2021a) about the positive impact of revenue growth on profitability.

To check the robustness of the main findings, several sensitivity tests were performed. Firstly, we controlled for the potential impact of endogeneity on our data following the work by Lee and Thong (2023), Yeh and Trejos (2015), Uyar et al. (2020), and Dimitropoulos and Koronios (2021b) by utilizing a 2SLS (2 stage least square) process. Since both the percentage of female directors on the board and the level of EBIT and Z-score could be endogenously determined by the firm, a 2SLS procedure was employed using the country level of the Gender Equality Index, produced by the European Institute for Gender Equality (EIGE), and the ratio of female-to-male participation in the labor force for each country in the sample as the instruments in the first-stage regression. As an additional control, we used the one-year lagged BGD as the instrument in the first-stage regression, but with qualitatively similar results. The second-stage regression for both models was re-estimated using the fitted values from the first stage instead of the BGD variable. To check the validity of the instruments, the AR(1) and AR(2) tests were performed, which rejected the null hypothesis, suggesting that the instruments are valid for our research setting. Moreover, the Hansen J-statistic of overidentifying restrictions was insignificant within conventional levels, suggesting that the instruments were completely exogenous. The results of this procedure (untabulated) yielded qualitatively similar findings to those in Table 10.3, verifying all research hypotheses and indicating that the main conclusions are not affected by the existence of endogeneity. Secondly, following Dimitropoulos and Koronios (2021a), both models were re-estimated after changing the definitions of the control variables. Specifically, LEV was re-estimated as the ratio of long-term debt to total assets, GROWTH as the ratio of market value to book value of equity (MV/BV), and EBIT was replaced by ROE, but the results remained similar after these alterations. Finally, following Uyar et al. (2020) both models were re-estimated using cross-section OLS estimation instead of the panel random effects. The results were qualitatively similar but with lower values of the respective coefficient and R^2s.

10.3 CONCLUSIONS

Using financial and sustainability performance data from an unbalanced sample of 579 unique listed hotel firms operating within 32 countries of the European continent over the period 2008–2019, this chapter aimed to examine the impact of sustainability performance and gender diversity on financial performance and distress risk. Empirical evidence corroborated the main research hypotheses that sustainability performance and board gender diversity contributed positively to financial performance and viability. Specifically, hotel firms with increased percentages of board gender diversity and enhanced sustainability performance experienced a larger positive effect on their financial performance and a reduction on their distress risk (higher Z-score), corroborating arguments in the literature referring to the resource-based view of an organization. This chapter is a response to the call for more research made by Russen et al. (2021) on the resource dependence theory and its implications for the association between sustainability, board gender diversity, and financial performance within the hospitality sector, and offers useful policy implications.

Firstly, the chapter extends prior research on related issues of women's leadership and upper-echelon positions within corporate boards and shows the interplay between sustainability performance and gender diversity as a driver of financial performance and viability (Lee and Thong, 2023; Uyar et al., 2020). Thus, when tourism corporations are in the process of nominating members to the board of directors, they should consider the balance between male and female representation, as a diversified board can provide crucial resources to the firm (Adams and Ferreira, 2009), contributing positively to the reduction of distress risk and even improving profitability. At the same time, this chapter can help European hospitality firms realize the relationship between their sustainability strategy and financial performance, thereby improving their sense of social and environmental responsibility for enhancing their company's concept of sustainability. Secondly, from a public policy perspective, the findings on the impact of sustainability performance on distress risk reduction could serve as an impetus for regulators to enhance sustainability-related disclosures for unlisted firms and even promote diversity on the board of directors as a factor that can provide more reliable information to investors and market participants, ensuring efficient economic decisions. Finally, from the investor's side, this research may signify that board gender diversity and sustainability performance could be important indicators of corporate risk and financial performance. Thus, investors should consider these two features when analyzing investment targets and their related risks and performance.

Nevertheless, this study does not come without limitations. Firstly, the sample period stops in 2019, so the analysis does not include the impact of the recent COVID-19 lockdowns and their effect on distress risk and financial performance. Future research can delve more into this issue and examine the impact of environmental or other economic crises on the relationship between sustainability performance and gender diversity and on profitability and distress risk. Secondly, the study covers only hotels and motels; thus, the findings could not be generalized to other service sectors. Future research can examine this issue further. Finally, the current chapter did not consider other features of the board, such as board members' experiences, academic backgrounds, or stock ownership by board members. These characteristics could provide additional insights into the effect of diversity and sustainability performance on profitability and viability.

REFERENCES

Adams, R. B., and Ferreira, D. (2009). Women in the boardroom and their impact on governance and performance. *Journal of Financial Economics*, *94*, 291–309. https://doi.org/10.1016/j.jfineco.2008.10.007.

Bernile, G., Bhagwat, V., and Yonker, S. (2018). Board diversity, firm risk, and corporate policies. *Journal of Financial Economics*, *127*, 588–612. https://doi.org/10.1016/j.jfineco.2017.12.009.

Chabowski, B., Chiang, W. C., Deng, K., and Sun, L. (2019). Environmental inefficiency and bond credit rating. *Journal of Economics and Business*, *101*, 17–37. https://doi.org/10.1016/j.jeconbus.2018.08.003.

Dimitropoulos, P., and Koronios, K. (2021a). *Corporate Environmental Responsibility, Accounting and Corporate Finance in the EU*. Cham: Springer Nature.

Dimitropoulos, P., and Koronios, K. (2021b). Board gender diversity and cash holdings: Empirical evidence from the European sport and leisure sector. *International Journal of Financial Studies*, *9*, 64. https://doi.org/10.3390/ijfs9040064.

Dimitropoulos, P. E., and Koronios, K. (2023). Corporate environmental performance and bond ratings: European evidence. In: Vrontis, D., Thrassou, A., Efthymiou, L., Weber, Y., Shams, S. M. R., and Tsoukatos, E. (eds.), *Business for Sustainability, Volume I* (Palgrave Studies in Cross-disciplinary Business Research, In Association with EuroMed Academy of Business). Cham: Palgrave Macmillan, 141–158.

Fatma, H. B., and Chouaibi, J. (2023). Gender diversity, financial performance, and the moderating effect of CSR: Empirical evidence from UK financial institutions. *Corporate Governance*, *23*(7), 1506–1525. https://doi.org/10.1108/CG-11-2022-0445.

García, C. J., and Herrero, B. (2021). Female directors, capital structure, and financial distress. *Journal of Business Research*, *136*, 592–601. https://doi.org/10.1016/j.jbusres.2021.07.061.

Ghaderi, Z., Mirzapour, M., Henderson, J. C., and Richardson, S. (2019). Corporate social responsibility and hotel performance: A view from Tehran, Iran. *Tourism Management Perspectives*, *29*(1), 41–47. https://doi.org/10.1016/j.tmp.2018.10.007.

Gröschl, S., and Arcot, S. (2014). Female hospitality executives and their effects on firm performance. *Tourism and Hospitality Research*, *14*(3), 143–151. https://doi.org/10.1177/1467358414538997.

Gupta, V. K., Mortal, S., Chakrabarty, B., Guo, X., and Turban, D. B. (2020). CFO gender and financial statement irregularities. *Academy of Management Journal*, *63*(3), 802–831. https://doi.org/10.5465/amj.2017.0713.

International Labour Organization (2024). World employment and social outlook: May 2024 update. https://doi.org/10.54394/HZFD7984.

Jiang, Y., Xue, X., and Xue, W. (2018). Proactive corporate environmental responsibility and financial performance: Evidence from Chinese energy enterprises. *Sustainability*, *10*, 964. https://doi.org/10.3390/su10040964.

Lee, K. W., and Thong, T. Y. (2023). Board gender diversity, firm performance and corporate financial distress risk: International evidence from tourism industry. *Equality, Diversity and Inclusion: An International Journal*, *42*(4), 530–550. https://doi.org/10.1108/EDI-11-2021-0283.

Li, Y., and Singal, M. (2017). CEO attributes and firm performance in the hospitality industry. *Journal of Hospitality Financial Management*, *25*,(2), 77–89. https://doi.org/10.1080/10913211.2017.1398941.

Liu, Y., Wei, Z., and Xie, F. (2014). Do women directors improve firm performance in China? *Journal of Corporate Finance*, *28*, 169–184. https://doi.org/10.1016/j.jcorpfin.2013.11.016.

Loukil, N., and Yousfi, O. (2016). Does gender diversity on corporate boards increase risk-taking? *Canadian Journal of Administrative Sciences*, *33*, 66–81. https://doi.org/10.1002/cjas.1326.

Luo, X. and Bhattacharya, C.B. (2006). Corporate social responsibility, customer satisfaction and market value. *Journal of Marketing*, *70*(1), 1–18.

Migliorelli, M., and Marini, V. (2020). Sustainability-related risks, risk management frameworks and non-financial disclosure. In: Migliorelli, M., and Dessertine, P. (eds), *Sustainability and Financial Risks* (Palgrave Studies in Impact Finance). Cham: Palgrave Macmillan, 93–118.

Oikonomou, I., Brooks, C., and Pavelin, S. (2014). The effects of corporate social performance on the cost of corporate debt and credit ratings. *The Financial Review*, *49*, 49–75. https://doi.org/10.1111/fire.12025.

Orlitzky, M., Schmidt, F. L., and Rynes, S. L. (2003). Corporate social and financial performance: A meta-analysis. *Organizational Studies*, *24*, 403–441. https://doi.org/10.1177/0170840603024003910.

Powell, M. and Ansic, D. (1997). Gender differences in risk behaviour in financial decision-making: An experimental analysis. *Journal of Economic Psychology*, *18*, 602–628. https://doi.org/10.1016/S0167-4870(97)00026-3.

Refinitiv (2021). Refinitiv Eikon Financial Solutions. https://www.refinitiv.com.

Revelli, C., and Viviani, J.-L. (2015). Financial performance of socially responsible investing (SRI): What have we learned? A meta-analysis. *Business Ethics, A European Review*, *24*(2), 158–185. https://doi.org/10.1111/beer.12076.

Rodríguez-Fernández, M., Sánchez-Teba, E. M., López-Toro, A. A., and Borrego-Domínguez, S. (2019). Influence of ESGC indicators on financial performance of listed travel and leisure companies. *Sustainability*, *11*, 5529. https://doi.org/10.3390/su11195529.

Russen, M., Dawson, M., and Madera, J. M. (2021). Gender diversity in hospitality and tourism top management teams: A systematic review of the last 10 years. *International Journal of Hospitality Management*, *95*, 102942. https://doi.org/10.1016/j.ijhm.2021.102942.

Russo, M. and Fouts, P. (1997). A resource-based perspective on corporate environmental performance. *Academy of Management Journal*, *40*(3), 534–559. http://www.jstor.org/stable/257052?origin=JSTOR-pdf.

Schröder, M. (2014). Financial effects of corporate social responsibility: A literature review. *Journal of Sustainable Finance & Investment*, *4*(4), 337–350. https://doi.org/10.1080/20430795.2014.971096.

Singal, M. (2014). The link between firm financial performance and investment in sustainable initiatives. *Cornell Hospitality Quarterly*, *55*(1), 19–30. https://doi.org/10.1177/1938965513505700.

Stellner, C., Klein, C., and Zwergel, B. (2015). Corporate social responsibility and Eurozone corporate bonds: The moderating role of country sustainability. *Journal of Banking & Finance*, *59*, 538–549. https://doi.org/10.1016/j.jbankfin.2015.04.032.

Su, C.-H., and Chen, C.-D. (2020). Does sustainability index matter to the hospitality industry? *Tourism Management*, *81*, 104158. https://doi.org/10.1016/j.tourman.2020.104158.

Turban, D., and Greening, D. W. (1996). Corporate social performance and organizational attractiveness to prospective employees. *Academy of Management Journal*, *40*(3), 658–672. https://doi.org/10.2307/257057.

Uyar, A., Kilic, M., Koseoglu, M. A., Kuzey, C., and Karaman, A. S. (2020). The link among board characteristics, corporate social responsibility performance, and financial performance: Evidence from the hospitality and tourism industry. *Tourism Management Perspectives*, *35*, 100714. https://doi.org/10.1016/j.tmp.2020.100714.

World Tourism Organization (2019). *Global Report on Women in Tourism – Second Edition*. Madrid: UNWTO.

Yeh, C. M., and Trejos, B. (2015). The influence of governance on tourism firm performance. *Current Issues in Tourism*, *18*(4), 299–314. https://doi.org/10.1080/13683500.2013.820258.

Index